A
Historical Guide
to James Baldwin

EDITED BY
DOUGLAS FIELD

A HISTORICAL GUIDE TO
James Baldwin

HISTORICAL GUIDES
TO AMERICAN AUTHORS

The Historical Guides to American Authors is an interdisciplinary, historically sensitive series that combines close attention to the United States' most widely read and studied authors with a strong sense of time, place, and history. Placing each writer in the context of the vibrant relationship between literature and society, volumes in this series contain historical essays written on subjects of contemporary social, political, and cultural relevance. Each volume also includes a capsule biography and illustrated chronology detailing important cultural events as they coincided with the author's life and works, while photographs and illustrations dating from the period capture the flavor of the author's time and social milieu. Equally accessible to students of literature and of life, the volumes offer a complete and rounded picture of each author in his or her America.

A Historical Guide to Ernest Hemingway
Edited by Linda Wagner-Martin

A Historical Guide to Walt Whitman
Edited by David S. Reynolds

A Historical Guide to Ralph Waldo Emerson
Edited by Joel Myerson

A Historical Guide to Nathaniel Hawthorne
Edited by Larry Reynolds

A Historical Guide to Edgar Allan Poe
Edited by J. Gerald Kennedy

A Historical Guide to Henry David Thoreau
Edited by William E. Cain

A Historical Guide to Mark Twain
Edited by Shelley Fisher Fishkin

A Historical Guide to Edith Wharton
Edited by Carol Singley

A Historical Guide to Langston Hughes
Edited by Steven C. Tracy

A Historical Guide to Emily Dickinson
Edited by Vivian R. Pollak

A Historical Guide to Ralph Ellison
Edited by Steven C. Tracy

A Historical Guide to James Baldwin
Edited by Douglas Field

A
Historical Guide
to James Baldwin

EDITED BY
DOUGLAS FIELD

OXFORD
UNIVERSITY PRESS
2009

OXFORD
UNIVERSITY PRESS

Oxford University Press, Inc., publishes works that further
Oxford University's objective of excellence
in research, scholarship, and education.

Oxford   New York
Auckland   Cape Town   Dar es Salaam   Hong Kong   Karachi
Kuala Lumpur   Madrid   Melbourne   Mexico City   Nairobi
New Delhi   Shanghai   Taipei   Toronto

With offices in
Argentina   Austria   Brazil   Chile   Czech Republic   France   Greece
Guatemala   Hungary   Italy   Japan   Poland   Portugal   Singapore
South Korea   Switzerland   Thailand   Turkey   Ukraine   Vietnam

Published by Oxford University Press, Inc.
198 Madison Avenue, New York, New York 10016

www.oup.com

Library of Congress Cataloging-in-Publication Data

A historical guide to James Baldwin / edited by Douglas Field.
  p. cm.—(Historical guides to American authors)
Includes bibliographical references and index.
ISBN 978-0-19-536653-2; 978-0-19-536654-9 (pbk.)
1.   Baldwin, James, 1924–1987—Criticism and interpretation.
2.   African Americans in literature. 3.   Literature and history—United
States—History—20th century. 4.   Literature and society—United
States—History—20th century. I.   Field, Douglas, 1974–
PS3552.A45Z697 2009
818'.5409—dc22   2008051796

1 3 5 7 9 8 6 4 2

For Harold Norse
(1916–2009)

Acknowledgments

The writers in this volume have all made significant contributions to the field of Baldwin studies and have been a pleasure to work with on this project. I would particularly like to thank Lynn Scott and Quentin Miller for their initial support of the project and to Steven C. Tracy, editor of several books in this series, whose sound advice and kind words spurred me on. I am grateful to the Research and Enterprise Committee at Staffordshire University for funding several trips abroad, which enabled me to gather material for this book. I would also like to thank Matthew Hollinshead at the Photography Department at Staffordshire University for helping me with some of the images.

James Campbell has been enormously generous, sharing material and allowing me to pester him with questions. His warmth has typified the camaraderie and kindness that friends of Baldwin have shown to me. I am also indebted to Engin Cezzar for allowing me to use several photographs; to Lucien Happersberger for his charming correspondence and permission to use a wonderful photograph; to George Solomos (Themistocles Hoetis) for allowing me to interview him and for generously allowing me use a number of photographs; to Harold Norse, poet and old friend of Baldwin's from the Greenwich Village days, who regaled me with wonderful tales of hanging out with Jimmy in the 1940s. I am also grateful to the Baldwin estate and the U.S. Postal Service for allowing me to use a copy of the Baldwin stamp. Thank you to the wonderful team at Oxford University Press. In particular, thank you to Shannon McLachlan, Christina Gibson, and Brendan O'Neill. Finally, thank you to Marie Crook for her patience, keen eye, and support.

Contents

A HISTORICAL GUIDE TO
James Baldwin

Introduction

Douglas Field

I

In 2001, eight critically acclaimed writers, including Amiri Baraka and Chinua Achebe, gathered at Lincoln Center in New York City to pay homage to the life and work of James Arthur Baldwin. Fourteen years after Baldwin's untimely death at the age of sixty-three, the writers assembled could not agree on his legacy or literary reputation. "It was hard to decide," the Irish novelist Colm Tóibín noted, "what part of him came first" (Tóibín 15). Was it, Tóibín pondered, his race or his sexuality? Should Baldwin be remembered for his eloquent early novels or his fiery and polemical essays? Was he a religious writer or an embittered secular artist who used the cadences of the King James Bible for aesthetic effect?

The discussion at Lincoln Center highlights the difficulties of defining this prodigious writer whose work spanned four decades, culminating in one hundred and twenty-four book reviews, six novels, seven works of nonfiction, two plays, a children's book, a scenario, a collection of short stories, and two books of poetry. Despite Tóibín's conclusions that the tributes at Lincoln Center pointed toward a Baldwin legacy that "is both powerful and fluid," and that Baldwin's work "fit[s] whatever category each reader requires," the writer's reputation has suffered from his refusal to adhere to a single ideology and his continued resistance to, and suspicion of, labels and categories (15). While Baldwin is often included as part of the canonical male African American triumvirate (along with Ralph Ellison and Richard Wright), much of his work remains neglected. Although his first novel, *Go Tell it on the Mountain* (1953), is often required reading in university courses, and although his short story "Sonny's Blues" is frequently anthologized, Baldwin's work is noticeably absent from many critical works on black literature and culture. While there has been something of a "Baldwin Renaissance" over the last few years, as Carol Henderson points out in her bibliographic essay in this collection, the author has also been "conspicuous by his absence," as Craig Werner notes elsewhere, from such important critical works as Henry Louis Gates, Jr.'s *The Signifying Monkey* (1988), Robert Stepto's *Behind the Veil* (1979), and Houston Baker's *Blues, Ideology, and Afro-American Literature* (1984) to name but a few (107). For many readers (and critics) Baldwin's work has confounded expectations, appearing at times troubling and inconsistent, as a brief overview illustrates.

While Baldwin's first novel, *Go Tell it on the Mountain* (1953), was hailed as a masterful exploration of black culture, his second novel, *Giovanni's Room* (1956), portrays a homosexual relationship in Paris with no African American characters. Although it was hailed as a seminal work of homosexual literature, Baldwin repeatedly steered readers away from interpreting *Giovanni's Room* as a work of gay fiction. While Baldwin is rightly acclaimed as a major writer of homosexual literature, only three of his published essays discuss homosexuality.[1]

In his first book of essays, *Notes of a Native Son* (1955), Baldwin forcefully distanced himself from the genre of protest fiction, insisting that he was an American, not an African American writer. Baldwin's first commercial success, *Another Country* (1962), bemused and frustrated critics—many of whom objected to what they saw as the writer's advocacy of love as a solution to civil rights issues. Yet, according to Amiri Baraka, Baldwin's politically engaged second play *Blues for Mister Charlie* (1964), "announced the Black Arts Movement" (105). Sidelined by a number of civil rights activists on account of his sexuality and pummeled by younger radical writers, Baldwin would become heavily involved with the Black Panthers. By the late 1960s, in despair after the assassinations of Malcolm X and Martin Luther King, Baldwin's pronouncements were bleak and controversial: "it is not necessary for a black man to hate a white man...in order to realize that he must kill him" (*No Name in the Street* 550). Baldwin's later fiction experimented with a female narrator (*If Beale Street Could Talk,* 1974) and a sweeping novel about a gospel singer that takes in London, Paris, Africa, and the American South (*Just Above My Head,* 1979).

Baldwin's literary, political, and ideological twists and turns have puzzled and frustrated literary critics who have sought to place him in one category or another. In particular, as both an African American and a gay author, Baldwin's work has suffered from critics who have attempted to privilege either his ethnicity or his sexuality. As Andrea Lowenstein noted in a pioneering essay, "James Baldwin and His Critics," published in *Gay Community News* (1980), Baldwin's racial and sexual identities have hampered his reputation over the years. "One wonders," Lowenstein writes, "whether, if Baldwin were *either* black or gay, more reviewers might be able to actually address his work itself." Instead, Lowenstein argues, Baldwin's "double minority status" is so "threatening" that "what is finally reviewed in the end is [sic] the critics' own fears and projections" (11). Although there are still some remarkable silences on Baldwin's sexuality, there has been a steady trickle of articles since the early 1980s examining the implications of Baldwin as both a black and a gay writer.[2] More recently, two notable collections of critical essays on Baldwin—Dwight McBride's *James Baldwin Now* (1999) and D. Quentin Miller's *Re-Viewing James Baldwin: Things Not Seen* (2000)—have done much to reinvigorate and establish a treatment of Baldwin's race *and* sexuality.

A further critical division in Baldwin's work is highlighted by the conflicting views on whether he is primarily an essayist or a novelist. Despite Baldwin's claim that he never perceived himself as an essayist, a number of critics have contrasted the secure legacy of his nonfiction with his dubious reputation as a novelist. "James Baldwin *was* literature for me," enthused Henry Louis Gates, Jr., adding, "especially the essay" (163). For many critics, such as Harold Bloom, "[w]hatever the ultimate canonical judgment upon James Baldwin's fiction may prove to be, his nonfictional work clearly has permanent status in American literature" (1). Similarly, by 1963, Irving Howe concluded that "[w]hatever his ultimate success or failure as a novelist, Baldwin has already secured his place as one of the two or three greatest essayists this country has ever produced" (135).

Baldwin's uncertain reputation as a novelist was ironically generated by the success of his first novel, *Go Tell it on the Mountain*, as illustrated by Stanley Crouch's conclusion that the "talent for writing fiction that Baldwin showed in his first novel...never achieved maturity" (235). Critics who were puzzled by his departure from black culture with *Giovanni's Room* largely pilloried *Another Country*, which, for many critics, signaled his demise as a novelist despite its commercial success. As Calvin C. Hernton noted, by 1964, Baldwin was "at the zenith (and decline) of his fame in America," with a number of African Americans already expressing "ambivalence" over his work (105). Morris Dickstein, for example, noted that, whilst *Another Country* was "shapeless," the "feelings were still vigorous and sharp," in contrast to Baldwin's fourth novel, *Tell Me How Long the Train's Been Gone* (1968), which Dickstein concluded was "a long, dismal failure" (166). For Dickstein, Baldwin the novelist "seemed to have lost all ability to command belief," a point echoed by Jean-François Gounard, who concluded that, although Baldwin was "an excellent essayist and a very good polemicist, by the late seventies Baldwin no longer seemed to know how to define a novel" (254).

The consensus that Baldwin had lost his footing by the mid-1960s is illustrated by criticism that points to an increasing lack of clarity and cohesion in his writing. As William Wasserstrom concluded, "not once during a career now ending its third decade, had James Baldwin lapsed in public fealty to a single idea," (74) a point that Baldwin made himself in the introduction to *The Price of the Ticket* (1985), a collection of his nonfiction. Reflecting on his early years as a Trotskyite, Baldwin concluded that it "was useful as I learned that it may be impossible to indoctrinate me" (xiii). As Quentin Miller points out in the introduction to *Re-Viewing James Baldwin*, this refusal to be pinned down, to "be labeled as a gay writer, a black writer, a protest writer, or a prophetic writer" has meant that "his legacy is not entirely stable" (4). For some critics, such as François Burgess, Baldwin's work was too far-reaching: "Alone among the Black contemporary writers, Baldwin could not or did not know how to find a central ideology that would give to his work coherence and unity" (quoted in Bobia 54). For other critics, such as Harold Cruse, Baldwin's work was weakened because he "does not know what he stands for, sociologically" (482). Perhaps most damning of all, some critics, such as Addison Gayle, criticized his writing for not showing "knowledge of the history and culture of black people," concluding that "[o]f black history, he is totally ignorant, and of black writers before Richard Wright, oblivious" (219). Howe pointed to Baldwin's "rifts in logic" (121), Albert Murray referred to the "exasperating confusion" in his writing (148), and a number of critics bemoaned, as Harold Cruse posited, the "tormented inconsistency that runs through much of Mr. Baldwin's work" (200).

Baldwin acknowledged that his work left him open to "a vast amount of misunderstanding," (*Rap on Race* 136) and even called himself "the perfectly impossible man" (Leeming "The White Problem": 20); however, while scholarship on Baldwin has criticized his writing for being too disparate, too disordered, this seeming lack of cohesion is central and internal to his writing. His work relentlessly calls for an interrogation and examination of complexity. "[A]ll theories are suspect," Baldwin wrote in his first collection of essays, adding that "one must find, therefore, one's own moral center and move through the world hoping that this center will guide one aright" ("Autobiographical Notes" 9). As if anticipating the difficulties in locating him, Baldwin insisted in "Everybody's Protest Novel"—the essay that marked his entrance into the literary world—that it is "[o]ur passion for categorization, life neatly fitted into pegs, [which] has led to an unforeseen, paradoxical distress; confusion, a breakdown in meaning" (15). In this essay Baldwin famously criticized the protest novel writer on the grounds of its "insistence that it is his categorization alone which is real and which cannot be transcended" (18).

Baldwin's repeated repudiation of labels and categorization courses through his work. In order to facilitate change, Baldwin declared to the poet Nikki Giovanni, "We have to make our own definitions and begin to rule the world that way" (*Dialogue* 34). Asked in 1979 what he hoped to achieve, Baldwin replied that he wished "to destroy that frame of reference for myself and for those coming after me" (Salaam 108). "I was not born to be what someone said I was. I was not born to be defined by someone else," Baldwin declared in his last interview, "but by myself and myself only" (Troupe 193).

By emphasizing the right and need to define oneself, Baldwin's writing builds on the pioneering work of Frederick Douglass, whose narratives speak of the cultural, political, and ideological imperatives of self-governance and self-definition. Douglass's narratives recount the history of a slave who has mastered language, and his polished rhetoric clearly identifies the transition from slave to free man or woman. In Baldwin's work, however, his characters are frequently shackled by the past, like Rufus Scott, the protagonist of *Another Country*, who is "bowed down with the memory of all that had happened" (49). In interviews, speeches, essays, and fiction, Baldwin evokes the past, reminding his white liberal readership of a brutal past of slavery and economic inequality, where African Americans and whites are caught in "history's ass-pocket" (*No Name in the Street* 481).

Baldwin—black, gay, expatriate writer—constantly battles in his works for selfhood, for identity, as the titles suggest: *Nobody Knows My Name, No Name in the Street*, "Stranger in the Village." Contrary to Darryl Pinckney's conclusion that Baldwin developed "a permanence of self that the insecurity of his social condition could not threaten" (64), this "permanence of self," is always precarious, unstable in his writing. Throughout his work Baldwin's use of personal pronouns are a battlefield, where the "I" is at times personal, even confessional, collective, transhistorical, or indeed ambiguous. Or, as Baldwin once said, "I't refers to "all those strangers called Jimmy Baldwin" (Auchinloss and Lynch 79).

Recent criticism, in particular Dwight McBride's introduction to *James Baldwin Now*, has attempted to capture and locate Baldwin's multifarious roles. Surveying the ways in which Baldwin's work has been categorized, McBride argues that, with cultural studies, it is now finally possible to recognize Baldwin as "an intricately negotiated amalgam of all those things [black, gay, expatriate, etc.]" (2). Whatever Baldwin's legacy becomes, his work still continues to speak across the borders of race, gender, sexuality, and religion. As the son of a preacher man, the grandson of a slave, and a witness to America, Baldwin's voice continues to cry out.

2

One of the challenges for readers and critics of Baldwin's writing has been to read his work in the context of the shifting decades from which his work emerged. Born before the Great Depression, Baldwin would die during Ronald Reagan's second term in office, having witnessed huge changes in the cultural and political climate spanning the Great Depression, World War II, the cold war, civil rights, Vietnam, and gay liberation. Or, to put it another way: Baldwin's early essays refer to Bessie Smith, his later work discusses Boy George.

Baldwin's very early years coincided with the Harlem Renaissance, an artistic movement at its peak in the mid to late 1920s. Despite the fact that he was taught by one of the leading poets, Countee Cullen, Baldwin rarely referred to the literary and artistic feats of his African American forebears. For Baldwin and his family, the achievements of the literati were far removed from the daily grind of feeding a quickly expanding family. "I hit the streets when I was seven," Baldwin recalled. "It was the middle of the Depression and I learned how to sing out of hard experience" ("Dark Days" 788). After three years as a Pentecostal preacher, Baldwin left the church to write, publishing his first major piece in the left-wing journal *The Nation* in 1947. Although not affiliated with any political party, Baldwin had a brief stint as a Trotskyite and wrote for several left-wing journals, including *New Leader.*

When Baldwin moved to Paris in 1948, he followed in the footsteps of a number of expatriate American writers, including Richard Wright, Chester Himes, and Gertrude Stein. Although he would remain abroad at the height of the cold war, Baldwin was attuned to the persecution of artists and homosexuals, referring to his "obsession with the McCarthy phenomenon" (*No Name in the Street* 466). As Carol Henderson points out in her bibliographic essay, Baldwin was subjected to many years of surveillance by the FBI from the early 1960s to the late 1970s (his file is more than 1,700 pages).[3]

The FBI's interest in Baldwin had much to do with his sexuality, but it also focused on his political activism. (And it's important to remember that Baldwin, unlike Ralph Ellison or Richard Wright, participated actively in the civil rights movement). By the early 1960s, particularly after the publication of *Another Country* and *The Fire Next Time*, Baldwin was one of the most photographed writers in America. Baldwin appeared frequently on prime-time radio and television, his face appeared on the cover of *Time* magazine, and many of his essays were widely available in publications such as the *New York Times*. For many critics, citing his third novel, *Another Country,* as his last accomplished novel, Baldwin's work suffered in part due to his twin roles as artist and celebrity. By the mid-1960s, Baldwin was not only in frequent demand as a writer and spokesman, but he was subject to scabrous attacks from younger black radicals such as Eldridge Cleaver and Amiri Baraka, who attacked the older writer on the grounds of his sexuality and "outmoded" political views.

While it would be hard to argue that Baldwin's last three novels are characterized by the poise and elegance of his early fiction, his later fictional works are beginning to receive the critical attention that they merit, as several of the collected essays here attest.[4] The tight modernist control of Baldwin's early fictional writing—the exquisite phrasing buttressed by precise punctuation—is less evident in works after *Giovanni's Room* (and certainly after *Another Country*). Yet to overlook Baldwin's later fiction because of its narrative bagginess or lack of editing is to miss his bold and innovative explorations of the blues, his tender and self-critical meditations on black radicalism (as well as the connections between black radical politics and homosexuality), his fierce critique of institutionalized religion (but insistence on the need for spirituality), and his use of gospel music as a symbol of love (including love between men). To read Baldwin's later work is to understand that he wasn't sufficiently institutionalized as a writer. In contrast to those writers who are at their desks by nine, Baldwin would sleep until midday after the rigors of entertaining and debating the night before (evenings that frequently spilled into the mornings). Although Baldwin's fiction after the mid-1960s lacks the sustained control of his early novels, there is much to rejoice in Baldwin's later writing: There may be more padding, but there are still breathtaking descriptions of dread, desire, and loss told through the syncopated prose of a writer who, although in need of tuning at times, could still bring the house down. As critics begin to dismantle the divisions that have characterized Baldwin scholarship (as black *or* gay, novelist *or* essayist), it is hoped that criticism will question the established narrative of Baldwin as an accomplished and talented writer who lost his way by the mid-1960s.

Baldwin's last novel of the 1960s, *Tell Me How Long the Train's Been Gone*, is the painful meditation of an aging artist who can watch—but can no longer participate—in the revolution. The novel is clearly autobiographical in places, but perhaps Baldwin was too harsh, too self-critical. Ever the prophet, Baldwin preempted numerous cultural, literary, and ideological changes in American life. As early as 1949, in an astonishingly bold essay on homosexuality, "Preservation of Innocence," Baldwin picks apart the terms *natural* and *unnatural* and then segues into a discussion of gender. Anticipating now-established theories of gender and performance by some forty years, Baldwin explores the roots of the "tough guy" in American culture with razor-sharp analysis. In "Encounter on the Seine," published in *Notes of a Native Son*, Baldwin observes how an encounter with an African "causes the Negro to recognize that that he is a hybrid" (89), a theory that, whilst not developed, hints at Homi Bhabha's much later work on hybridity. In Baldwin's last novel, *Just Above My Head*, the narrator records how he "was traveling before the days of electronic surveillance, before the hijackers and terrorists arrived" (350), a description which, though about a different era of terrorism, reads as a prophetic and chilling reminder of the current political climate.

3

The U.S. Postal Service's issuance of a James Baldwin stamp in 2004 went some way toward recognizing the late, great author. (As an early transatlantic commuter and avid traveler, Baldwin would no doubt have enjoyed his image adorning mail across the United States and globe.) And yet nowhere, not even in Harlem, as Herb Boyd notes in his biography of Baldwin, is there a "statue...school, park, place, square, or street named after James Baldwin" (179). Baldwin, it seems, still has "no name in the street."

The aim of this collection, however, is not to memorialize Baldwin's life and work but to reexamine his fiction and nonfiction in the context of the historical, political, and cultural eras that shaped his writing. The essays collected here, written by leading Baldwin scholars, are original essays on key aspects of the author's life and work, including the significance of his transatlantic identity and the ways in which religion, music, civil rights, and sexuality impacted on his career. The collection does not attempt to discuss every major work by Baldwin (to do so would require several volumes) but rather to situate his fiction and nonfiction in the turbulent decades of the 1940s to the 1980s. Some of the essays here touch on more familiar works by Baldwin, whilst others draw on less well-known works with the hope that readers will return to—or seek out—essays, short stories, poems, plays, or novels from his prodigious oeuvre. To read Baldwin's work is to be reminded of his mesmerizing talent as a writer and the ways in which his work not only reflected his times, but also helped shape them.

Randall Kenan's incisive biographical chapter gives a vivid sense of Baldwin's complicated life and career, from his teenage years as a preacher to his final years in Paris, from his battles with his preacher stepfather to his struggles and successes as a prodigious writer. As Kenan astutely observes, Baldwin was intimately attuned to turbulent political shifts, particularly during the civil rights era, when his visits to the South meant that he "identified with the shared history," "thirst for freedom," and "religious passion of African American activists."

Clarence E. Hardy III's chapter, "James Baldwin as Religious Writer: The Burdens and Gifts of Black Evangelicalism," examines Baldwin's complicated relationship to religion. Hardy convincingly argues that Baldwin, although not a believer in the traditional sense of the word, "was still a religious writer." Hardy argues that Baldwin's writing, even when far removed from the theme of his evangelical upbringing, is characterized by his preoccupation with religion. As Hardy argues, "religion and Baldwin's complicated relationship with it best illuminates what makes his work distinctive." In his thought-provoking chapter, a complicated and fascinating portrait of Baldwin is revealed as Hardy explores the ways in which the author not only employed the rhythms and heritage of his religious upbringing for aesthetic purposes, but grappled with religion throughout his life.

Baldwin's preoccupation with religion is intimately connected to his love of music. From his recollections of the saints singing in *The Fire Next Time* to the gospel singer of his last novel, music and musicians chime throughout Baldwin's fiction and nonfiction. In "Using the Blues: Baldwin and Music," D. Quentin Miller explores Baldwin's fascination with gospel, blues, jazz, and classical music to argue that music—in particular, the blues—was, for the author, "a key to unlock the mysteries of his identity as an exile, an artist, a black American in a racially hostile era, and a boy preacher who turned against his church." Baldwin, as Miller articulates, grew up with the development of jazz, and his work, particularly his later fiction, explores the ways in which music has the ability to communicate, heal, and provoke.

In "James Baldwin and Sexuality: *Lieux de Mémoire* within a Usable Past," Justin A. Joyce and Dwight A. McBride contextualize Baldwin's critical insights into sexuality. In order to locate Baldwin within an African American cultural critique and to situate the significance of the challenge he posed to that heritage, Joyce and McBride trace a genealogy of the disavowal of black queers in representations of the African American community by moving beyond Baldwin to consider the generation of writers that preceded him (Langston Hughes, Alain Locke, Claude McKay). By expanding the discussion of Baldwin to include artists of the Harlem Renaissance, the chapter brings together a set of related concerns about the state of African American studies, the state of Baldwin scholarship, the complicated relationship Baldwin exhibits to identity politics, and how that complexity presages the need for a critical sensibility evident in black queer studies. Though some attention is paid to *Another Country*, emphasis is placed upon *Giovanni's Room*, a text whose reception and scholarly history strongly illustrates the ritualistic quality of James Baldwin and his work as sites for mobilizing discourses of sexuality in the African Americanist critique.

In "Challenging the American Conscience, Re-imagining American Identity: James Baldwin and the Civil Rights Movement," Lynn Orilla Scott focuses on Baldwin's fifteen-year engagement with the civil rights and Black Power movements. Although a number of critics have suggested that Baldwin's work suffered as a consequence of his roles as writer and public intellectual, the writer's contribution to and involvement in the civil rights movement has not been examined in depth. Using a wide range of sources (including interviews and recordings in addition to Baldwin's fiction and nonfiction), Scott inaugurates a detailed examination of the writer's passionate engagement with the movement, not just as a writer but as a speaker and witness to the violent confrontations of the 1960s.

Baldwin's commitment to the civil rights movement—which included several visits to the American South—is even more remarkable given that the author spent so many years in France and Turkey. In her chapter "'In the Same Boat': James Baldwin and the Other Atlantic," Magdalena J. Zaborowska explores Baldwin's seldom-noted preoccupation with the themes of migration in his work. As Zaborowska argues, a closer look at Baldwin's work reveals not only the author's "frequent use of the motifs of departure, passage, arrival, [and] acculturation," but also demonstrates writing that is keenly attuned to the representation and articulation of racialized identities. Baldwin, the writer from Harlem, becomes, as Zaborowska suggests, a writer whose work is concerned with circum-Atlantic themes that enrich an understanding of a multidimensional American identity.

Finally, in "The Price of the Ticket: Baldwin Criticism in Perspective," Carol E. Henderson provides a succinct overview of Baldwin's literary reputation in the United States and abroad. Henderson charts how Baldwin's work slid in and out of critical favor from the 1950s to the 1990s, when renewed interest in the author inaugurated what Henderson calls the "Baldwin Renaissance." By examining Baldwin's reception over four decades, Henderson's chapter also serves as a useful barometer of U.S. literary, political, and cultural shifts. In addition, Henderson presents an indispensable guide not only to Baldwin's work, but also to key secondary reading in books and journal articles.

NOTES

1. The essays are "Preservation of Innocence," first published in *Zero* (1949), omitted from *The Price of the Ticket,* and not published until 1989 in *Out/Look* 2.2 (Fall 1989): 40–45; "The Male Prison," first published as "Gide as Husband and Homosexual," in *New Leader* (December 13, 1954); and "Freaks and the American Ideal of Manhood," first published in *Playboy* (January 1985) and reprinted as "Here Be Dragons," in *The Price of the Ticket: Collected Nonfiction, 1948–1985* (New York: St. Martin's/Marek, 1985). All three essays are published in *James Baldwin: Collected Essays,* edited by Toni Morrison (New York: Library of America, 1998).

2. Emmanuel Nelson's criticism pioneered a discussion of Baldwin's work in relation to his race and sexuality. See, in particular, "John Rechy, James Baldwin and the American Double Minority Literature," *Journal of American Culture* 6.2 (1983): 70–74, and "Critical Deviance: Homophobia and the Reception of James Baldwin's Fiction," *Journal of American Culture* 14.3 (1991): 91–96.

3. For an excellent account of Baldwin's FBI files, see James Campbell, "I Heard It Through the Grapevine: James Baldwin and the FBI," first published in *Granta* 73 (Spring 2001) and republished in Campbell's *Syncopations: Beats, New Yorkers, and Writers in the Dark* (Berkeley: University of California Press, 2008), 73–102.

4. See, in particular, Lynn Orilla Scott, *James Baldwin's Later Fiction: Witness to the Journey* (East Lansing: Michigan State University Press, 2002).

WORKS CITED

Auchinloss, Eve, and Nancy Lynch. "Disturber of the Peace: James Baldwin—An Interview." In *Conversations with Baldwin*, edited by Fred L. Standley and Louis H. Pratt. Jackson: University Press of Mississippi, 1989. 64–82.

Baldwin, James. "Everybody's Protest Novel." 1949. Reprinted in *James Baldwin: Collected Essays*, edited by Toni Morrison. New York: Library of America, 1998. 11–18.

———. "Preservation of Innocence." 1949. Reprinted in *James Baldwin: Collected Essays*, edited by Toni Morrison. New York: Library of America, 1998. 594–600.

———. "Encounter on the Seine" (Originally published as "The Negro in Paris"). 1950. Reprinted in *James Baldwin: Collected Essays*, edited by Toni Morrison. New York: Library of America, 1998. 85–90.

———. "Autobiographical Notes." 1955. Reprinted in *James Baldwin: Collected Essays*, edited by Toni Morrison. New York: Library of America, 1998. 5–9.

———. *Notes of a Native Son*. 1955. Reprinted in *James Baldwin: Collected Essays, edited by Toni Morrison*. New York: Library of America, 1988. 5–129.

———. *Nobody Knows My Name: More Notes of a Native Son*. 1961. London: Penguin, 1961.

———. *Another Country*. 1962. London: Penguin, 1990.

———. *The Fire Next Time*. 1963. London: Penguin, 1964.

———. "The Use of the Blues." *Playboy* (January 1964): 131–32, 240–41.

———. "Nothing Personal." 1964. Reprinted in *The Price of the Ticket: Collected Nonfiction, 1948–1985*. New York: St. Martin's/Marek, 1985. 381–93.

————. "God's Country." *New York Review of Books* 8 (March 23, 1967): 20.

————, and Margaret Mead. *A Rap on Race*. New York: Dell, 1971.

————. *No Name in the Street*. 1972. Reprinted in *The Price of the Ticket: Collected Nonfiction, 1948–1985*. New York: St. Martin's/Marek, 1985. 449–552.

————, and Nikki Giovanni. *A Dialogue*. Foreword by Ida Lewis. Afterword by Orde Coombs. London: Michael Joseph, 1975.

————. *Just Above My Head*. 1979. London: Penguin, 1994.

————. "Dark Days." 1980. Reprinted in *James Baldwin: Collected Essays*, edited by Toni Morrison. New York: Library of America, 1998. 788–98.

————. *The Price of the Ticket: Collected Nonfiction, 1948–1985*. New York: St. Martin's/Marek, 1985.

Baraka, Amiri. *Eulogies*. New York: Marsilio Publishers, 1996.

Bloom, Harold. "Introduction." In *James Baldwin: Modern Critical Views*, edited by Harold Bloom. New York: Chelsea House Publishers, 1986. 1–9.

Bobia, Rosa. *The Critical Reception of James Baldwin in France*. New York: Peter Lang, 1997.

Boyd, Herb. *Baldwin's Harlem: A Biography of James Baldwin*. New York: Atria Books, 2008.

Campbell, James. "I Heard it Through the Grapevine: James Baldwin and the FBI." *Syncopations: Beats, New Yorkers, and Writers in the Dark*. Berkeley and Los Angeles, California: University of California Press, 2008. 73–102.

Crouch, Stanley. "The Rage of Race." In *Notes of a Hanging Judge: Essays and Reviews, 1979–1989*. New York: Oxford University Press, 1990. 231–36.

Cruse, Harold. *The Crisis of the Negro Intellectual: A Historical Analysis of the Failure of Black Leadership*. 1967. Reprinted with a foreword by Bazel E. Ellen and Ernest J. Wilson III. New York: Quill, 1984.

Dickstein, Morris. *Gates of Eden: American Culture in the Sixties*. New York: Basic Books, 1977.

Gates, Jr., Henry Louis. "An Interview with Josephine Baker and James Baldwin." In *James Baldwin: The Legacy*, edited by Quincy Troupe. New York: Simon & Schuster, 1989. 161–72.

Gayle, Jr., Addison. *The Way of the New World: The Black Novel in America*. New York: Anchor Press/Doubleday, 1975.

Gounard, Jean-François. *The Racial Problem in the Works of Richard Wright and James Baldwin*, translated by Joseph J. Rodgers, Jr. Foreword by Jean F. Béranger. London: Greenwood Press, 1992.

Hernton, Calvin C. *White Papers For White Americans*. New York: Doubleday, 1966.

Howe, Irving. "Black Boys and Native Sons." In *Selected Writings, 1950–1990*. San Diego: Harcourt Brace Jovanovich, 1990. 119–39.

Leeming, David. "The White Problem." In "Home and Away: Twentieth Century Masters Tribute to James Baldwin," edited by M. Mark. Special issue, *Pen America: A Journal for Writers and Readers* 1.2 (Fall 2001): 19–23.

Lowenstein, Andrea. "James Baldwin and His Critics." *Gay Community News* (February 9, 1980): 10, 11, 17.

McBride, Dwight A., ed. *James Baldwin Now*. New York: New York University Press, 1999.

Miller, D. Quentin, ed. *Re-Viewing James Baldwin: Things Not Seen*. Foreword by David Leeming. Philadelphia: Temple University Press, 2000.

Murray, Albert. *The Omni-Americans: New Perspectives on Black Experience and American Culture*. New York: Outerbridge & Dienstfrey, 1970.

Nelson, Emmanuel. "John Rechy, James Baldwin and the American Double Minority Literature." *Journal of American Culture* 6.2 (1983): 70–74.

———. "Critical Deviance: Homophobia and the Reception of James Baldwin's Fiction." *Journal of American Culture* 14.3 (1991): 91–96.

Pinckney, Darryl. "The Magic of James Baldwin." *New York Review of Books* (November 19, 1998): 64–74.

Salaam, Kalamu ya. "James Baldwin: Looking Towards the Eighties." *Black Collegian* 10.2 (October–November 1979): 105–10.

Scott, Lynn Orilla. *James Baldwin's Later Fiction: Witness to the Journey*. East Lansing: Michigan State University Press, 2002.

Tóibín, Colm. "The Last Witness." *London Review of Books* 23.18 (September 20, 2001): 15–20.

Traylor, Eleanor. "On Solid Ground." In "Home and Away: Twentieth Century Masters Tribute to James Baldwin," edited by M. Mark. Special issue, *Pen America: A Journal for Writers and Readers* 1.2 (Fall 2001): 35–37.

Troupe, Quincy. "The Last Interview." In *James Baldwin: The Legacy,* edited by Quincy Troupe. New York: Simon & Schuster, 1989. 186–212.

Wasserstrom, William. "James Baldwin: Stepping Out of the Promise." In *Black Fiction: New Studies in the Afro-American Novel Since 1945,* edited by A. Robert Lee. New York: Barnes & Noble Books, 1980. 74–96.

Werner, Craig. "James Baldwin: Politics and the Gospel Impulse." *New Politics* 2.2 (1989): 106–24.

James Baldwin, 1924–1987

A Brief Biography

Randall Kenan

In death James Baldwin received something that seemed to have eluded him for several decades: recognition as one of the greatest writers America has produced.

Once upon a time, in the early 1960s, he was hailed as the voice of the civil rights movement; his books were best sellers; his image was emblazoned on the covers of national magazines; he was interviewed on television and radio; politicians and leaders sought his advice. Then, in the late 1970s and 1980s, he became viewed essentially as an exile, living on a bucolic estate in the south of France, the diminishing voice of a bygone era, slowly growing faint, less relevant, out of touch with mainstream Reagan America. His last major work was published in 1979. While his importance as a public figure had never been in doubt, the literary merit of his work and its continued aesthetic relevance was up for debate.

But now, in early December 1987, at New York City's Cathedral of St. John the Divine—the largest Gothic cathedral in America—a great gathering of literary figures came to bid James Baldwin farewell, and an estimated five thousand people gathered in the streets. The event was notable not only for the attendees, but for the air of celebration, including much music— one of James Baldwin's abiding loves—spirituals and jazz and gospel, beginning with the rumble of a Yoruba death drum and ending with a recording of the author singing "Precious Lord," played on loudspeakers for the congregation. Along with the famous musicians and figures Baldwin called friends were the poets Maya Angelou and Amiri Baraka, novelist Paule Marshall, and many others.

His close friend, Pulitzer Prize winning novelist, William Styron said of Baldwin:

> Night after night Jimmy and I talked, drinking whisky through the hours until the chill dawn, and I understood that I was in the company of as marvelous an intelligence as I was ever likely to encounter.... He was spell-binding, and he told me more about the frustrations and anguish of being a black man in America than I had known until then, or perhaps wanted to know. (Troupe 45)

Another close friend and novelist, future Nobel laureate Toni Morrison, said of Baldwin that day:

> No one possessed or inhabited language for me the way you did. You made American English honest—genuinely inter-national. You exposed its secrets and reshaped it until it was truly modern dialogic, representative, humane. You stripped it of ease and false comfort and fake innocence and evasion and hypocrisy. And in place of deviousness was clarity. In place of soft plump lies was a lean, targeted power. In place of intellectual disingenuousness was what you called "exasperating egocentricity," you gave us undecorated truth. You replaced lumbering platitudes with an upright elegance. (Troupe 76)

The gathering wanted to acknowledge Baldwin's importance as a human being first and also as a friend and a great writer. The audience was reminded of Baldwin's importance as a literary voice in a time when African American letters were marginalized, in a time when the battle for civil rights shone an international light on the plight of the American Negro, thus giving Baldwin's eloquence and passion a rare platform. The critic

Horace A. Porter was present at the ceremony and would later write about it, quite vividly and movingly, in the epilogue to his 1989 book, *Stealing the Fire: The Art and Protest of James Baldwin*:

> The event had been breathtaking for me, the presumptuous literary critic. [One of Baldwin's early character's] hilltop fantasy, his glowing American dream, in Central Park had been made real.... Baldwin had prophetically spelled out, in his beginning, his magnificent end: "He would be, of all, the mightiest, the most beloved, the Lord's anointed; and he would live in this shining city which his ancestors had seen with longing from far away. For it was his; the inhabitants of the city had told him it was his; he had but to run down, crying, and they would take him to their hearts and show him wonders his eyes had never seen." (180)

If Martin Luther King Jr. had been the civil rights movement's leader, James Baldwin had been its prophet, like a figure from the Old Testament. Small, dark, an electrifying speaker, he functioned early in his literary journey much like Jeremiah calling out his nation's crimes and predicting a coming conflagration. His accomplishments—six novels and six notable works of nonfiction, as well as plays and short stories and other forms—would have been impressive for an American artist of any color.

But well before the late 1970s, certain critical refrains about his work began to recur: Baldwin has not lived up to his original promise as a novelist; Baldwin has squandered his vast talent on mere journalistic and essay writing, when he should have sequestered himself in an ivory tower and focused on purely aesthetic pursuits; in the long run Baldwin will best be remembered for his eloquent essays, but not for his fiction.

Baldwin's death in the late 1980s, however, began another stage in his literary journey. Without his physical presence, his writing would have to speak for itself. Critical essays, memoirs, and biographies began to emerge in the wake of his death. Was James Baldwin's writing as important as his message? Outside the tumultuous times in which it was conceived, does his fiction have any artistic resonance? The noted literary critic Harold Bloom had written just before Baldwin's death in 1986:

> Whatever the ultimate canonical judgment upon James Baldwin's fiction may prove to be, his nonfictional work clearly has permanent status in American literature. Baldwin seems to me the most considerable moral essayist now writing in the United States, and is comparable to George Orwell as a prose Protestant in stance....Unlike Emerson, Baldwin lacks the luxury of detachment, since he speaks, not for a displaced Yankee majority, but for a sexual minority within a racial minority, indeed for an aesthetic minority among black homosexuals. (1)

The publication in 1998 of two volumes of Baldwin's work by the Library of America was the most canonical recognition that Baldwin's work had yet received. This nonprofit institution annually publishes a few handsome volumes by the United States' most enduring writers and has come the closest to establishing an agreed-upon national literary canon. Their publication of *James Baldwin: Collected Essays* and *James Baldwin: Early Novels and Stories* seems to have permanently placed Baldwin among writers like William Faulkner, Edith Wharton, John Steinbeck, Robert Frost, Thomas Paine, Thomas Jefferson, Ralph Waldo Emerson, his beloved Henry James, and many others. Perhaps the more dismissive voices had been a tad premature.

And, in 2004, an even clearer sign of canonical acceptance was Baldwin's inclusion on a U.S. Postal Service first-class stamp. The image was a painting by the artist Thomas Blackshear II, based on a black-and-white photograph taken in 1938. As a vice president of the U.S. Postal Service said about Baldwin in a 2004 news release: "His fervent voice in 20th century American literature forced us to think about issues affecting our great nation, and his leadership in the civil rights movement continues to be an inspiration today" (United States Postal Service Press Release. July 8, 2004. Stamp News Release Number: 04–045).

James Arthur Baldwin was born on August 2, 1924, at Harlem Hospital in New York City. His mother, Emma Berdis Jones, was unmarried, and had moved to New York from Deals Island, Maryland, just after World War I. (Baldwin did not learn of his illegitimacy until his teenage years.)

In 1927 Berdis married David Baldwin, a laborer and Baptist preacher, originally from Bunkie, Louisiana, who had come to New York in 1919. Baldwin would later write of the man he called his father:" No one, including my father, seems to have known exactly how old he was, but his mother had been born in slavery" (*Price of the Ticket* 128). David Baldwin's mother, Barbara, lived with the family in Harlem until her death in 1930; from her, young James heard many stories of the post–Civil War South, stories that captured his imagination. These stories of hardships and fear and lynching gave the boy a horror-story vision of this place called the South.

David and Berdis Baldwin would have eight children altogether: three boys (James, George, Wilmer, and David) and five girls (Barbara, Gloria, Ruth, Elizabeth, and Paula Maria). David's eldest son, (by another woman) Samuel, was driven away from the family by his father in 1932.

While working at a bottle factory on Long Island, David Baldwin would preach in storefront churches throughout Harlem on Sundays and on weeknights as well. This period being the height of the Great Depression, he never managed to earn sufficient money for his family—Berdis worked as a cleaning woman and a laundress—and his frustrations mounted, year by year. He became a hard, difficult, and bitter man. The family moved frequently, from apartment to apartment all over Harlem, often unable to afford the rent. Many times the family had to go on charity relief. At Thanksgiving, James and his brother George would queue on the street outside the famed Cotton Club for free turkey dinners. "I began to wonder what it could have been like for such a man to have had nine children whom he could barely feed. He used to make little jokes about our poverty, which never, of course, seemed very funny to us; they could not have seemed funny to him, either." (*PT* 130).

David Baldwin's bitterness was usually visited upon his children. He would beat them upon little or no provocation, and James received the most severe punishments—often, he felt, due to his illegitimacy. David Baldwin called James the ugliest child he had ever seen, and nicknamed him Frog Eyes. But Baldwin was certain David Baldwin loved his children, though at times they were too frightened of him to realize it or to return his affections.

> He could be chilling in the pulpit and indescribably cruel in his personal life and he was certainly the most bitter man I have ever met; yet it must be said that there was something else in him, buried in him, which lent him his tremendous power and, even, a rather crushing charm....He claimed to be proud of his blackness but it had also been the cause of much humiliation and it had fixed bleak boundaries to his life. (*PT* 128–29)

Many was the night James Baldwin cried himself to sleep.

His mother soon noticed that Jimmy—as he was called by his family—was a remarkably smart child. He began reading early and often. As the oldest child he was expected to help with his younger siblings, which he did with great cheer, but he always found time to read. As a boy he had already developed a serious taste for Charles Dickens, Fyodor Dostoyevsky, and what he would later call his favorite book for many years, *Uncle Tom's Cabin* by Harriet Beecher Stowe. "I read books like they were some weird kind of food" (Weatherby 15). But David Baldwin greatly disfavored Jimmy's insatiable thirst for book-learning. The minister distrusted the secular world at large, and felt that to foster intellectual ambition in a black boy was to doom him to failure and disappointment. David Baldwin was only happy when he saw James reading the Bible.

Baldwin would go on to impress his teachers at Frederick Douglass Junior High School, among whom was the celebrated African American poet Countee Cullen. Baldwin wrote many stories and essays and articles for the school magazine, *The Douglass Pilot*.

At the age of fourteen, Baldwin became a young minister at the Fireside Pentecostal Assembly, a storefront church in Harlem. Loud, chaotic, full of music and prayers and personal testimonies, this world had enormous impact on James Baldwin. It was an escape, in some ways, from his harrowing home-life. Each Sunday and on certain weeknights, he would speak—preach—extemporaneously, drawing on an already formidable knowledge of the Bible and on what in the argot of Pentecostalism is called "the spirit," or divine inspiration, the Holy Spirit speaking through an individual, directly to the parishioners.

> That was the most frightening time of my life, and quite the most dishonest, and the resulting hysteria lent great passion to my sermons—for a while. I relished the attention and the relative immunity from punishment that my new status gave me.... The church was very exciting. It took a long time for me to disengage myself from this excitement, and on the blindest, most visceral level, I never really have.... There was no music like that music, no drama like the drama of the saints rejoicing, the sinners moaning, the tambourines racing, and all those voices coming together and crying holy unto the Lord. (*PT* 345)

Though this activity pleased his father, it also would become a sore spot between them, as, week-by-week, young preacher James Baldwin began to eclipse his father in the pulpit.

This is the world he would later write about with such vivid tenderness in his first novel, *Go Tell It on the Mountain* (1953), an achingly autobiographical work. In that book young John Grimes grows up in poverty in a large family in Harlem and, at fourteen, becomes a child minister. Grimes is even called Frog Eyes in the novel. The book is one of our best evocations of African-American interwar life and of the world of the so-called Holy Rollers, a world of religious ecstasy and transplanted Southern culture. Baldwin would later say of that world: "I was born into a Southern community displaced into the streets of New York. And what did we bring with us? What did my father bring with him? He brought with him his Bible. He, and others like him, with their Bibles and their hymn books, managed to rent a space which had been a store and took out the fixtures, built a pulpit, got a piano, a tambourine—and it became a church" (Campbell 9).

For high school James Baldwin attended the notable DeWitt Clinton High School in the Bronx, a public school known for producing a great stream of outstanding Americans: statesmen, scientists, captains of industry, publishers, authors. Outside Harlem for the first time, Baldwin had to deal with people from many other backgrounds and cultures, a great many of whom were the sons and daughters of European immigrants. In their midst he stood out for being exceptionally dark, exceptionally poor, the only child minister—and also exceptionally gifted. This was also the time Baldwin began to explore his sexuality, realizing he was probably gay. Though he dated girls, he told a friend at the time that he hadn't made up his mind yet about his sexuality, though a great many, including his own mother, already assumed he was gay. "Honey, I knew when Jimmy was a little boy," his brother David once told a biographer. "Of course we just knew" (Weatherby 15).

In truth, Baldwin was a so-so student, despising math and often failing to study, usually because of his father's harangues or because he was spending so much time in the pulpit, which kept him from his homework, and also working a part-time job to help out his family. Nonetheless, it was clear that Baldwin showed huge talent as a writer, contributing stories, poems and plays to the school's magazine, *The Magpie*, which he served as editor in his senior year. One of his closest friends at the time, Emile Capouya, who would go on to become an important editor and publisher, recalled that Baldwin was "an obvious genius. He was also very holy in those days" (Weatherby 24).

Around this time, during his last years in high school, the many conflicting elements in his life began to come to a head for James Baldwin. He met two men who would cause him to confront deep truths about himself and to ask himself about his future and about his destiny. One of these men was the African American artist Beauford Delaney, an accomplished painter and portraitist. He was gay. The thirty-nine-year-old Delaney lived in a studio in New York's Greenwich Village, and Baldwin visited him there often. Baldwin would later say that Delaney taught him how to "see." "I repeat that Beauford never gave me any lectures, but he didn't have to—he expected me to accept and respect the value placed upon me" (*PT* xii). Delaney would remain a lifelong friend and mentor.

Of the other man, Baldwin would later write in the essay "Here Be Dragons":

> Shortly after I turned sixteen, a Harlem racketeer, a man of about thirty-eight, fell in love with me, and I will be grateful to that man until the day I die. I showed him all my poetry, because I had no one else in Harlem to show it to, and even now, I sometimes wonder what on earth his friends could have been thinking, confronted with stingy-brimmed, mustachioed, razor-toting Poppa and skinny, popeyed Me when he walked me (rarely) into various shady joints, I drinking ginger ale, he drinking brandy. (*PT* 681)

Baldwin was beginning to see the church as a Band-Aid for the ills of racial discrimination and poverty and injustice. "I became more guilty and more frightened, and kept all this bottled up inside me, and naturally, inescapably, one night, when this woman had finished preaching, everything came roaring, screaming, crying out.... All I really remember is the pain, the unspeakable pain; it was as though I were yelling up to Heaven and Heaven would not hear me" (*PT* 343–4). His new appreciation for how important art was in his life, his recognition of his sexuality, and his growing ambivalence with the church led Baldwin, in 1941, to preach his last sermon. He had retired as a preacher at the tender age of seventeen, but his ministry, in many ways, was just getting underway.

The ensuing years were difficult for Baldwin, but crucial for his later development. He moved away from his father's home, though continuing to contribute money to the family. He worked for a time in Belle Mead, New Jersey, laying railroad track for $80 a week—a relatively good-paying job for a college-less young man in 1941. But Baldwin found the world of work and racial codes and segregation oppressive in the extreme, and he tried to battle it head-on by going into segregated restaurants and Whites Only venues, by confronting individuals directly, and by other acts of civil disobedience. He would write about his state of mind at the time in "Notes of a Native Son" as "some dread, chronic disease...[a] rage in the blood....I saw nothing very clearly but I did see this: that my life, my real life, was in danger, and not from anything other people might do but from the hatred I carried in my own heart" (*PT* 135). Altogether these events ultimately led to his firing after close to a year of struggle. Despite the initial shock and aggravation of being jobless, Baldwin in many ways saw his dismissal as a blessing, and decided to redouble his efforts in the world of writing.

Soon after Baldwin's return to Harlem, David Baldwin died, having been institutionalized in July 1943, quite mad with paranoia. He finally succumbed to tuberculosis. That same day his youngest daughter, Paula Maria, was born.

Three days later, while David Baldwin's funeral was being held, a riot broke out in Harlem. Baldwin would use this strange confluence of events to write one of his most powerful essays, "Notes of a Native Son." Surely one of the best essays Baldwin ever wrote—from a writer who excelled at the art form—it crystallized his greatest strengths as an essay writer: the sermonic tone; the mastery of complex syntax, with long, baroque, often periodic sentences; the use of autobiographical material to launch into larger societal themes; and the preoccupation not only with race, but with the overarching themes of Christianity—love and what it costs, justice, redemption, and an abiding sense of hope for the future in the face of seemingly dire circumstances.

But more than anything else, "Notes of a Native Son" is an attempt to reconcile with his father in death, to understand the hatred James Baldwin carried around in his own heart, and to see how that anger was not his alone:

> None of this was doing anybody any good. It would have been better to have left the plate glass as it had been and the goods lying in the stores....Harlem had needed something to smash. To smash something is the ghetto's chronic need. Most of the time it is the members of the ghetto who smash each other, and themselves. But as long as the ghetto walls

are standing there will always come a moment when these outlets do not work. (*PT* 144)

And later, like the minister he would remain, Baldwin concluded:

It began to seem that one would have to hold in the mind forever two ideas which seemed to be in opposition. The first idea was acceptance, the acceptance, totally without rancor, of life as it is, and men as they are: in the light of this idea, it goes without saying that injustice is a commonplace. But this did not mean that one could be complacent, for the second idea was of equal power: that one must never, in one's own life, accept these injustices as commonplace but must fight them with all one's strength. This fight begins, however, in the heart and it now had been laid to my charge to keep my own heart free of hatred and despair. (*PT* 145)

Baldwin moved to Greenwich Village and embarked on his new life as a writer while keeping body and soul together by working as a waiter. He thrived on the bohemian world of artists and actors and general wartime revelers at liberty in the big city. He also began in earnest to work on his first novel, which he called "Crying Holy."

During this time Baldwin made some of his most important alliances and friendships. One was with a young actor from the Midwest named Marlon Brando, who would become his roommate and lifelong friend. Baldwin would later tell his biographer: "I think I was about twenty so it was probably 1944. . . . I had never met any white man like Marlon. He was immensely talented—a real creative force—and totally unconventional and independent, a beautiful cat" (Weatherby 57). The other was with the most famous and successful African American writer in America, Richard Wright, author of the best-selling and award-winning novel *Native Son* (1940).

The native Mississippian was living in Brooklyn at the time, and welcomed Baldwin at his home. Baldwin impressed Wright, who agreed to read the pages from his novel-in-progress. Through Wright's intervention, Baldwin was awarded a Eugene F. Saxon

Fellowship of $500, and Wright's publisher, Harper & Brothers, optioned the novel for possible publication. But after months of work, the novel did not come together, and the publisher passed on the manuscript. Nor could he find other publishers to take it. This rejection sent Baldwin into a deep depression.

But the conviviality and encouragement of Greenwich Village soon revived Baldwin, and he set about proving himself as a writer. With the help of journalists and editors with whom he socialized in his downtown life, he eventually got magazine assignments. His first professional published work was a review of a collection of Maxim Gorki's short stories that appeared in the April 12, 1947, issue of the *Nation* magazine. He would write book reviews for the *Nation* and the *New Leader*. Baldwin's first full-length essay—"Harlem Ghetto: Winter 1948," addressing the idea of black anti-Semitism—came out in the February 1948 issue of *Commentary*. His first work of professional fiction was published ten months later, "Previous Condition," in the same magazine. Baldwin was gaining the attention and respect from some of New York's most important intellectuals, people like Sol Levitas, Lionel Trilling, Randall Jarrell, and Elliott Cohen. Baldwin worried that the accolades he received were not just due to his status as a brilliant, young writer who had not gone to college, but to the fact that he was black. He also worried that he was being boxed into writing mostly on African American themes.

In 1940 Baldwin had received a $1,500 Rosenwald Fellowship, based on an idea for a nonfiction book that never came to fruition. This further failure, and his inability to successfully bring together his novel, caused Baldwin continued frustration and even more bitterness toward American society. When the man he considered his best friend, Eugene Worth, committed suicide by jumping from the George Washington Bridge, Baldwin blamed that, too, on racism and the way the United States was bent on the dehumanization of black men. He would later tell the *Paris Review* about this time: "I still had to deal with the streets and the authorities and the cold. I knew what it meant to be white and I knew what it meant to be a nigger, and I knew what was going to happen to me. My luck was running out. I was going to jail, I was going to kill somebody or be killed" (Standley and Pratt 233). Baldwin decided to leave the country.

With what was left from his fellowship money, he purchased a one-way ticket to France. On November 11, 1948, he arrived in Paris with only $40 to his name.

At the time, among African Americans, France had a reputation as welcoming black artists with open arms. The great artiste Josephine Baker, great jazz musicians like Sidney Bechet, novelists (including now Richard Wright), and scores of others were known to be flourishing in Paris. The cost of living was cheap; the food was grand; there was no segregation. But Baldwin, who knew very few people in Paris and had little prospects (he spoke no French at the time), found his situation became quickly dire.

Though his $40 only lasted three days, his friends helped Baldwin find a cheap hotel, and took him about to all the cafes and bars and restaurants and introduced him to important members of what was famously known as the American colony in Paris: writers, artists, journalists, aspiring artists, and artists manque, a heady bohemian world of expatriates, many of whom were World War II veterans now exploring this grand old world so distinct and multifarious compared to the small-town provincialism of the United States.

On his first day in Paris, Baldwin was reacquainted with Richard Wright at the famed Deux Magots café. Wright greeted him, "Hey boy." Wright had quickly become the darling of the French intellectual set, then ruled by the philosophers Jean-Paul Sartre and Simone de Beauvoir. Baldwin developed a distaste for the much-vaunted clique straight away, feeling that they were condescending to Wright and other blacks, treating them as exotic curiosities rather than as equals.

Before long Baldwin became dependent on the American colony, often borrowing money for the bare necessities: food and drink and rent. As a result he found himself resented and resentful for his dependence. The little money he was able to make at odd jobs flew out of his hands; after selling the little he had of worth, he found himself penniless and ill in the cold Parisian winter. Soon he came down with pneumonia and survived only through the largesse of the Corsican woman who owned the

hotel where he was staying. She fed him, nursed him, and for-
gave his bills.

Baldwin soon came to realize that though French society did
not traffic in the same racial prejudice as his homeland, class and
social status, and even race, very much remained as factors to be
negotiated in Europe. The Arabs of Algeria and other Africans
from the French colonies were at the bottom of the French
social and economic ladder, and, as Baldwin soon discovered,
they suffered in much the way his people suffered in America.
"In France, the Algerian is the nigger" (Standley and Pratt 152).
Baldwin identified with this segment of society and would come
to live in what was known as the Arab quarter of Paris. Baldwin
even spent a few days in prison in 1949, an experience he'd later
write about in the essay "Equal in Paris."

As one could imagine, Baldwin got little novel-writing done
during this difficult time, but he did manage to finish an essay
for the English-language magazine *Zero*. One of his seminal literary essays, "Everybody's Protest Novel," reassessed his once-
favorite novel, *Uncle Tom's Cabin*. His thinking had changed over
the years, and he now felt the book was more agitprop than art.
It was a badly written book, he said, whose main aim was the
abolition of slavery, laudable but not enough to qualify as art
in his opinion. The characters were cardboard, the language
was subpar. What was needed, according to Baldwin, was an
art that addressed blackfolk as full and complex human beings,
not as ideas. "In overlooking, denying, evading his complexity—
which is nothing more than the disquieting complexity of ourselves—we are diminished and we perish; only within the web
of ambiguity, paradox, this hunger, danger, darkness, can we
find at once ourselves and the power that will free us from ourselves" (PT 33). To create art, Baldwin says, is the true business of
the novelist; to do otherwise is to reduce people to wooden characters and to reduce the truth. As an example of this sort of protest writing, Baldwin singles out Richard Wright and his *Native
Son* character Bigger Thomas. In the novel the young black man
accidentally kills a young white woman, is put on trial, and ultimately is sentenced to death. His case becomes a cause célèbre
among the political leftists, and, in the novel, Bigger Thomas

has a revelation about his place in society and the cause of all his troubles: racism. The solution: socialism. (Wright's involvement with the American socialist movement has been well documented.) Bigger Thomas, according to Baldwin is "Uncle Tom's descendant, flesh of his flesh, so exactly apposite a portrait that, when the books are placed together, it seems that the contemporary Negro novelist and the dead New England woman are locked together in a deadly timeless battle" (*PT* 33). Baldwin was looking for transcendence in his novels, not political protest.

On the same day the essay was published, Baldwin happened to run into Richard Wright in a café, and the two got into a row. Baldwin denied that he had meant Wright harm, but Wright felt his young protégé had sought to injure him and damage his reputation. "It never occurred to me," Baldwin would later write. "I thought I was being a bright honors student. I thought we could have a discussion about that. His reaction made me reexamine everything" (*PT* 271).

(Baldwin would go on to write two more essays about Wright and his so-called protest fiction: "Many Thousands Gone," in 1951, and "Alas, Poor Richard," published in 1961, after Wright's death. The latter was Baldwin's attempt to explain himself, to reconcile what looked like not only ingratitude but a personal vendetta. "We had not become friends, because I was really too young to be his friend and adored him too much and was too afraid of him" [*PT* 271]. The underlying psychological tension between the two writers remains apparent, despite Baldwin's protestations to the contrary. He admits in the essay that Wright had become a father figure to him; perhaps, in the depths of his psyche, Baldwin was ridding himself of another oppressive father. Wright and Baldwin never reconciled.)

Baldwin's circumstances changed dramatically when, in the late winter of 1949, he met an attractive young Swiss of seventeen named Lucien Happersberger. Tall and slim and very charming, he had run away from his bourgeois family to become an artist. Also with next to no money, Happersberger became an ally of Baldwin's. Though both of the young men had been seeing men and women, a bond developed between them—two rascals on the make in postwar Paris—a bond that buoyed Baldwin. They would meet each day, pool their little money, swap stories, drink together, encourage each other.

But by late 1951 Baldwin seemed at his wit's end. His health was on the brink of collapse, emotionally he was exhausted, and though he wanted nothing more than to finish his novel, his great dream, he seemed incapable of doing so. Happersberger took the reins and spirited Baldwin away to his family's chalet in the Swiss alpine village of Loèche-les-Bains. Baldwin would later write about this time in his essay "Stranger in the Village (1953)." He recounts that he had never felt more out of place or more exotic; the six hundred villagers would come up to touch him and rub his hair, making him feel even stranger. "In all this, in which it must be conceded there was the charm of genuine wonder and in which there was certainly no element of intentional unkindness, there was yet no suggestion that I was human: I was simply a living wonder" (PT 81).

Yet the landscape, which Baldwin found "bleak" and "forbidding," helped him concentrate his mind and focus on his main work at hand—that and a weekly fifty franc stipend from Lucien's father. Baldwin would play two Bessie Smith records over and over again and write. Three months later he had completed the novel he'd begun back in Greenwich Village about John Grimes and his Holy Roller family back in Harlem. He now called the book Go Tell it on the Mountain.

In February 1952 Baldwin sent his completed novel to a New York agent named Helen Strauss, and a few weeks later he got word that the publisher, Alfred A. Knopf—a company that had done well with a number of African American writers during the Harlem Renaissance—was interested in the book and in meeting with James Baldwin. With $500 he borrowed from his old roommate Marlon Brando, now a Broadway success and visiting Paris, Baldwin sailed back to New York in April, after four years of scrambling to survive.

Though Knopf was interested in publishing the novel and offered him a $1,000 advance, the editors wanted some significant changes made before they could publish the manuscript. Baldwin would later say that he felt the editors didn't understand the book very well and that he regretted making some of

the changes—like taking out any explicit reference to the protagonist's sexuality and slicing much of the religious material.
Nonetheless, he was in no position to refuse such an offer, and,
after returning to France, made the changes. At long last, the
book was finally accepted.

Considered by many critics to be Baldwin's best work of
fiction, *Go Tell it on the Mountain* (named after an old African
American spiritual) faithfully and lovingly recreates the Harlem
of his youth. The protagonist of the novel, John Grimes, remains
one of Baldwin's most impressive fictional characters, a stand-in
for himself, yet fully realized as a fourteen-year-old boy. The elements of Baldwin's youth are all there—the Pentecostal storefront churches, the large family, his embittered father (Gabriel in
the novel), the history of the South he had learned at his grandmother's knee, his own attraction to the Christian message, and
the tug of the secular world. The novel's language, though rich
and often lyrical, is marked by a vivid and concrete style that
has been compared at times to Hemingway, but also gives way
at times to the biblical rhetorical flashes with which Baldwin
would come to be so deeply associated. (Hemingway's own debt
to the King James version of the Bible has been often noted.) As
compelling as the Harlem sections of the novel are, the middle
section, "The Prayers of the Saints"—three chapters that tell the
stories of Gabriel, Florence, and Elizabeth, the father, mother,
and aunt of young John—is perhaps the most successful. Their
stories closely follow that of the adults who raised Baldwin, but
these chapters are also marvels of characterization and evoke
a world Baldwin did not know firsthand. A testament to his
abilities to imagine and shape a fictional world, the book would
establish him as a fine and serious novelist.

When the book came out in May 1953, the reception was
extremely positive. It was called by the *New York Times* "a striking first novel." *Time* magazine's reviewer said the church scenes
were as "compelling as anything that has turned up in a novel
this year." *The Saturday Review*: "Masterful." And *Commentary*'s
writer praised it as "[t]he most important novel written about the
American Negro" (Weatherby 104). On the strength of his first
novel, Baldwin received a prestigious Guggenheim Fellowship.

Next to be published, in 1955 by Beacon Press of Boston, was a collection of Baldwin's essays. *Notes of a Native Son* consisted of five older essays and five new essays written for the book, including the landmark title essay. The book contained his essay on Beecher Stowe and Wright, "Everybody's Protest Novel"; a review about the all-black musical *Carmen Jones*; essays about race and politics such as "The Harlem Ghetto" and "Journey to Atlanta"; and essays about Paris and black identity—most notably "A Question of Identity," where he talks about his kinship with Henry James and explores the idea of the being an expatriate: "If the American found in Europe only confusion, it would obviously be infinitely wiser for him to remain home. Hidden, however, in the heart of the confusion he encounters here is that which he came so blindly seeking: the terms on which he is related to his country, and his world" (*PT* 99).

The book received even more enthusiastic praise than had his novel. The great poet Langston Hughes (who had not been a fan of *Go Tell it on the Mountain*, which he found too precious in its prose) lauded Baldwin for being a "straight-from-the-shoulder writer" and found the book of essays both amusing and important. Ironically, Hughes also warned Baldwin against being too obsessed with matters of race and challenged him to "look at life purely as himself and for himself" (Campbell 94). A reviewer in *Commonweal* called Baldwin "the most eloquent Negro writing today" (Leeming 105).

From his school days, Baldwin had harbored ambitions of becoming a successful playwright. He had even studied drama while living in Greenwich Village. He now turned his hand at a play, which he finished in a few months. Like his first novel, *The Amen Corner* was centered around the minister Sister Margaret Alexander (a character heavily influenced by some of the powerful church mothers of his youth, particular one Mother Horn). Sister Margaret is torn between her husband, a jazz musician in trouble with the law, her son who is in danger of going wayward, and the imperatives of her ministry about the sins of the secular world. The play revisits the old obsessions of Baldwin's fire-and-brimstone Harlem youth, as well as gives voice to some of his most soaring rhetoric in the form of set pieces. Despite

discouragement from his agent and chilly responses from producers and directors in New York—African American plays were
considered hard sells for the theater-going public—Baldwin per-
severed. In 1954 a production went on in Washington, D.C., at
Howard University, a historically black college. Baldwin came
to Washington to aid the director, a poet, playwright, and university professor named Owen Dodson. This academic setting
was a heady brew for Baldwin, who remained insecure because
of his lack of a college education. But the students revered him
and hung on his every word, and Baldwin came away feeling
positive about the entire experience. In May 1955, the play ran for
ten nights to good notices, though it failed to gain the attention
of mainstream theater producers who were still not convinced
of the financial efficacy of the Negro theater.

James Baldwin's next literary adventure would not go so
swimmingly. For the last few years, he had been working on a
novel about two white men locked in a tumultuous love affair
in France. Baldwin dared to write from the point of view of a
Caucasian; moreover, he had the temerity to write about homosexuality with the suggestion that it was acceptable and on par
with heterosexuality. The one act was considered highly offen-
sive, the other unacceptable and illegal in most of the United
States.

His agent, Helen Strauss, suggested that he burn the manuscript, and their working relationship came to an end. Alfred
A. Knopf, his publisher, reacted with great distaste and firmly
rejected the book. A publisher in the United Kingdom, Michael
Joseph, felt differently, undeterred by the controversial material,
and published *Giovanni's Room* in 1956. An American publisher,
Dial Press, decided to take the chance as well.

In truth the book's tone is restrained, and the sexual content
is minimal at best. The novel is essentially a love story. A young
American, David, living in the world of the post–World War II
expatriates, falls in love with Giovanni, an Italian barkeeper in
Paris. But love is never easy. The prose here is poetic and rich;
the structure is nonlinear; and the relatively brief first-person
narrative remains a highlight of Baldwin's efforts as a writer of
modernist fiction.

The book received high praise, despite the fears of so many. Writing in the *New York Times*, Granville Hicks said of the book: "Mr. Baldwin writes of these matters with an unusual degree of candor and yet with such dignity and intensity that he is saved from sensationalism." Philip Rahv of the *Partisan Review* wrote: "It has been a long time since I have read anything as good by a younger American writer" (Weatherby 129).

Nine years after having left America, at long last, James Baldwin had attained a degree of success that had seemed out of his reach only three years before. He had the resources to travel back and forth to Europe and explore the continent beyond France. Magazines were giving him lucrative assignments for articles and essays.

During this time—a time in which the freedom movement among African Americans was reaching a fevered pitch, with landmark Supreme Court cases and sit-ins and boycotts, with the federal government's moves to force desegregation, and with local governments' resisting such moves—Baldwin began to write about what was becoming known as the civil rights movement, the latter-day culmination of actions that had begun after Emancipation in 1863.

His first visit to the American South was to Charlotte, North Carolina, in 1957. *Harper's* magazine had commissioned him to write about the federally mandated integration of schools. The initial goal was to have at least four black children in each all-white school. The article, "A Hard Kind of Courage" (the name was changed to "A Fly in the Buttermilk" when collected in *Nobody Knows My Name*), recreates the feelings of tension and violence in the air as black students were forced to walk gauntlets of jeering white students—and sometimes parents—while spit and stones were hurled at them.

Baldwin would also go to Little Rock, Arkansas, to cover the school desegregation there, and to Atlanta, Georgia, where he met the Reverend Martin Luther King Jr. for the first time. Baldwin instantly fell under King's spell, as so many had and would. They spoke the same King James biblical language and the language of American Protestants. King was not only exceptionally charming and intelligent, but carried a message of nonviolent protest and love, ideas that appealed mightily to Baldwin.

> But the Reverend King is not like any preacher I have ever met before. For one thing, to state it baldly, I liked him. It is rare that one likes a world-famous man—by the time they become world-famous they rarely like themselves, which may account for his antipathy. Yet King is immediately and tremendously winning, there is really no other word for it. (PT 145)

Baldwin would travel to Montgomery, Alabama, and hear King preach at the Dexter Avenue Baptist Church, and he got to see the damage done by bombs thrown at King's home.

During these visits to the South—Baldwin would travel to most of the southern states and write about his experiences there—he began to formulate and write about the kinship he felt with southern blacks, and his connection to them and to the land in which they fought. No longer did he see himself as simply a denizen of Harlem, but as a black American. He identified with the shared history, the fear; he identified with the religious passion; he identified with the thirst for freedom. In many ways writing firsthand about the people and their struggle during the civil rights movement deepened, enriched, and focused Baldwin's voice in a way that might not have happened without those eyewitness experiences. He had found a role he was uniquely gifted to do.

Baldwin wrote and spoke more and helped raise money for civil rights groups like the Southern Christian Leadership Council, the National Association for the Advancement of Colored People, the Student Non-Violent Coordination Committee, and many others. The time he had spent in his youth as a minister had prepared him abundantly to orate with great power and passion, and audiences responded to him with great enthusiasm. Many people in the media would begin to call James Baldwin the spokesman of the civil rights movement—though he held no elected office, ran no organization, and led no marches or actions. Baldwin himself denied any such lofty title: "I'm still trying to speak just for me, not for twenty million people," he told journalist and critic Nat Hentoff in 1963 (Standley and Pratt 33). These activities also maintained a constant tension with his writing that harkened back to his criticisms of Richard Wright: Should Baldwin be more focused on making art and spend less time writing about race and politics? Or did he have a responsibility to give voice to the struggles he was witnessing?

This period was one of the most productive of James Baldwin's life. He kept a small apartment now on Horatio Street, in Greenwich Village. Along with the fundraisers, television shows, and radio interviews he did, he also wrote a stage adaptation of *Giovanni's Room*; a great many magazine assignments and essays; short stories; and an ambitious third novel that was a cauldron for all his ideas on interracial and bisexual love.

His next published book, however, was another work of nonfiction, a book that gathered the best of his writings about the civil rights movement, as well as essays about culture and art. The thirteen pieces covered a wide range of topics, from eyewitness reports of the segregated South and civil rights actions to essays about Harlem, André Gide, Nobel laureate William Faulkner, Ingmar Bergman, Norman Mailer (with whom he had an ongoing argument which he wrote about in an essay entitled, "The Black Boy Looks at the White Boy"), and his once-mentor, Richard Wright.

Nobody Knows My Name: More Notes of a Native Son came out in 1961 to excellent reviews and became Baldwin's first best seller—a rarity for a collection of essays—a status that endured for over six months. Esteemed literary critic Alfred Kazin wrote: "This is the book of a deeply troubled man. The spiritual autobiography of someone who hopes, by confronting more than one beast on his way, to see whether his fear is entirely necessary" (Leeming 186). Without argument, James Baldwin was now the best-known and most important black writer in America.

This escalating fame made Baldwin's life resemble that of a popular entertainer more than that of a serious writer. Now there were more parties, more commitments for fundraisers, more media interviews, more late nights in restaurants and bars. Baldwin's heavy drinking became legendary. He tried to escape

New York and the social swirl, going to work at his Dial Press editor's home on one occasion and on another at the Connecticut home of friend and novelist William Styron. But, as Baldwin would put it, "People always seemed to know where I was hiding my typewriter. They were always dropping by at all times of the day and night. . . . I had to get away" (Weatherby 177).

Back in Paris he found the situation was no less hectic, and he simply enjoyed socializing too much to turn a deaf ear to knocks at the door inviting him to come out and play. It would be in Istanbul, Turkey, in a rented apartment overlooking the Bosporus, where he would finally find enough space and time to concentrate on his work. On December 10, 1961, he finished the novel that had been haunting him for six years.

His most complex work to date, *Another Country* (1962) really did try to bind together all the various strains of Baldwin's major obsessions: race, gender, sexuality, social class—black men, white men, black women, white woman. It was his artistic manifesto about the demons and angels at war in America: Dickensian in scope, Balzacian in social scale, and Jamesian in architecture. It included some of the best prose he had written to date. Set largely in Baldwin's bohemian, late-1950s New York, *Another Country* embraces Harlem, Greenwich Village, and the American colony of Paris. In many ways the most important character in the novel is the city of his birth. The final chapter begins:

> The sun struck, on steel, on bronze, on stone, on glass, on the gray water far beneath them, on the turret tops and the flashing windshields of crawling cars, on the incredible highways, stretching and snarling and turning for mile upon mile upon mile, on the houses, square and high, low and gabled, and on their howling antennae, on the sparse, weak trees, and on those towers, in the distance, on the city of New York. (363)

Aside from the city, the five main characters—who are not just ideas, but fully formed individuals—mirror that spectrum: Rufus Scott is a black jazz drummer; his sister, Ida, is a radiant jazz singer; Vivaldo Moore, a white man and an unpublished novelist, is Ida's love; but Eric, a white man and an actor is also the lover of both Vivaldo and Rufus; in turn, Eric's married lover is Cass, a white woman. This is a multivalent cast of characters, indeed, mixed and matched and made to love and hate one another in intriguing, often illuminating duets and trios, dramatic, melodramatic, and as compelling as any nineteenth-century novel of social mores.

Just as when he was a child minister, Baldwin's main theme in the book is love and its complicated, demanding, confusing, but ultimately salvific power: Love is the only answer to this racial mess we've gotten ourselves into. Significantly, the character who appears to be the main character in the novel, Rufus, a fiercely attractive and troubled black man, commits suicide after commanding the stage for over the first fifth of the novel—a bold and risky move on Baldwin's part. It is a loud echo of his friend Eugene Worth's suicide and, perhaps, represents Baldwin's attempt to make sense of that traumatic experience:

> He stood at the center of the bridge and it was freezing cold. He raised his eyes to heaven. He thought, You bastard, you motherfucking bastard. Ain't I your baby, too? He began to cry. Something in Rufus which could not break shook him like a rag doll and splashed salt water all over his face and filled his throat and his nostrils with anguish. He knew the pain would never stop. He could never go down into the city again. He dropped his head as though someone had struck him and looked down at the water. It was cold and the water was cold. (78)

Hence the characters left in Rufus's wake are called not to make hollow paeans to romantic love, but to grapple with actual connections, actual lives, the messy business of actual flesh and blood, love and death. The characters suffer, and ultimately Baldwin is too much of a realist to tie up all the knots in a soaringly romantic fashion. But he does leave them with glimmers of possibility, and leaves the reader to ponder about such hopes. Fear is the killer, Baldwin says; love takes courage and hard work.

When *Another Country* was published in 1962, it became his greatest success commercially. Though the reviews were not uniformly glowing (some would call it pornography—it was banned in Louisiana for being obscene), most found the book a fascinating success, published in a time when its topics were on everyone's lips. The writer for the *New York Times* wrote that "forty years after T. S. Eliot published 'The Waste Land' in verse Mr. Baldwin has given us a prose version of human desolation in a very different manner and with far less obscure symbolism" (Leeming 205). *Time* magazine hailed Baldwin as "one of the brashest, brightest, most promising young writers in America." Mark Shorer said it was "one of the most powerful novels of our time" (Weatherby 190). All the reviews were not glowing—in fact, an equal number of reviews declared it poorly written, loosely constructed, tedious, and too sex-filled. Norman Mailer, in an essay later to appear in his infamous collection *Advertisements for Myself*, suggested that Saul Bellow had done more to illuminate the African American psyche than had Baldwin.

Regardless, the book remained near the top of best-seller lists for weeks in 1962, and in 1963, when the paperback was released, it became the second largest-selling book of that year.

At the suggestion of William Shawn, the longtime editor of *The New Yorker*, James Baldwin wrote a piece about the Nation of Islam, commonly known as the Black Muslim movement. The most popular leader of the group was a young man of great charisma, Malcolm X, who was gaining great attention for his fiery speeches and controversial ideas (he was not an advocate of nonviolence at the time) and who was often seen to be in opposition with Martin Luther King Jr. But the head of the organization was a man named Elijah Muhammad, one of the founders of the organization, which combined strains of traditional Islam with a mantra of black pride, racial separatism, and economic self-sufficiency. Baldwin visited the Honorable Elijah Muhammed at his mansion in Chicago in August 1961.

The resulting article, "Down at the Cross," is an extended sermon of sorts, a grand, sweeping manifesto about America's racial strife that crystallized Baldwin's major ideas in one place. Baldwin used the opportunity of writing about the Nation of Islam to bring to bear his own autobiography, providing insights into Protestant Christianity and how it came to succor his own psyche just as the Nation of Islam succored the black youth who were joining the new religious movement in droves. He wrote of the moral appeal and justification of much of the bellicose rhetoric used by the Honorable Elijah Muhhamed and by Malcolm X; he wrote of the causes of hatred and the need for pride; and he wrote of his admiration for the discipline that the Black Muslims promoted. But in the end, Baldwin found himself disagreeing with the Nation of Islam's tracts and foresaw doom down that road. He believed that to embrace the same hatred and to call for the same separatism that white supremacists advocated would be to learn nothing from the ongoing civil rights movement. "Whoever debases others is debasing himself," Baldwin writes. He then becomes a prophet for what must occur to heal the racial wounds of America:

> The only thing white people have that black people need, or should want, is power—and no one holds power forever. White people cannot, in the generality, be taken as models of how to live. Rather, the white man is himself in sore need of new standards, which will release him from his confusion and place him once again in the fruitful communion with the depths of his own being. And I repeat: The price of liberation of the white people is the liberation of the blacks—the total liberation, in the cities, in the towns, before the law, and in the mind. (PT 375)

The onus of solving this problem lay at the feet of not only black America, but also white America. Together, black folk and white folk had to face—fully face—the ills of the past and do the work of re-creating American society as a whole. To fail, Baldwin writes, would be catastrophic: "Any attempt we make to oppose these outbursts of energy is tantamount to signing our death warrant" (PT 373). He ends his peroration with a resounding optimism, a sense of the possible:

> If we—and now I mean the relatively conscious whites and the relatively conscious blacks, who must, like lovers, insist on, or create, the consciousness of the others—do not falter

in our duty now, we may be able, handful that we are, to end the racial nightmare, and achieve our country, and change the history of the world. If we do not now dare everything, the fulfillment of that prophecy, re-created from the Bible in song by a slave, is upon us: "God gave Noah the rainbow sign, No more water, the fire next time!" (*PT* 379)

The 20,000-word essay, entitled "Letter from a Region of My Mind," was published in its entirety, taking up most of *The New Yorker*'s November 17, 1962, issue. The article caused a great stir, selling out at the newsstands almost instantly, and Baldwin's publisher, Dial Press, moved with great haste to publish it in book form. With the addition of a brief letter to his nephew, "My Dungeon Shook," originally published in *The Progressive*, as the introduction, the book, *The Fire This Time*, was one of the biggest sellers of 1963. Baldwin received $65,000 for the paperback edition, which was also a huge best seller. *Time* magazine put James Baldwin on its cover: "In the United States today there is not another writer, black or white, who expresses with such poignancy and abrasiveness the dark realities of the racial ferment in North and South" (Weatherby 205).

That year Baldwin—who was now, despite his protestations, considered a significant voice for black America—was involved in a much talked about meeting with Robert Kennedy, U.S. attorney general and brother of the president. Kennedy had called for a meeting with Baldwin and other black leaders, and they met on May 24, 1963, at a Kennedy family apartment in New York. In addition to Baldwin, those present included Kenneth Clark, noted educator and psychologist; Edwin Berry, director of the Chicago Urban League; Lorraine Hansberry, the playwright of *A Raisin in the Sun*; the singers and actors Lena Horne and Harry Belafonte; Clarence Jones, one of Martin Luther King's attorneys; and, significantly, Jerome Smith, a young black activist who had been badly beaten during civil rights protests in the South. Martin Luther King Jr. had been invited, but was unable to attend on such short notice.

It is important to note that the legacy of Robert Kennedy—his remembrance after his assassination in 1968—has tended to focus largely on his final years, when he had become deeply interested in the plight of the poor and disenfranchised, in social justice and equality. In truth Robert Kennedy underwent one of the most dramatic public transformations in U.S. political history. He had begun his journey as a reportedly haughty and arrogant millionaire's son, working for Senator Joe McCarthy as assistant counsel of the Senate Permanent Subcommittee on Investigations in the 1950s. As attorney general, he had discouraged the president, his brother, from getting too deeply involved in the civil rights movement—this was the Robert Kennedy who met with these prominent African Americans in 1963.

The meeting did not go well. Kennedy wanted specific ideas on how to relieve poverty in northern cities, but the participants lectured the attorney general about the gamut of problems faced by black folks throughout the country and accused him and his brother of moving too slowly and not doing enough. The argument got heated. Kennedy felt personally attacked and reacted with anger, becoming more and more defensive. At one point Smith told the attorney general not only that he was disaffected with the idea of nonviolence, but that if ever called to fight for his country he would "never! never! never!" do it (Weatherby 223). Kennedy attacked the young man's patriotism, which in turn provoked shouts in defense from the other black people in the room. Robert Kennedy would later tell his biographer, Arthur Schlesinger: "They seemed possessed. They reacted as a unit. It was impossible to make contact with them." The meeting ended in frustration and hurt feelings, with little solved and with much bewilderment (Weatherby 224). Baldwin later spoke with the *New York Times* about the meeting and put an upbeat spin on what had been a fraught encounter, saying that he felt the attorney general had his heart in the right place. "Despair is a sin," he said. "I believe that. It is easy to be bleak about the human race, but there are people who have proved to me that we can be better than we are" (Weatherby 228).

Later that year, Medgar Evers, a leader of the National Association for the Advancement of Colored People in Jackson, Mississippi, about whom Baldwin had written about in *Notes of A Native Son*, was assassinated in his front yard. President John F. Kennedy went on television that night to underscore his commitment to civil rights. In November of that year, the president himself was assassinated. Baldwin lamented the killing: "You could argue with him. He could hear. He began to see. There was no reason for him, a Boston millionaire's son, to know more about blacks than anybody else. But he could listen" (Weatherby 234). Baldwin, whose views about the racial problems of America had always centered around the notions of mutual comity, recognition, and reasoning, was finding it hard to keep his head high. Earlier that same year, on August 28, 1963, he had attended the famous March on Washington for Jobs and Freedom. Initially he had been slated to speak before Martin Luther King Jr., but, for no given reason, was taken off the list of speakers. Baldwin took the exclusion personally, wondering if it were due to his open homosexuality, no doubt an affront to many of the members of the archly religious and largely conservative Southern Christian Leadership Conference (SCLC), one of the main sponsors of the event. (Ironically, the main organizer, without whom many believe the march might not have been a success, was a man named Bayard Rustin, also gay and also a thorn in the side of the SCLC, but whom the Reverend King found indispensable.)

But successes were still in store for Baldwin. His first Broadway production was mounted in April 1964. *Blues for Mister Charlie* is baldly political, but no less effective for being so. It is the story of the murder of a young black man and its aftermath in 1955 Mississippi. His killer, a white racist, is acquitted by an all white jury. Directed by Burgess Meredith and starring Rip Torn, the play ran for four months.

Baldwin's first and only collection of short stories, *Going to Meet the Man*, was published in 1965. Though the reviews were not his best, a few of the eight stories would go on to become anthology standards. "Sonny's Blues" is the story of two brothers, one a talented jazz musician. "This Morning, This Evening, So Soon," considered to be Baldwin's best short story, a form he did not practice much, is about a black jazz singer in the world of post–World War II Europe, a world Baldwin had come to know intimately. The title story, something of a tour de force, is written from the point of view of a racist white sheriff in the

American South, again showing Baldwin's daring as an artist straddling the line between politics and art.

That same year another event shook Baldwin deeply. He had come to know and admire Malcolm X, who himself had been undergoing something of a transformation from the firebrand of the civil rights movement toward a more traditional embrace of Islam and a more peaceful approach to racial problems. He no longer referred to white people as white devils. Malcolm X had shown up at one of Baldwin's lectures, and the two had become friends. "He was one of the gentlest people I have ever met" (PT 498).

Baldwin would write of Malcolm X in his memoir *No Name in the Street*:

> Malcolm was not a racist, not even when he thought he was. His intelligence was more complex than that; furthermore, if he had been a racist, not many in this racist country would have considered him dangerous. . . . What made him unfamiliar and dangerous was not his hatred for white people, but his love for blacks, his apprehension of the horror of the black condition, and the reasons for it, and his determination so to work on their hearts and minds that they would be enabled to see their condition and change it themselves. (PT 499)

When Malcolm X was shot while speaking at the Audubon Ballroom in Harlem on February 21, 1965, Baldwin found it difficult to sound hopeful about the future. Some confusion followed his remarks to the press when he learned in London of Malcolm's death. Though the killers were known to be members of the Nation of Islam, Baldwin told reporters: "Whatever hand pulled the trigger did not buy the bullet. That bullet was forged in the crucible of the West, that death was dictated by the most successful conspiracy in the history of the world, and its name is white supremacy" (Weatherby 264). By pointing to the heart of what Baldwin saw as the problem, he allowed himself to be misinterpreted. This misunderstanding marks a significant change in Baldwin's relationship with the press. As the situation in America became more stormy, Baldwin's rhetoric became less about love and more about hellfire and retribution.

The year 1968 challenged Baldwin in significant ways. His second Broadway production, the play he had written in the 1950s, *The Amen Corner*, closed after a brief run. The reviews were not flattering. *Tell Me How Long the Train's Been Gone*—a book he struggled to write amid the constant speaking engagements, parties, and fundraising—was published in June of that year. Its main character, Leo Proudhammer, is from a background similar to Baldwin's own. He is also black and bisexual, as well as being a big success as an actor. Leo seems to be a further stand-in for Baldwin as a case study in the problems success brings for a black artist, the tension between creating art and being involved in the work of civil rights.

In this fourth novel, set in Baldwin's familiar Harlem and Greenwich Village, Leo is involved in a love triangle with a southern white woman, Barbara, and a fiery young black activist, Christopher. With overtones of Shakespeare's Othello (and Iago), the two men wind up together and, Baldwin suggests, perhaps become involved in the more militant wing of the civil rights movement. At the end of the novel the two men discuss the future:

> "Guns," said Christopher. "We need guns."...
> "Yes," I said. Then, "But all I want is for you to live."
> "Alone?" he asked...."Alone?" he repeated. "Walking over the bodies of the dead? Is that what you want for me, Leo? Is that what you mean when you say you want me to live?...and I know you love me and you don't want no blood on my hands—dig—but if you don't want me to keep on going under the feet of horses, then I think you got to agree that we need us some guns. Right?" (*Tell Me How Long the Train's Been Gone* 369–70)

The reviews were mixed. Some called it a "masterpiece" (*Commentary*); others dismissed the book variously for being navel-gazing, out-of-touch with mainstream black life, poorly written, too political at times, and a work of propaganda and for having flat characters (for some reason the first-person narrative bothered many reviewers as being inappropriate for the needs of the story) (Weatherby 282). Baldwin, in essence, was being accused of what he had faulted Harriet Beecher Stowe for doing in *Uncle Tom's Cabin.*

Baldwin's concern over the reception of his novel was eclipsed by the assassination of Martin Luther King in April 1968. He had been in Palms Springs, California, at the time, working on a screenplay about the life of Malcolm X. (Never produced, the screenplay was published in 1972 as *One Day, When I Was Lost.*) He writes in *No Name in the Street* about the moment he heard the news:

> Billy Dee Williams had come to town, and he was staying at the house....The phone had been brought out to the pool, and now it rang. Billy was on the other side of the pool, doing what I took to be African improvisations to the sound of Aretha Franklin. And I picked up the phone.
> It was David Moses....He said, "Jimmy—? Martin's just been shot," and I don't think I said anything, or felt anything....I remember weeping, briefly, more in helpless rage than in sorrow, and Billy trying to comfort me. (*PT* 528–29)

As so many Americans at the time, Baldwin took the assassination particularly hard. He felt he might never write again. His bitterness toward America now reached a volcanic level, and it came out in interviews. Not long after King's funeral, Baldwin left the country, thinking, perhaps, that he might never return.

But now neither Paris nor Istanbul gave him much peace. England and Italy were no better. He was hounded by fans and reporters; he was expected to keep up a brisk social life. After falling ill in 1970—he was hospitalized for ten days—he went with friends to a tiny southern French village, Saint-Paul-de-Vence, about ten miles from the port city of Nice. There he found a 300-year-old farmhouse, remade as a twelve-room inn, set amid acres of gardens and forests, with an arresting view of the mountains. He began to rent out the inn, room by room, and eventually purchased it entire. He was forty-seven, and he had finally found his home.

Though now living abroad again, Baldwin felt very much a part of what was going on back home. Despite an increasingly bitter tone, he continued to weigh in on the American political and social scene. He wrote about the court cases of activist Angela Davis; he wrote in favor of the Black Panthers (who, interestingly enough, had denounced Baldwin as being a gay Uncle Tom); and he sent money to causes. "I am *not* in exile," he told the *Black Scholar* in 1973, "and I am *not* in paradise. It rains down here too" (Standley and Pratt 154).

His next two published works were something of a departure for him. The first, *A Rap on Race* (1971), was the transcript of a long conversation with the noted anthropologist and author Margaret Mead. (Two years later he had a similar conversation with the young black poet Nikki Giovanni, which was published as, simply, *A Dialogue*.) The second, *No Name in the Street*, (1972) was more conventional, a memoir of his years in the civil rights movement, which, in 1972, was both close and distant. His portraits of Malcolm X and Martin Luther King Jr. are poignant and vivid, and the entire reflection is full of wistfulness. It did not have the resounding tone of his earlier nonfiction, and, in fact, admitted to a creeping despair about American's future:

> To be an Afro-American, or an American black, is to be in the situation, intolerably exaggerated, of all those who have ever found themselves part of a civilization which they could in no wise honorably defend—which they were compelled, indeed, endlessly to attack and condemn—and who yet spoke out of the most passionate love, hoping to make the kingdom new, to make it honorable and worthy of life. (*PT* 521)

The style often seems forced. Though providing rare glimpses into its subjects by an extraordinary witness, though the insights are undeniably compelling, the book received some rather stinging reviews. Baldwin was accused of resorting to empty rhetoric, of rambling, and of succumbing to bitterness and pessimism, of lacking passion.

His 1974 novel, *If Beale Street Could Talk*, did not fair much better with the critics. The love story of Fonny and Tish, two young black lovers—him a sculptor falsely imprisoned, she pregnant with his child, hard-up for money and trying to get him released—is at heart as much about the precariousness of the American judicial system for black men as it is about love. It can also be read as a justification for Baldwin's mounting anger toward his homeland. Some hope ultimately prevails in the book, in the form of a child, but this is more a hope for the future, while the adults toil on in a system that does not care about them as human beings. Though the book got some of Baldwin's best reviews in a decade, an almost equal number attacked the novel as being slight and nostalgic and out of step with the times.

Baldwin's output for the balance of the decade continued on an uneven footing. *The Devil Finds Work* (1976) was a combination of memoir and film criticism that received bewildered notices; it remains, perhaps, one of his most misunderstood works of non-fiction. Idiosyncratic, well-versed in current films and actors, it is laced with strong opinion and pithy insights, as in Baldwin's assessment of 1973's *The Exorcist*:

> I can only say that Satan was never like that when he crossed my path (for one thing, the evil one never so rudely under-estimated me). His concerns were more various, and his methods more subtle. *The Exorcist* is not in the least concerned with damnation, an abysm far beyond the confines of its imagination, but with property, with safety, tax shelters, stocks and bonds, rising and falling markets, the continued invulnerability of a certain class of people, and the continued sanctification of a certain history. (PT 633)

The book is in many ways unprecedented and a harbinger of a new literary form—something unexpected from a writer of Baldwin's pigeon-holed reputation as a social-realist writer. In the same year, he also tried his hand at children's literature, with *Little Man Little Man, A Story of Childhood*.

Baldwin was enjoying his newfound home in the south of France. Though he would travel frequently to the United States and elsewhere for speeches and readings, his social hub now centered around Saint-Paul-de-Vence. (In 1976, Morehouse University, a traditionally black college and the alma mater of Martin Luther King Jr., gave Baldwin an honorary doctorate.) Young men came and young men went, though none took up full-time residence for any length. His family visited often for long stays, as well as Lucien Happersberger, who remained his lifelong friend, despite occasional troubles and disputes. The locals of Provence became exceedingly delighted by their famous new residence and enjoyed his company and presence and protected him from nosey outsiders.

During this period, a young African American student, studying at Cambridge University and working as a summer correspondent for *Time* magazine, interviewed Baldwin in the south of France. The student was Henry Louis Gates, Jr., the future African American literary scholar, author, encyclopedia compiler, documentarian, and Harvard University professor. The 1973 interview became an event not simply because Baldwin had been one of Gates's literary heroes ("I am about to confess something that literary critics should not confess: James Baldwin *was* literature for me, especially the essay" [Troupe 163]), but because they were later joined by the great singer, dancer, star of stage and screen Josephine Baker—or "Jo," to Baldwin. Gates turned in a long, fascinating joint interview with both of them, covering a wide range of issues, but focusing mainly on race relations in the United States and what it means to be an African American expatriate in Europe. *Time* declined the article, which was finally published in 1985. But the get-together made enough of an impact on Baldwin that he wrote a play inspired by the meeting, "The Welcome Table." Baldwin had hoped either Lena Horne or Ruby Dee would play the female lead, but the play went unproduced before his death (Leeming, 381).

Just Above My Head, James Baldwin's last novel, was published by Dial Press in 1979. It is Baldwin's longest novel, and is a fictional portrait of a life that hews closely to Baldwin's own experiences. The main character is Arthur Montana, a successful gospel singer, who is black and gay. The book is narrated by Arthur's brother, Hall. The story goes back to Hall and Arthur's days as boys in the storefront churches of Harlem and revisits the potency of Pentecostalism in their formative years; it follows Arthur to France in the postwar years; and through him tours the civil rights–embattled South. Increasingly, Montana must confront his position in society, the demands of success, the imperatives of politics, the need to create art. Though Baldwin had written about same-sex love before, *Just above My Head* contains perhaps his most explicit rendering, but not just about the glands, but also about the emotion, and positively so. Equally rapturous is the book's obsession with Baldwin's other great love, music. Blues, gospel, jazz—the entire gamut of African American musical expression is celebrated in this sprawling novel, which some critics have classified as a jazz novel, whose architecture is heavily influenced by the notion of improvisation and rifting upon the scales and notes of a song:

> The song does not belong to the singer. The singer is found by the song. Ain't no singer, anywhere, ever *made up* a song— that's not possible. He *hears* something. I really believe, at the bottom of *my* balls, baby, that something hears *him*, something says, come here! and jumps on him just exactly like you jump on a piano or a sax or a violin or a drum and you make it sing the song you hear: and you love it, and you take care of it, better than you take care of yourself, can you dig it? but you don't have no mercy on it. You can't have mercy! That sound you hear, that sound you try to pitch with the *utmost* precision—and did you hear me? Wow!—is the sound of millions and millions and, who knows, now, listening, where life is, where is death? (*Just Above My Head* 552)

The book spent thirty-seven weeks on the *Washington Post* best-seller list, became a featured alternate selection of the Book-of-the-Month Club, and the paperback rights were sold for $305,000. The reviews were not overwhelmingly positive, but it was warmly received, as if to say Baldwin was back on track toward fulfilling the literary promise he had shown as a fiction writer from the beginning, having been sidetracked by so much urgently calling nonfiction.

By the early 1980s, Baldwin's health was in decline. He continued to socialize frequently and to drink and smoke heavily, which resulted in a series of hospital stays and collapses. At one point he had a mild heart attack, but ignored his doctor's insistence that he slow down and take better care of himself. Stubbornly, he continued on, and accepted a guest lectureship at five colleges affiliated with the University of Massachusetts. (Many of the young black students he worked with have gone on to have stellar careers, including the Pulitzer Prize–winning playwright Suzanne Lori-Parks.) While in Massachusetts he was given a major party for his sixtieth birthday in Amherst, attended by a great many literary luminaries and friends, including Maya Angelou and historian/editor Lerone Bennett. "I've learned one thing," Baldwin said at the end of the night, "Never avoid the truth about yourself" (Weatherby 357).

In the early 1980s, *Playboy* magazine had assigned Baldwin to write about the troubling missing and murdered children cases in Atlanta. Between the summer of 1979 and the spring of 1982 over twenty-nine children, adolescents, and adults were killed or went missing. In May 1981 a suspect was apprehended, Wayne Williams, a twenty-two-year-old African American; he was indicted and tried, based on extremely technical forensic and circumstantial evidence. The idea that this ne'er-do-well, living at home with his parents, ungainfully employed, could have committed so many murders and have avoided detection for over two years seemed implausible to many. Ultimately Williams was convicted for only two murders, but was portrayed in the media as having been the overall culprit.

James Baldwin was not alone in seriously doubting William's culpability in so many of the murders, as well as the motives of the Georgia judicial system in its attempt to quickly turn the cases into history, wanting to get the blight on the "city too busy to hate" fast behind them. Baldwin expanded his article into *The Evidence of Things Not Seen* (1985), which Dial Press, his publisher for the last several decades, tellingly turned down. Though the long essay demonstrates some of Baldwin's skill with language, it falls down as an act of reportage. (Baldwin's strength had never been as a reporter; in truth, his power came from his passion and eloquent eyewitnessing, not from digging for the facts.) His use of his autobiography and personal reflections seems self-indulgent and irrelevant here. Essentially, he only had a gut reaction that Wayne Williams was not the scourge of Atlanta—intuition and common sense—but that's about all the book amounted to: an emotional reaction to a tragic and unsolved mystery. The book fared poorly in the bookstores.

In 1985, along with *Jimmy's Blues*, which was a collection of Baldwin's selected poems (not a genre associated with Baldwin; this collection would not give him much entrée as a formal poet), *The Price of the Ticket* was published. A massive collection of every one of his essays, from 1948 to 1985, arranged in chronological order, it stood as a testament to Baldwin's achievement over the years, a treasury of the art of the essay. However, the book only received nods of recognition from the press, as if to say: Oh, yes, there was once this important writer named James Baldwin. The preface, however, of the same name as the book, rises to some of Baldwin's best writing ever.

France continued to honor Baldwin. In 1986, President François Mitterand, made him a commander of the Legion d'Honneur, France's highest honor for a civilian. He continued to work on plays and a major novel he had conceived back in the 1950s.

A few months later, Baldwin was diagnosed with cancer of the esophagus, but doctors had caught it too late. He spent the spring and summer of 1987 in Saint-Paul-de-Vence, growing increasingly ill. He died on December 1, in the presence of his brother David and his old friend Lucien Happersberger.

In the decades since James Baldwin's death, his literary assessment has undergone interesting and far-flung changes. Immediately after his death, many laudatory and sober articles, memoirs, and critical works ensued, marking him as an important literary American figure. In the intervening years, though his work remained in print, his place seemed unsure. A major, authorized biography was published by his first publisher, Alfred A. Knopf, in 1994, written by David Leming, who had once been Baldwin's personal secretary and who had remained a close friend. By the turn of the century, his reputation had grown with enduring seminars and continued critical work, capped by the publication in The Library of America editions of his nonfiction and early fiction in 1998.

For a period, many considered his essays to be his major legacy, but his novels, stories, and plays are receiving serious attention as well.

It is telling that we are now at a time when the American literary establishment is reassessing nonfiction's relationship to fiction. Which is the superior form? Can a great work of nonfiction compare to a great novel? A great essay to a great short story? Is David Thoreau as great an artist as Herman Melville? It is a time when Gore Vidal is hailed for his nonfiction and essentially dismissed for his many novels; when Norman Mailer wins two Pulitzer Prizes for nonfiction, but considers his novels *The Naked and the Dead* and *Ancient Evenings* to be his greatest contributions to posterity; when Joan Didion's nonfiction vies for parity with any fiction written in the post–World War II era. James Baldwin's legacy seems tailor-made for this literary debate. Whatever the outcome, decades and decades hence, his output, his skill, his subject matter, and his underlying ability to communicate his passion will surely remain a legitimate oeuvre for deserved and continued attention.

WORKS CITED

Baldwin, James. *The Price of the Ticket: Collected Nonfiction, 1948–1985.* New York: St. Martin's/Marek, 1985.

Bloom, Harold, ed. *James Baldwin.* New York: Chelsea House, 1986.

Campbell, James. *Talking at the Gates: A Life of James Baldwin.* New York: Viking, 1991.

Leeming, David A. *James Baldwin: A Biography.* New York: Alfred A. Knopf, 1994.

Porter, Horace A. *Stealing the Fire: The Art and Protest of James Baldwin.* Middletown, Conn.: Wesleyan University Press, 1989.

Standley, Fred L., and Louis H. Pratt, eds. *Conversations with James Baldwin.* Jackson: University Press of Mississippi, 1989.

Troupe, Quincy, ed. *James Baldwin: The Legacy.* New York: Touchstone/Simon & Schuster, 1989.

Weatherby, James J. *James Baldwin: Artist on Fire.* New York: Donald I. Fine, 1989.

James Baldwin as Religious Writer

The Burdens and Gifts of Black Evangelicalism

Clarence E. Hardy III

Just a few years before his death, in an essay that introduced his most important nonfiction in *The Price of the Ticket* (1985), James Baldwin remembered how he "got started" as a writer. His three years in Harlem's Pentecostal churches and his brief career as a teenage preacher had indelibly shaped his memories of a tumultuous adolescence and defined his first steps into adulthood as he struggled to launch his writing career. "Indeed, my departure from the pulpit," Baldwin recalled, "and my leaving home were almost simultaneous" (xvi).

But the "white world" he entered upon leaving both faith and family was still "alien and mainly hostile territory" (xvi). Greenwich Village in lower Manhattan was nearly as alienating for the budding new artist as Harlem had been when he was simply the son of a failed local evangelist. It was only after he left his country of birth altogether for Europe that he could finish his first novel, *Go Tell it on the Mountain* (1953). And ironically, just like his fictional alter ego, John Grimes, in that semiautobiographical novel, it was Baldwin's initial embrace of religion that marked his own first steps beyond the life he knew at home and the compelling but destructive father who so dominated his inner life. A few years before he left his Harlem home, the young Baldwin embraced a Pentecostal faith that not only differed

from the faith of his father, who was a some-time Baptist minister from New Orleans, but also provided the boy preacher with
a level of success that had always eluded his father.[1]

But neither outward success, though unprecedented in his
family, nor this fervently apocalyptic brand of Christian faith
quietened young Baldwin's inner turmoil. In the past when he
was troubled, he had sought "refuge" on a special hill in Central
Park where he could see the entire "sweep of New York" from
his own Harlem to "the white city downtown" (Eckman 35).
Baldwin would place this same hill, which had offered him a
measure of respite, into his first novel, so that his fictional
counterpart, John Grimes, could find a place to ponder his own
future. There John wondered whether "the way of the cross"
was simply empty rhetoric that gave hungry black boys like him
"a belly filled with wind" while others who "did not fear God"
could eat to their "heart's content" (*Go Tell It on the Mountain* 34).
While nothing matched the intensity and passion Baldwin found
in the music and preaching of Pentecostal churches, when he,
like John Grimes, saw the religious drama of sin and salvation
up close it seemed empty and manipulative. "Being in the pulpit
was like being in the theatre," Baldwin confessed, "I was behind
the scenes and knew how the illusion was worked" (*Fire Next
Time* 55). And so only a year after he started preaching Baldwin
felt his faith slowly "crumbling" as he "began to read again" and
return to the world of books he had seemingly left behind (51).
When Baldwin started, he preached "once a week" on Saturday
afternoons and occasionally on Sunday (Eckman 61). But as he
took fewer engagements and "preached as rarely as possible," he
began to see religion as a phase he needed to end if he wanted
to become the writer he hoped to be. And when to his surprise
his father asked the younger Baldwin whether he would "rather
write than preach," an increasingly wayward son answered:
"Yes" (*Notes of a Native Son* 90).

But what are we to make of the religion of Baldwin's teenage years and its role in his career as a novelist and social critic?
Should we simply see his religious past as an interesting detour
or unnecessary prelude to a largely secular career? While scholars, until relatively recently, have generally overlooked the

importance of his religious past in interpreting his literary work, Baldwin himself described it as having significant influence.[2] As Baldwin writes at the beginning of his first collection of essays, *Notes of a Native Son* (1955): "I hazard that the King James Bible, the rhetoric of the store-front [Pentecostal] church, something ironic and violence and perpetually understated in Negro speech—and something of Dickens' love for bravura—have something to do with me today" (2). But, in truth, his religious inheritance did not simply provide a rhythm of speech or a style of rhetoric; it also helped him pursue the very essence of what he described as the "business of the writer" in a culture like that of the United States, where religion's influence predominates. For Baldwin the writer's essential vocation was "to examine attitudes, to go beneath the surface, to tap the source," (3) and his former life as a boy preacher helped him to see just how intertwined Christianity was with social power in the United States and how it shaped citizens' view of each other and the broader world.

In fact, it is Baldwin's twin exile—from the country of his birth and the church of his youth—that has shaped the very contours of his best literary efforts in both fiction and nonfiction. For Baldwin the sense of exile that black people felt in the face of Africa defines what it means to be American. "This depthless alienation from oneself and one's people is," Baldwin writes, "in sum, the American experience" (*Notes of a Native Son* 104). Some critics in recent years have focused on how Baldwin's expatriate status in particular not only gives coherence to his work that helped define black identity in postwar America, but also links Baldwin to a broader cultural modernism represented in the figures of F. Scott Fitzgerald, Marcel Proust, and James Joyce.[3] They note how Baldwin, inspired by authors like Henry James, "distill[ed] from his private experience of the expatriate condition" what became "a paradigm for [viewing] the alienating effects of American life," including how race has bedeviled the broader culture (Tomlinson 135–36). No matter how central black people have been to the development of Western culture, their status as outsiders continues to define their identity and their relationship to the larger society. As Baldwin himself argued: "[T]he most crucial time in my own development came when I

was forced to recognize that I was a kind of bastard of the West"
(*Notes of a Native Son* 4).

Well-known Baldwin critic Trudier Harris has demonstrated
how Baldwin's alienation from his religious past was analogous
to his alienation from his country of birth. Both forms of alienation linked him to the work of other writers who explored what
it meant to be an expatriate. Baldwin's struggle over his black
evangelical heritage connects him to the very beginnings of
black literature, where "the appeal of Christianity was [always]
one of the primary preoccupations" (Harris 18). At the same
time, his alienation with this same heritage linked him in the
postwar period with writers like Lorraine Hansberry, who along
with Baldwin represented what Harris calls "Christianity's last
stand," marking the moment when black evangelical culture
no longer dominated the black literary landscape (21). As Harris
writes: "What would have been blasphemy for Baldwin's characters becomes for his [literary] descendants [like Ntozake Shange
and Toni Morrison] a way of creating space for black women to
grow, to know and define themselves" without the threat of a
Christian god who damns them for their efforts (21).

Although Baldwin had detached himself from the church and
paved the way for black writers unencumbered with the legacy
of evangelical Christianity, he was still a religious writer. He
continued throughout his career to shape his memories of his
black evangelical heritage into meaningful art and insightful
social criticism. The Pentecostal churches of his youth were an
obvious source for Baldwin. They offered a compelling cultural
backdrop that he could exploit and vibrant characters to popu-
late some of his most enduring works of fiction. Black religious
culture provided more than a ready-made milieu: scholars have
begun in recent years to demonstrate how Baldwin adapted its
aesthetic aspects even for his fiction set in environments far
beyond the church walls. When Baldwin, for example, deploys
the religious language of his evangelical heritage to describe
physical intimacy in *Another Country* (1962) and *If Beale Street
Could Talk* (1974), sex holds a sacramental power over lovers,
bodily cementing various partners across race and gender. In his
descriptions of physical intimacy, by invoking religious language

with its inherent ambiguity and indeterminacy, Baldwin manages to suggest the mystery at the core of all human relationships and the instability that marks all sexual (and racial) identities (Hardy 66–67). As literary critic Kevin Ohi suggests in his analysis of Baldwin's *Another Country*: "[S]elf-revelation almost always appears in the novel as a poignantly yearned-for impossibility. Revelation appears only in the guise of its failure" (264).

Baldwin can be considered a religious writer not because he was a believer (he wasn't, in any traditional sense) or because he was able to adapt the cultural forms of black religious culture for secular purposes, but instead because religion and Baldwin's complicated relationship with it best illuminates what makes his work distinctive. At the same time, Baldwin's struggle with (evangelical) Christianity represents how black culture and the nature of black identity evolved in postwar urban America. Ironically, from the beginning, editors and agents questioned why he had to include "all that come-to-Jesus stuff" in his work. Although they recognized that "a Negro evangelist and his family" had to talk in a "come-to Jesus" idiom in *Go Tell It* to make the world Baldwin describes a credible one, they wanted the new author to "take it [i.e., the religious language] out" (*Amen Corner* xiv). Baldwin refused. But despite his refusal to excise the rhythms and substance of religion from his literary imagination, scholars, until recently, only seemed to appreciate religion's influence on Baldwin's life and work in the narrowest of senses. As literary scholar Michael Cobb argues: "People refused (and still refuse) to engage his religious discourse critically and thus read the religious as a belief system that Baldwin must eventually abandon in favor of his more secular concerns" (294).

What Baldwin, in fact, offers is inside knowledge of how religious people think and act. He understood, perhaps only as a religious outsider who once believed could, the architecture of religious thought and how it shaped black people's collective aspirations and their connections to the larger society and world. In much of his early work, Baldwin describes a Christianity that equates the black with the ugly and damned, even as it paradoxically provides the rhetorical and institutional space for black resistance and black humanity. And even in the often-incendiary

The Fire Next Time (1963), where his condemnation of his experience within Christianity is at its most strident, Baldwin demonstrates the continued vitality of black Christianity's moral voice by translating its religious language into a secular one. Martin Luther King's calls for his fellow ministers and nonviolent activists "to redeem the soul of America" (Fairclough 32) became, in Baldwin's hands, a broader plea to "relatively conscious whites and the relatively conscious blacks" to come together "like lovers" to "create" a new "consciousness" (*Fire Next Time* 141). Despite rejecting traditional Christian beliefs and institutions, Baldwin found that his religious heritage provided him a vocabulary to engage areas as varied as sex and politics. It provided a perch from which to condemn both a wayward nation and Christianity itself for betraying the sons and daughters of African slaves. In reckoning with his lost faith, Baldwin managed in his literary work to illuminate both the possibilities and restrictive limitations of evangelical culture in black American life, even as he defined much of what was best in his own art and social criticism.

Reckoning with (the Loss of) Faith in Life and Art

At first, before his one-time religious devotion became a principal source for his early writings, the bouts of religious ecstasy Baldwin found in a Pentecostal churches in Harlem provided an escape from the temptations of lust and danger that often filled his teenage summer days and suggested a profound connection between the human impulse for sex and religion. Baldwin was fourteen: the ever-present "whores, pimps and racketeers" had become "a personal menace," and suddenly Baldwin found himself deeply afraid of both "the evil within" and "the evil without" (*Fire Next Time* 28). When Baldwin along with his boyhood friend Arthur Moore arrived at Mount Calvary Assembly Hall of the Pentecostal Faith Church for All Nations, he didn't know that "the strangest sensation" he had ever experienced would provide temporary relief from his inner turmoil. One moment he was clapping and singing and in the next he was flat on his back with the "lights beating down" on his face while surrounded by Pentecostal believers (44–45). While "the anguish" of his conversion left him "utterly drained and exhausted," it also "released" him the "guilty torment" that had bedeviled him for several months; the guilt and fear that he had "bottled up inside" all summer long came "roaring, screaming, crying out" just when the pastor finished preaching (44, 47).

Rosa Artimus Horn, the South Carolina native and pastor who presided over Mount Calvary and Baldwin's anguished conversion, was truly an imposing presence for an impressionable young Baldwin. In his first play, *The Amen Corner* (1968), this "proud and handsome woman" became the basis for the protagonist Margaret Alexander, who, like Horn, resided in rooms attached to her church (Eckman 59). And when Baldwin later became a preacher in his own right for a different Pentecostal church, Horn's example helped him connect the rituals of religion to that of theater. His sense of the theatrical and his ability to write plays was birthed in Horn's church. "I was armed, I knew, in attempting to write the play," Baldwin argued in introductory notes for *The Amen Corner*, "by the fact that I was born in the church." Like many anthropologists, Baldwin believed that "the *communion* which is theatre" initially emerged "out of the ritual of the church" (*Amen Corner* xvi).

But what did this connection between churches and theater illuminate about the nature and limitations of religious speech and practice? "[M]averick freak poets and visionaries" serve both the church and the theater and are produced "by our [human] need and out of an impulse more mysterious than our desire" (*Devil Finds Work* 31). But when Baldwin compared the church to the theater in *The Devil Finds Work* (1976), the church was found wanting. For Baldwin true theater was created in the tension between the "real and the imagined" that rooted the creative imagination in the real bodies of actors on stage instead of in the ephemeral hopes of a religious world that no longer seemed relevant or true to modern people (30). "[W]e are *all* each other's flesh and blood," Baldwin argued. "This is a truth which is very difficult for the theater to deny, and when it attempts to do so the same thing happens to the theater as happens to the church;

it becomes sterile and irrelevant" (30–31). As a cultural critic, Baldwin simply makes explicit what was long reflected in his earliest fiction. In those early stories Baldwin depicts black churches as sterile repositories of illusions where ministers preach about a love largely absent from the church.

Even so, Baldwin treasured the opportunity for the intensely felt human connection that the theaters of stage and pulpit offered those who witnessed their dramatic aspects, even if—or perhaps precisely if—this connection is cemented against the desires of those involved. In his plays at least, and perhaps in his other literary work, Baldwin hoped to engender the same kinds of involuntary responses as Rosa Horn helped prompt in him decades before. "[W]hat I wanted to do in the theatre," Baldwin writes in his introductory notes for *The Amen Corner*, "was to recreate moments I remembered as a boy preacher, to involve the people even against their will, to shake them up, and hopefully to change them" (*Amen Corner* xvi). But if religious language forges these involuntary but powerful connections between people, what precisely, in Baldwin's mind, makes it bloodless? What truth does religion ultimately deny?

Although Baldwin in *The Fire Next Time* and *The Devil Finds Work* portrayed his teenage ministry as a fraudulent hustle, his closest associates consistently described him as sincere in his religious devotion when he first converted. Although his mother was "shocked" when he announced he wanted to become a preacher, she simply "knew he was sincere" (Eckman 61). And Arthur Moore, the boyhood friend who accompanied him to Horn's church, attested to how "devout" the young Baldwin was: he attended church services several times a week and abstained from smoking, movies, and dancing as Pentecostal churches demanded (Eckman 61). But no matter how sincere his devotion, the religious strictures he rigorously followed simply made his own body, now alive with desire, feel like a stranger to him.

Baldwin, like John Grimes, his alter ego in his first novel, saw how his body, viewed from within religion's rules against sexual desire, seemed both "treacherous and bewildering" (30) "For John, as for Baldwin," literary critic Peter Powers writes, "the Holiness tradition of the Christian church pits desire against duty" (787).

The scene in *Go Tell It on the Mountain* that best illustrates the interwoven character of Christianity, (sexual) shame, and poverty is where the young John "with shame and horror" cleans the grimy, narrow room his mother assigns him and confronts his own feelings of bitterness and defilement. In this room, dirt "triumphed beneath the sink" and "roaches spawned" no matter how hard John cleaned (21). This grimy room, symbolically tied so firmly to the limitations and restrictions for black life, is of course almost mockingly decorated with Christian plaques of Scripture verses that celebrate the possibility of salvation. As John cleans the grimy, narrow room, he curses with an "angry hardness of heart" beneath his breath at his Sisyphean task: *"He who is filthy, let him be filthy still"* (22). As long as John stays within this reality that his religion endorses, his body is condemned and his sexual desires are damned as sinful. And Baldwin himself, ultimately, could not escape his desires or himself, and so he "abandoned" his church and his place in the community "in order not to betray myself or the ministry" (*Price of the Ticket* xvi). His own body filled with (sexual) desires was the fundamental and ever-present truth he felt Christianity ignored.

Baldwin of course rarely engaged in Christian doctrine after leaving the church, but his religious experiences of physical denial drove him to question in quite specific terms the Christian conception of the body and sex. Baldwin believed that Saint Paul's injunctions to "mortify" the flesh created a schizophrenic "Christian personality...at war with itself" over the issue of sex ("White Racism or World Community?" 440). And since a person's "sexuality" could, in Baldwin's view, only "be divorced or distanced from the idea of the self...with great violence," he saw Christian myths like the Virgin Birth with its implicit denial of sex as entirely absurd ("Here Be Dragons" 678). As Baldwin asked pointedly in a conversation with poet Nikki Giovanni: "What is wrong with a man and a woman sleeping together, making love to each other and having a baby like everybody else? Why does the son of God have to be born immaculately?" (*Dialogue* 38).

What Baldwin offered in place of traditional Christianity was a religious language that directly invoked and even celebrated the body and undid the very category of religion by describing as sacred what had been seen as dirty and profane. Particularly in his references to music, even in his earliest writings, Baldwin found kinship between religious pursuits and sexual play. In his first novel, Baldwin manages to describe the juke joints as places where the sacred and profane meet and move together in the gyrations of women who have a love for "sin" and for the movement of their sensuous bodies. Through the eyes of Gabriel, John Grimes's father, Baldwin describes how in the "smoke-filled, gin-heavy dance halls" of Louisiana women were "twisting their bodies into lewd hallelujahs" (136–37). In Baldwin's later novels, truth is rooted in the miracle of the bodily connection of sex and cannot be denied by religion or any other human force. In *Another Country* (1962), the "[sexual] act of love" is described as a "confession" because the body cannot "lie about itself. . . . it cannot lie about the force which drives it" (180). And early in Baldwin's last novel, *Just Above My Head* (1979), the narrator, Hall Montana, describes his deep love for his wife's body after another bout of sexual activity. Smelling her lingering fragrance on the bed sheets, he muses: "Every inch of her body is a miracle for me; maybe because her body has taught me so much about the miracle of my own" (24). For Baldwin, the flesh and spirit are indivisible. As Baldwin said in Sweden before the World Council of Churches in 1968: "From my point of view, it seems to me the flesh and the spirit are one; it seems to me that when you mortify the one, you have mortified the other" (*No Name in the Street* 54).

The celebration of sexual intimacy as sacred represents the concrete unraveling of a religious posture that mortifies the flesh it should venerate and that treasures safety over necessary risk. In the United States, Baldwin believes "safety" is the "real meaning of the word 'religious'" (*Fire Next Time* 27). The religious posture Baldwin embraced at fourteen seeks to rescue its adherents from the (sexual) desires they fear within and exclude those they fear and hate from without. Baldwin questioned just how exclusionary black evangelicals wanted to be. He asked: "Was Heaven, then to be merely another ghetto?" Baldwin wondered why the love the church preached was partial and "salvation stopped at the church door." Injunctions to love everybody, Baldwin argued, seemed to "appl[y] only to those who believed as we did" (*Fire Next Time* 57–58).

From the beginning, despite his trenchant criticisms of religious institutions that failed to encourage followers to love fully, Baldwin struggled to develop a language of love that was religious and did not exclude anyone. Even in *The Amen Corner,* where Baldwin purposely highlighted the limitations of religious institutions after critics mistook his evocative descriptions of black Pentecostals for approval, Baldwin embraced a religious language of love and grace unmoored from religious institutions yet still inspired by religious tradition.[4] Near the play's resolution Baldwin explicitly pits the workings of love against the rigidities of the institutional church. Only when the minister and protagonist in the play, Margaret, leaves her pulpit for perhaps the last time does she reckon with the expansiveness of love that goes far beyond the church as a human institution. "I'm just now finding out what it means to love the Lord," she confesses. "It ain't all in the singing and the shouting" (*Amen Corner* 88). Instead, Margaret suggests that to love God is to love absolutely everyone without reservation and to "suffer with them and rejoice with them and never count the cost" (88).

But despite his ultimate rejection of Christianity, the notion of Christian love still animates Baldwin's moral vision as witnessed in Margaret's declaration that now she knows "what it means to love the Lord" (88). From his ambiguous relationship with Christianity, we see within Baldwin's focus on religion the emergence of a new "religious" language that reaches beyond the institutional confines of church bodies and challenges a nation that claims to worship and follow the Christian god. Critic Stanley Macebuh suggests that much of Baldwin's early work pivots around his "alienation from God and society" to establish a new "religion of love." The next section will explore how Baldwin comes "to grips with," in Macebuh's words, "the more public aspects" of what had been primarily a "theological preoccupation" in the social criticism he offers in the wake of the civil rights movement in the 1960s and 1970s (67). In wrestling with religion in personal terms, Baldwin manages not only to grapple with much of what most defines racial identity, but to establish the basis for his broader critical analysis of American nationalism.

The Plagues That Define (Black) America

The very ambiguity that defined how Baldwin viewed religion in the intimately personal terms of sex and sexual identity also defined how he understood religion's place in societal terms that encompassed both black people and the larger nation. At first glance, churches as depicted in *The Amen Corner*—and in most of Baldwin's early fiction—are simply a menace to the full and free flourishing of human life. The life of the protagonist, Margaret, demonstrates how religious institutions limit individuals and foster a self-loathing that damages their ability to love without fear and the terror of loneliness. In his notes for the play, Baldwin describes Margaret as "in the church because her society has left her no other place to go." But her success in accepting her tragic condition despite having "lost everything" represents the "historical triumph of the Negro people in this country" (xvi). In Margaret's ultimate determination to love despite the costs even as the church, in which she has housed her hopes, cannot help her achieve her fullest potential, Baldwin sees the collective suffering and aspirations of black people whose religion helps define their humanity even as it limits their ultimate possibilities.

But Baldwin's exploration of the interwoven character of Christianity and black self-loathing began, of course, a few years before *The Amen Corner* was published. In his 1949 commentary on Harriet Beecher Stowe's *Uncle Tom's Cabin*, "Everybody's Protest Novel," Baldwin describes the difficulties black Christians have in navigating a religion where "black is the color of evil" and black worshippers ask God in hymns to "wash" them "whiter than snow"; he describes how they appear to venerate a god who "made" them, "but not in His image" (*Notes of a Native Son* 16). Trapped within a world Christianity helped create, black people are forced to see themselves not only as unwanted by their fellow countrymen but also as personifications of evil and intrinsically unworthy before an uncaring god. In *Go Tell It on the Mountain*, just four short years later, this same Christian god finds expression in the character of John's father, Gabriel Grimes, whom Stanley Macebuh would describe as the "personification of the vengeful God of Baldwin's fundamentalist Christian imagination" (51). Baldwin, indeed, acknowledged in a 1984 interview that his first novel was about "my relationship to my father and to the church" (Elgrably and Plimpton 240). In the novel Baldwin implicitly couples themes of race and religion in the body and life of the young John Grimes as seen from the perspective of his wayward father, Gabriel. The two times when John is seen through the eyes of Gabriel, John takes on the visage of Satan. When John looks in a mirror hours before his conversion, he remembers that his father, Gabriel, "had always said that his face was the face of Satan" (27). In the moments just before his son's conversion, Gabriel "had never seen such a look on John's face before: Satan, at that moment, stared out of John's eyes" (150).

At the novel's end it may be unclear how John will handle the burdens of being a black Christian, but in the play *Blues for Mister Charlie* (1964), loosely based on the lynching death of Emmett Till in 1955, Baldwin is much more explicit about the dilemmas the Christian faith has created for black people, both individually and collectively. Baldwin, in fact, chooses to define the United States around what he describes as the twin plagues of race and religion and examines how Christianity has damaged those whom it defines and curses as black. The play takes place in Plaguetown, U.S.A., because in Baldwin's words: "The plague is race, the plague is our concept of Christianity, and this raging plague has the power to destroy every human relationship" (7). In Baldwin's view, both race and religion, dependent on the ability to label and exclude categories of people, inevitably fracture the potential for human relationships. At the same time, Baldwin acknowledges that it is only within these conceptions of race and religion that black people have managed to affirm any sense of their own humanity at all.

Meridian, a disillusioned minister who struggles with his religious heritage as he copes with the loss of his son, Richard, illuminates the conundrum that Christian identity has become for black people in the United States. Richard is brutally murdered at the beginning of the play. Toward the end of the first act, speaking to a local white liberal reporter, Meridian says:

> I'm a Christian. I've been a Christian all my life, like my Mama and Daddy before me and like their Mama and Daddy before them. Of course, if you go back far enough, you get to a point *before* Christ, if you see what I mean, B.C.—and at that point, I've been thinking black people weren't raised to turn the other cheek, and in the hope of heaven. No, then they didn't have to take low. Before Christ. They walked around just as good as anybody else, and when they died, they didn't go to heaven, they went to join their ancestors. He was a sinner, so he must have gone to hell—if we're going to believe what the Bible says. (56)

Even though he is a Christian preacher, Meridian wonders aloud whether the gospel that he preaches has been more a curse than a blessing. Richard, as a sinner, has been consigned to hell and forever lost to his father. Meridian asks whether his religion gives him any real capacity to fight back and maintain a semblance of dignity in the face of the white terrorism that has already murdered his son. And yet, in the next moment, Meridian sees no dignity outside of the faith: "[W]ould I have *been* such a Christian if I hadn't been born black? Maybe I *had* to become a Christian in order to have any dignity at all" (56).

For Baldwin, black people are people who collectively find themselves in exile, even as they sing hymns, preach sermons, and desperately hold on to their dignity in the face of doubt. Gabriel in *Go Tell It on the Mountain* disdainfully describes black people as a bastard people who appeal to a god who does not answer because they have no alternative. As Baldwin writes in Gabriel's voice: "Behind them was darkness, nothing but the darkness, and all around them destruction, and before them nothing but the fire—a bastard people, far from God, singing and crying in the wilderness" (137). What is whispered in the recesses of Gabriel's mind became visible in the tortured prayers of Meridian in *Blues for Mister Charlie*. Invoking the famous question of Psalm 137—"How shall we sing the Lord's song in a strange land?"—a favorite biblical text of Baldwin's own father, Meridian begins his prayer before his congregation by confessing his heavy heart and then cries aloud to God:

> It is not only that our lives, from day to day and every hour of each day, are menaced by the people among whom you have set us down. We have borne all these things, my Lord, and we have done what the prophets of old could not do, we have sung the Lord's song in a strange land. In a strange land! What was the sin committed by our forefathers in the time that has vanished on the other side of the flood, which has had to be expiated by chains, by the lash, by hunger and thirst, by slaughter, by fire, by the rope, by the knife, and for so many generations, on these wild shores, in this strange land? (104)

After hurling these complaints to a silent god, Meridian hears the younger generation ask him "which road to follow" (105). Instead of giving them a clear answer, he tells them instead "to trust the great gift of life, learn to love one another and dare to walk the earth like men" (105–6). And, although his prayers appear to go unanswered, Meridian affirms his determination to continue. Despite his exilic status and the alienation he feels, Meridian works to forge human relationships in the quest for dignity that he will pursue, whether he hears from God or not. He continues to proclaim his place in the United States and (perhaps) in Christianity: "I will not abandon the land—this strange land, which is my home" (105).

Although Baldwin's struggles with the Christian god are much more public and explicit in *Blues* than in his early writing, in the end, no matter how far he moves from the confines of the church of his youth, his struggle with the Christian god continues to define his identity. One can almost feel the texture of Baldwin's long-strained relationship with black evangelical culture amid a dialogue between Mother Henry and her grandson, the young Richard, just before he is murdered. During the course of their conversation, Mother Henry tells her wayward grandson that she was determined to take care of her husband

and "raise my children in the fear of God." Richard immediately challenges his grandmother with a short "You know I don't believe in God, Grandmama." And Mother Henry responds, perhaps gingerly, "You don't know what you talking about. Ain't no way possible for you not to believe in God. You doubt me, you just try holding your breath long enough to die" (31–32). The plague Baldwin described in his notes for *Blues* had come to define black people collectively in Meridian's prayer had already come to define his son, a nonbeliever, whose death his father so deeply mourned. Baldwin's struggle with God defined much of Baldwin's work and life, whether he wanted it to or not. No matter how fiercely he resisted the struggle against Christianity, his profound connection with his religious heritage always emerged. Only Baldwin's death in southern France in 1987 could end the skirmish that began in the streets of Harlem against the Christian god.

"Born in a Christian Nation"

At the same time as he wrestled with the nature of black religious identity in *Blues for Mister Charlie*, Baldwin viewed the instability inherent in all forms of human identity as a basis to challenge a society that conceived itself as Christian. He would make this challenge especially in his groundbreaking *The Fire Next Time*. But even earlier, in a little noticed essay, "Preservation of Innocence" (1949), published four years before *Go Tell It on the Mountain*, Baldwin pondered how the notion of "nature" has been used to exclude the reality of same-sex desire and intimacy he felt and shared. "[W]henever nature is invoked to support our human divisions," Baldwin warned, we are "right to be suspicious" (594). This suspicion framed Baldwin's description of the origins of the sacred in the human imagination and how human beings use religion to categorize and exclude one another:

> I suspect that he [God] sprang into being on the cold, black day when we discovered that nature cared nothing for us. His advent, which alone had the power to save us from nature and

ourselves, also created self-awareness. . . . It marked the death
of innocence; it set up the duality of good-and evil. . . . [T]he
homosexual did not exist; nor properly speaking did the heterosexual. We are all in a state of nature. (596)

Without nature's validation, and in the course of struggle and
suffering, human communities imagine a god—an imaginary
entity Baldwin calls "man's most intense creation" (596)—who
rushes forward to establish rigid rules, labels, and categories
such as homosexuality and heterosexuality to comfort those
frightened at the sheer messiness and complexity of life. His
tone, throughout the essay, with its harsh depiction of the limitations and repression of church mores is strikingly similar to
the tone in *The Amen Corner.* Pressed against the rigidities of
traditional sexual morality, Baldwin sees this Christian god not
only as a human-created illusion that supplies refuge from a
hostile world, but also as a tyrant. This autocratic ruler in the
heavens is born in our fear of death, which becomes a symbol
of our capacity for self-loathing and for damning various kinds
of sexual intimacy and identity. "[I]t is not in the sight of nature
that the homosexual is condemned," Baldwin writes, "but in the
sight of God" (596).

In *The Fire Next Time* Baldwin opens the second essay, "Down
at the Cross," with a declaration that he was "born in a Christian
nation," (27) and offers a theological reading that depicts white
Americans as trapped within a God-given "purity" that helps
them avoid recognizing just how unstable and fluid racial and
sexual identities are. In order to escape the terror that the fear of
death and loneliness can bring, they engage, as Baldwin explains
in a later 1984 interview, in a self-repression that also restricts and
excludes others ("Go the Way Your Blood Beats" 177). Baldwin's
willingness to challenge notions of purity not only unravels traditional conceptions of religion, but also provides a basis for a religious writer to confront United States—"a nation with the soul
of a church" (Mead 262). Baldwin even affirmed before an international church conference that his very credential for speaking
about the effects of religious rhetoric and identity was that he was
"not a theologian in any way whatever," but someone who has

in fact left the "pulpit" ("White Racism or World Community?" 435). His apostasy propels his social criticism when he observes in his *No Name in the Street* (1972): "If [white] Americans were not so terrified of their private selves, they would never have need to invent and could never have become so dependent on what they still call 'the Negro problem.' This problem, which they invented in order to safeguard their purity, has made of them criminals and monsters, and it is destroying them" (54). In *The Fire Next Time* Baldwin believes that a continued white "intransigence and ignorance" made cosmic "vengeance [as] inevitable" as the natural law of gravity (140–41).

But Baldwin's turn toward the faceless deity of natural law signals just how much he was willing to divest himself of the adornment that often comes with religious rhetoric, while still retaining its power to criticize a society steeped in religion. He is a theologian of the body without a god, challenging the twin foundations of race and religion in a nation seemingly established on (racial) exclusion and (sexual) self-denial. But despite Baldwin's reduction of a personal god (who labels and excludes) to a joyless force of nature, his language is charged with an almost mechanistic moral force that renders fiery judgment on the United States. As Baldwin writes in *The Fire Next Time*: "Time catches up with kingdoms and crushes them, gets its teeth into doctrines and rends them; time reveals the foundations on which any kingdom rests and eats at those foundations, and it destroys doctrines by proving them to be untrue" (72). The burdens of his religious heritage shaped his art and granted him insight into the very structure of traditional religious and racial thinking. At the same time, it allowed Baldwin to contend that history will judge America even if God does not. Baldwin predicted that the "Christian world" would reveal itself "as morally bankrupt and politically unstable" over time (*Fire Next Time* 73). Baldwin renders judgment on American society not through the invocation of a brooding Christian god, but through the blind inexorability of history that will undo white racial identities that are just as fluid as black identities.

So, in fact, religion was not simply a detour or even a necessary prelude to a secular career. In many ways it defined Baldwin's work. Baldwin was religious, first, because his social criticism recognized and challenged the theological basis for the white social identity that animated American society and the static racial categories that structured it. "[W]hite Americans do not believe in death," Baldwin writes in *The Fire Next Time*, "and this is why the darkness of my [black] skin so intimates them" (124). And Baldwin recognizes just how ensconced white Americans have been in notions of purity and how blind they have been that their notions of self are tied to those (black people) whom they do not see. For Baldwin, white social identities are rooted in a god-complex, where people obsessed with their own purity desperately deny their own mortality and fear of black people.

But more fundamentally, Baldwin is a religious writer because he was, in fact, a writer in exile from the church he once served, just like he was in exile from the country of his birth. Baldwin often defined himself through his sense of alienation and his distance from settled categories and expectations. He defined himself, indeed, as an exile even before he had left the country of his birth. As he told anthropologist Margaret Mead in an interview published as *A Rap on Race* (1971): "I was an exile long before I went away" (220). For Baldwin his choice to leave was not entirely his own. "I left because I wanted to live," he told Mead. "But the fact is that I am an exile because I can't live in America under the terms on which Americans offer me my life" (221). But despite these constant declarations of distance, his passionate talk of exile and alienation conveyed a fierce kinship to the land that had betrayed him. Forcefully claiming the country he left, Baldwin argued: "My country drove me out. The Americans drove me out of my country" (221). Baldwin seemed to acknowledge throughout their conversation Mead's point that he had "never left [his country] in spirit" (221). Even though he lived outside of America nearly as long as he lived within its borders, Baldwin became the most peculiarly American of authors; in the same way, Baldwin's fiercely felt exile from the church actually represents his firm connection to the faith he left behind. In his constant struggles with the Christian god, he revealed himself to be the most peculiarly religious of black writers in the postwar era.

NOTES

1. James Baldwin was born James Jones to the then-unwed Berdis Jones in Harlem Hospital in 1924 and had no biological connection with David Baldwin, the man who married his mother in 1927. I will refer to his stepfather as his father, just as Baldwin usually did, unless James Baldwin's status as a child born outside of wedlock is pertinent and under discussion.

2. There are, of course, some notable examples of scholars who have examined the significance of Baldwin's religious past. See, in particular, Trudier Harris, Stanley Macebuh, Michael Lynch, Sondra O'Neale, and Peter Kerry Powers, whose critical studies are included in the list of works cited.

3. For recent work that focuses on exile and Baldwin's expatriate status as central to his work and connected to global modernism, see Bryan R. Washington, *The Politics of Exile,* and Cyraina E. Johnson-Roullier, *Reading on the Edge.*

4. I find Barbara Olson's argument persuasive. In an article in the *African American Review,* she argues that Baldwin wrote *The Amen Corner* in part because he wanted to make the ambiguous attitude toward black evangelical culture revealed in *Go Tell It on the Mountain* more stark by more clearly "indict[ing] the church he had left in anger and disgust at age 17" (296).

WORKS CITED

Baldwin, James. *Amen Corner.* New York: Dial, 1968.
———. *Another Country.* New York: Dial, 1962.
———. *Blues for Mister Charlie.* New York: Dial, 1964.
———. *The Devil Finds Work: An Essay.* New York: Delta Trade Paperbacks, 1976.
———. *The Fire Next Time.* New York: Dial, 1963.
———. *Go Tell It on the Mountain.* New York: Knopf, 1953.
———. "Here Be Dragons." In *The Price of the Ticket: Collected Nonfiction, 1948–1985.* New York: St. Martin's/Marek, 1985. 677–90.
———. *Just Above My Head.* New York: Dial, 1979.
———. *Notes of a Native Son.* Boston: Beacon, 1955.
———, and Margaret Mead. *A Rap on Race.* Philadelphia: J. B. Lippincott, 1971.
———. *No Name in the Street.* New York: Dial, 1972.

————, and Nikki Giovanni. *A Dialogue*. Philadelphia: J. B Lippincott, 1973.

————. "Preservation of Innocence." In *James Baldwin: Collected Essays*, edited by Toni Morrison. New York: Library of America, 1998. 594–600.

————. *The Price the Ticket: Collected Nonfiction, 1948–1985*. New York: St. Martin's/Marek, 1985.

————. "Go the Way Your Blood Beats: An Interview with James Baldwin." Interiewed by Richard Goldstein. In *James Baldwin: The Legacy*, edited by Quincy Troupe. New York: Touchstone/Simon & Schuster, 1989. 173–85.

————. "White Racism or World Community?" In *The Price of the Ticket: Collected Nonfiction, 1948–1985*. New York: St. Martin's/Marek, 1985. 435–42.

Cobb, Michael L. "Pulpitic Publicity: James Baldwin and the Queer Uses of Religious Words." *GLQ: A Journal of Lesbian and Gay Studies* 7.2 (April 2001): 285–312.

Eckman, Fern Marja. *The Furious Passage of James Baldwin*. New York: M. Evans, 1966.

Elgrably, Jordan, and George Plimpton. "The Art of Fiction LXXVIII: James Baldwin. In *Conversations with James Baldwin*," edited by Fred Standley and Louis Pratt. Jackson: University Press of Mississippi, 1989. 232–54.

Fairclough, Adam. *To Redeem the Soul of America: The Southern Christian Leadership Conference and Martin Luther King, Jr.* Athens: University of Georgia Press, 1987.

Hardy, Clarence. *James Baldwin's God: Sex, Hope and Crisis in Black Holiness Culture*. Knoxville: University of Tennessee Press, 2003.

Harris, Trudier, "Introduction." In *New Essays on* Go Tell It on the Mountain, edited by Trudier Harris. New York: Cambridge University Press, 1996.

Johnson-Roullier, Cyraina E. *Reading on the Edge: Exiles, Modernities, and Cultural Transformation in Proust, Joyce, and Baldwin*. Albany: State University of New York Press, 2000.

Lynch, Michael F. "A Glimpse of the Hidden God: Dialectical Vision in Baldwin's *Go Tell It on the Mountain*." In *New Essays on* Go Tell It on the Mountain, edited by Trudier Harris. New York: Cambridge University Press, 1996. 29–57.

Macebuh, Stanley. *James Baldwin: A Critical Study*. New York: The Third Press, 1973.

Mead, Sidney E. "The 'Nation with the Soul of a Church." *Church History* 36.3 (September 1967): 262–83.

Ohi, Kevin. "'I'm not the Boy You Want': Sexuality, 'Race,' and Thwarted Revelation in Baldwin's *Another Country.*" *African American Review* 33.2 (Summer 1999): 261–81.

Olsen, Barbara K. "'Come-to-Jesus Stuff' in James Baldwin's *Go Tell It on the Mountain* and *The Amen Corner.*" *African American Review* 31.2 (Summer 1997): 295–301.

O'Neale, Sondra. "Fathers, Gods, and Religion: Perceptions of Christianity and Ethnic Faith in James Baldwin." In *Critical Essays on James Baldwin,* edited by Fred L. Standley and Nancy V. Burt. Boston: G. K. Hall, 1988. 125–43.

Powers, Peter Kerry. "The Treacherous Body: Isolation, Confession, and Community in James Baldwin." *American Literature* 77.4 (December 2005): 787–813.

Tomlinson, Robert. "'Payin' One's Dues': Expatriation as Personal Experience and Paradigm in the Works of James Baldwin." *African American Review* 33.1 (Spring 1999): 135–48.

Washington, Bryan R. *The Politics of Exile: Ideology in Henry James, F. Scott Fitzgerald, and James Baldwin.* Boston: Northeastern University Press, 1995.

Using the Blues

James Baldwin and Music

D. Quentin Miller

All I know about music is that not
many people ever really hear it. And
even then, on the rare occasions when
something opens within, and the
music enters, what we mainly hear,
or hear corroborated, are personal,
private, vanishing evocations. But the
man who creates the music is hearing
something else, is dealing with the
roar rising from the void and imposing order on it as it hits the air.

—James Baldwin, "Sonny's Blues" (1957)

American music underwent profound changes in the twentieth century. With the advent of recording and the rise of
radio and film, music was widely accessible and no longer strictly
dependent on local, live performance. Its accessibility helped listeners appreciate and explore its diversity: folk-music traditions
merged with European-derived classical traditions and challenged the dominance of the classical tradition. One indigenous
American form that was a product of such a merging was jazz,
an amalgam of the blues, gospel, and classical music. These four
musical categories—jazz, blues, gospel, and classical—recur

within James Baldwin's work and reveal his complexity as they signify racial identity, artistic identity, and national identity. Part of Baldwin's quest was to use music, especially the blues, as a key to unlock the mysteries of his identity as an exile, an artist, a black American in a racially hostile era, and a boy preacher who turned against his church.

In addition to music as a motif, the musician is a recurrent character in Baldwin's work, an alter ego for the author himself and a symbolic figure who was called to carry the burden of his race and to expose it in a public arena. Baldwin became especially interested in the thrills and dangers of musical performance in his contemporary world. He was conscious of the difference between music as performance and music as entertainment—conscious, in other words, of the tension between the artist and the commercial demands imposed by his audience. As a result of this tension, music informs Baldwin's fiction in three main ways: (1) characters listen to music to provide inspiration, clarity for their experiences, or space for contemplation; (2) characters perform or participate in the performance of music; and (3) narrators blend song lyrics fluidly with prose to connect individual experience to a broader cultural experience. The popularization and evolution of blues and jazz in the twentieth century focused on prominent vocalists, whose careers were widely accessible in the age of film, radio, and television. These vocalists give Baldwin models for his tragic heroes, and they provide him with a soundtrack that links the dramas he stages to a long history of African American suffering, relief, exuberance, and despair.

Baldwin's birth in Harlem in 1924 coincided with the period of high modernism in the arts, when artists in all genres embraced formal experimentation and invented a new aesthetic that reimagined perception, recast the function of art, and rethought the very nature of reality. This was also the era when jazz began to gain respect as a unique, syncretic art, not just a form of popular entertainment. While Debussy and Stravinsky experimented with atonal orchestral music that sometimes shocked audiences with its apparent vulgarity and evident violence, Louis Armstrong, Bessie Smith, and Duke Ellington were bringing jazz and blues into prominence, making this new form accessible to audiences who were dancing while they listened. As with Debussy and Stravinsky, audiences also expressed some degree of shock at the popularity of jazz because it was assumed to be sensual, even overtly sexual: the word *jazz* is itself a euphemism for sex. By the middle of the twentieth century, when Baldwin was in the process of becoming the most prominent African American writer of his time, jazz and the blues were receiving unprecedented critical acclaim and attention, both as complex musical forms in their own right and as two of the richest expressions of the African American experience. A host of periodicals about jazz and the blues were initiated during this period, from the founding of *Down Beat* magazine in 1935 to the publication of *Jazz Times* in 1970. Innovations like bebop and fusion allowed jazz performers such as Miles Davis and Herbie Hancock to cross between musical genres, anticipating and perhaps even catalyzing the popularity of variations of rock music in the late twentieth century. At the heart of both forms was the essential impulse of spontaneity and improvisation. Blues, according to Baldwin in his uncollected essay "The Uses of the Blues," refers to "the experience of life, or the state of being, out of which blues come" and "the toughness that manages to make this experience articulate" (131).

Emphasizing improvisation and technical mastery, jazz and the blues, especially when they flourished in the 1920s, provided a metaphor for African American liberation: here was the freedom blacks had been promised for over half a century but had been denied because of segregation and other forms of discrimination. The artistic freedom of the jazz performer appealed to black artists in all media during the so-called New Negro Renaissance, because it was an exuberant new genre that grew out of a very old one; as LeRoi Jones (Amiri Baraka) points out in his book *Blues People*, early twentieth-century jazz developed out of a blues tradition that had its roots in slave songs and field hollers: "Blues is the parent of all legitimate jazz, and it is impossible to say exactly how old blues is—certainly no older than the presence of Negroes in the United States" (17). The work of Langston Hughes, Baldwin's literary predecessor from Harlem, represents a sustained and conscious effort to bring the rhythms and structure of jazz and the blues into poetry. One of Hughes's most famous poems, "The Weary Blues" (1925), can be read as a companion piece to Baldwin's most famous story, "Sonny's Blues," for both describe the torment of the black musician and the tenuous, complex relationship he has with his listener. Hughes was keenly aware of the potential for African American literature to celebrate its rich musical heritage, but Baldwin did not necessarily think his predecessor succeeded. In one of his infamous battles with the giants of American literature, Baldwin reviewed the collected poems of Hughes negatively, pointing to their "fake simplicity" and claiming that, although Hughes had recognized the importance of music to African American experience, "he has not forced [it] to the realm of art where [its] meaning would become clear and overwhelming" ("Sermons and Blues" BR6). This salvo becomes one way for the young Baldwin to set his own goals: the meaning of black music had to become "clear and overwhelming" in his own work, or he would fail by his own standards.

Classical Music, Recorded and Live

In Baldwin's earliest work, the importance of African American music and of live musical performance is not as evident as it would be in later works. In the middle of the twentieth century, the accessibility of music underwent an enormous shift due to the flourishing of two technologies: recording and radio. In the late 1930s, as Baldwin came of age and the Great Depression waned, the radio and the phonograph were becoming ubiquitous appliances in American living rooms. The impact of this development on the cultural meaning of music cannot be underestimated. Half a century earlier, when the only way to hear music was to be in the same room as the musicians, performance was fundamental. The experience of listening to prerecorded music—on a phonograph, at a movie, or on radio—suggests a kind of mechanical detachment between audience and artist, but also the possibility for endless repetition, for hearing a song over and over again until it is within one's head. The distinction between recorded and live music provides an analogy to Baldwin's multiple roles: he divided his time between writing in private, even in exile in foreign countries, and speaking and lecturing to live audiences, especially during the early 1960s, when he was most involved with the struggle for civil rights. There is a clear difference between writing and public speaking, just as there is a difference between recorded music and live performance. Recording music and writing both allow for revision, both are accomplished in private settings, and the products of both can be returned to and examined repeatedly; live music and public speaking are spontaneous and interactive. In his early phase, after forsaking his role as a boy preacher, Baldwin wished to be a writer only; he had not yet discovered his public-speaking voice outside the church.

The cultural shift marked by the advent of recorded music is enormous: suddenly, music could be played repeatedly and broadcast across vast spaces. Yet the emotional impact of live performance is more profound. Baldwin's work explores both of these facets of music intensely: radios, jukeboxes, and phonographs are ubiquitous in his fiction and drama, but so are musicians. As a way of merging these two facets of music, he repeatedly holds up models of singers with whom most of his readers will be familiar because of their widespread popularity, such as Bessie Smith, Billie Holiday, Ray Charles, and Aretha Franklin. These vocal giants of the twentieth century are familiar to all Americans, and their triumphs and tragedies have been woven into the American story. On a more personal level, Baldwin focuses on local, individual performances—by his brother David, whose experience singing in a gospel quartet is described in the essay "Journey to Atlanta" and rendered in fiction in the novel *Just Above My Head* (1979); by Luke and David in the play *The Amen Corner* (1955); by Sonny in "Sonny's Blues"; by Leo Proudhammer in *Tell Me How Long the Train's Been Gone* (1968); and by Ida in *Another Country* (1962), to name just a few. These descriptions highlight the condition of the musician who pours his or her soul out for just a few people, not with any illusions of widespread fame, but simply because he or she has to. Baldwin himself had some experience with musical performance: even before he entered high school, he received a letter from the mayor of New York for writing his middle school's alma mater (Leeming 13), and he also performed in his church as a youth and in a Greenwich Village restaurant as a singing waiter in his teenage years, an experience which he reworks in *Tell Me How Long the Train's Been Gone.*[1] In a 1980 interview Baldwin says, "I grew up with music...more than with any other language. In a way the music I grew up with saved my life" (Standley and Pratt 190).

The pure artist who "is dealing with the roar rising from the void and imposing order on it as it hits the air," according to Sonny, is awe-inspiring, but also volatile. Music, if it is any good, involves a tremendous amount of risk and vulnerability. The marginalized musicians and other artists and performers in Baldwin's work—black, gay, poor, addicted, or any combination—are doubly at risk, and their music reveals the precariousness of their lives. Baldwin harshly judges his characters who refuse to take risks, who choose safety over vulnerability, even when such characters closely resemble the author himself. In Baldwin's first published short story, "Previous Condition" (1948), the protagonist Peter is paralyzed by his rejection of the poverty and lack of promise of Harlem on the one hand and his ejection from the white world of high art and glamour on the other. As the story opens Peter is listening to "the Breakfast Symphony. They were playing Beethoven....I listened to Ludwig and I watched the [cigarette] smoke rise to the dirty ceiling. Under Ludwig's drums and horns I listened to hear footsteps on the stairs" (85). The footsteps belong to the landlady who is about to evict him because white neighbors have complained about the presence of a black tenant.

Beethoven's music represents a few things here: passionate, intense art that can captivate Peter's attention, the high sophistication associated with the white world and European culture more specifically, and the deeply felt discouragement of a black man trying to enter that world. Peter regards classical music as a ticket out of the ghetto, but it is temporary, or illusory, as such. This moment listening to the Breakfast Symphony (which in the mid-century was broadcast daily on New York's WQXR) is part of a pattern: Peter describes how he and his white friends

Jules and Ida would attend classical summer concerts, and the experience is nearly euphoric:

> There were pauses in the music for the rushing, calling, halting piano. Everything would stop except the climbing soloist; he would reach a height and everything would join him, the violins first and then the horns; and then the deep blue bass and the flute and the bitter trampling drums; beating, beating and mounting together and stopping with a crash like daybreak. When I first heard the *Messiah* I was alone; my blood bubbled like fire and wine; I cried; like an infant crying for its mother's milk; or a sinner running to meet Jesus. (90)

This description merges, or at least alludes to, three types of music that influence Baldwin: it is classical music, but there is a deep "blue" bass at the heart of it, and Peter's simile at the end ("a sinner running to meet Jesus") signifies gospel. The profundity of Peter's listening experience is striking; it reveals how Baldwin clearly aspired to move his readers and audiences through a similar kind of passionate intensity and how the fictional Peter desperately wants access to the world that produces such music.

Peter identifies himself as an actor even though he realizes, "I'm not tall and I'm not good looking and I can't sing or dance and I'm not white" (84).These physical attributes, especially the last one, amount to the "previous condition" of the title, which explains his paralysis and his belief that he's "got no story" at the end, when he is listening to Ella Fitzgerald on the jukebox of a Harlem bar (100). The classical music that so moves Peter has always been and remains primarily a white European form. In Baldwin's essay "Autobiographical Notes," the introduction to his first essay collection, he describes himself as "a kind of bastard of the West," who recognizes that "Shakespeare, Bach, and Rembrandt" are "not really [his] creations, they did not contain [his] history" (*Notes of a Native Son* 6–7). Like Peter, part of Baldwin's racial self-doubt stems from this disconnection between the works of art he admires and those produced by his race for which he has not yet gained a full appreciation in the first decade of his career; Baldwin says, with a great deal of bitterness, that while he "hated and feared white people" for discriminating against him, he also "despised [black people], possibly because they failed to produce Rembrandt" (7), or Bach if we follow the other examples. Peter's bitterness in "Previous Condition" is evident along these lines: If Beethoven is unavailable to him either as a model or as a way to validate himself, he will have to look elsewhere for musical inspiration.

Bessie Smith and Other Inspirations

Thus Baldwin, while completing his first-novel manuscript (*Go Tell It on the Mountain*) in the Swiss village of Loèche-les-Bains, does not find himself listening to Beethoven, but rather to Bessie Smith, the so-called Empress of the Blues. From the moment when Baldwin's identity as a writer was quickening, the blues, rather than Beethoven, inspires him. In his essay "The Discovery of What It Means to Be an American," he writes, "It was Bessie Smith, through her tone and her cadence, who helped me to dig back to the way I myself must have spoken when I was a pickaninny, and to remember the things I had heard and seen and felt. I had buried them very deep. I had never listened to Bessie Smith in America (in the same way that, for years, I would not touch watermelon), but in Europe she helped to reconcile me to being a 'nigger'" (*Nobody Knows My Name* 18). Baldwin had regarded the blues as a kind of racial cliché, but as he responds to his calling to become a writer, he experiences a liberation: listening to the blues helps him to get his work done and puts him in touch with the core identity he had repressed. He elaborates on Bessie Smith's influence on him in a 1961 interview with Studs Terkel:

I finally realized that one of the reasons that I couldn't finish this novel was that I was ashamed of where I came from and where I had been. I was ashamed of the life in the Negro church, ashamed of my father, ashamed of the Blues, ashamed of Jazz, and, of course, ashamed of watermelon: all of these stereotypes that the country inflicts on Negroes, that we all eat watermelon or we all do nothing but sing the Blues. . . . Bessie had the beat. . . . I played Bessie every day. . . . I corrected things [in the novel] according to what I was able to hear when Bessie sang, and when James P. Johnson plays. It's that *tone*, that sound, which is in me. (4–5)

Here he is not only discovering what it means to be an American, but what it means to be black *and* what it means to be an artist. Listening to music allows him to discover a sound that is within him. In a sense, he is becoming someone who is able to perform music, someone who is "dealing with the roar rising from the void," by training himself to become one of the few who really hears music, who allows something to "open within."

In his published conversation with Margaret Mead, *A Rap on Race* (1972), Baldwin further amplifies and clarifies the relationship of his exile in Europe, his calling to become a writer, and his discovery of Bessie Smith; he says, "I began to think in French. I began to understand the English language better than I ever had before; I began to understand the English language which I came out of, the language that produced Ray Charles or Bessie Smith or which produced all the poets who produced me" (40). These two vocalists, along with Billie Holiday, become recurrent touchstones in Baldwin's allusions to popular black musicians in his work. All three vocalists represent a variation on the blues in different contexts and from different eras. Bessie Smith is the oldest of the three figures and the first to influence Baldwin. Smith was one of the most famous blues singers of the 1920s—the decade of Baldwin's birth—so she can be seen as part of his origin story, something that he has to "dig back to," as he says. Her bisexuality and her alcoholism likely augmented his interest in her, but her intense, soulful voice and her tragic premature death in a car crash were also paradigms for the musicians in Baldwin's fiction. Like Baldwin, Smith was born in poverty and rose to early success and prominence. By 1924, in fact, she was the highest paid black entertainer of her time (Albertson 10), before the advent of the movies diminished the popularity of live musical performance.

Gospel, According to James

Though he was born in Harlem at the pinnacle of the Harlem
Renaissance, Baldwin spent his formative years in the confines of
a fundamentalist church that considered jazz the devil's music,
allied with gambling, drinking, drugs, and sex—the other sins
on the streets of Harlem. The only music the young Baldwin
would have known, in the 1930s, was what we have come to
call gospel. Derived from spirituals, gospel music has much in
common musically with the very same musical forms (jazz and
the blues) considered sinful by the church elders. Mellonee V.
Burnim draws a distinction between spirituals, which evolved
in the nineteenth century, and gospel, which "emerged during
the first quarter of the twentieth century among members of
the urban working class—the lower economic and educational
strata of the Black community" (51). This was clearly the milieu of
Baldwin's youth. Foregrounding passionate vocal performance
that reveals deep sorrow and joy, gospel is a form of the blues in
a religious idiom, encouraging both solo performance and group
participation. There is also a classical tradition embedded in gospel: sacred music (from the English Renaissance on) developed
into church hymns, the lyrics of which merged with the gospel
repertoire. In *Blues People* LeRoi Jones describes the relationship between classical white songs and black gospel this way:
"The melodies of many of the white Christian and European
religious songs which the Negroes incorporated into their worship remained the same, but the Negroes changed the rhythms
and harmonies of these songs to suit themselves. The very fact
that the Negroes sang these songs in their peculiar way, with not
only the idiosyncratic American idiom of early Negro speech but
the inflection, rhythm, and stress of that speech, also served to
shape the borrowed songs to a strictly Negro idiom" (46). This
idiom had much in common with the secular music that was
evolving outside the church walls; as Jones writes, "The Negro's
religious music contained the same 'rags,' 'blue notes' and 'stop
times' as were emphasized later and to a much greater extent in
jazz" (47).

Baldwin's break from the church, so well documented in his writings and in Baldwin criticism, has an evident metaphor in his treatment of music: one might assume that he leaves gospel behind to explore secular forms of music, especially the blues. Hence, one might observe how the title of his first book is a gospel lyric—*Go Tell It on the Mountain* (1953)—but the titles of his later books and individual works explicitly reference the blues: the story "Sonny's Blues" (1957); the poetry collection *Jimmy's Blues* (1985); the play *Blues for Mister Charlie* (1964); the novel *If Beale Street Could Talk* (1974), the title of which alludes to the Memphis street known as the "birthplace of the blues"—the examples are myriad. And yet the titles of Baldwin's most famous essay collection, *The Fire Next Time* (1963), and his final novel, *Just Above My Head*, are derived from gospel lyrics. Clearly, the division between the blues and gospel, as well as their relationship to classical music, are, like everything in Baldwin, too complex to be expressed in a simple formula. The boundaries between sacred and secular, between popular and classical, between traditionally white and traditionally black musical forms prove to be fluid in Baldwin's work, just as they were fluid in the most daring and experimental musical works of the period. Duke Ellington's attempts to merge jazz and classical music in a sacred context in the three works *In the Beginning God* (1965), *Second Sacred Concert* (1968), and *Third Sacred Concert* (1973) can perhaps be seen analogously to Baldwin's most experimental, challenging novels: *Another Country*, *Tell Me How Long the Train's Been Gone*, and *Just Above My Head*. All three of these novels display the complex pattern between the three chief forms of music influencing Baldwin's world: gospel/sacred, classical/high art, and blues/popular.

Baldwin's ambivalent response to fame is one of the reasons he sympathized with Bessie Smith and became inspired by her, but he was also undoubtedly drawn to her as a raw blues voice, a voice he had heard before in a religious context in the form of gospel. His first story might have showcased the Breakfast Symphony, but his first novel reveals the deep influence of gospel on Baldwin's aesthetic and on his thinking. John Grimes, the protagonist of *Go Tell It on the Mountain*, understands this influence

and feels its weight: "The Sunday morning service began when
Brother Elisha sat down at the piano and raised a song. This
moment and this music had been with John, so it seemed, since
he had first drawn breath" (14). While Bessie Smith might have
been in Baldwin's blood before he was born, gospel music seems
as though it was his nourishment from birth, and it is directly
responsible for his faith:

> Elisha hit the keys, beginning at once to sing, and everybody
> joined him, clapping their hands, and rising, and beating the
> tambourines.
>   The song might be: *Down at the cross where my Saviour
> died!*
>   Or: *Jesus, I'll never forget how you set me free!*
>   Or: *Lord, hold my hand while I run this race!*
>   They sang with all the strength that was in them, and
> clapped their hands for joy. There had never been a time
> when John had not sat watching the saints rejoice with terror
> in his heart, and wonder. Their singing caused him to believe
> in the presence of the Lord; indeed, it was no longer a ques-
> tion of belief, because they made that presence real. (14–15)

This passage goes on to describe how this singing leads to the
clapping of hands, beating of feet, and dancing that signal religious ecstasy. John has yet to feel the presence of God within
himself, but he is convinced that music is evidence that God
exists, and that he will join in the chorus with the same fervor.

The relationship between performer and audience in gospel
is fluid. In Baldwin's novel, Elisha strikes a chord on the piano
to signal the beginning of a song that everyone knows. A gospel
performance is often initiated or guided by a single instrument
like a piano or an organ, but its core is harmonized vocal performance accompanied by a beat, kept through clapping or with
handheld percussive instruments like tambourines. One mem-
ber of the chorus will frequently sing solo, breaking away from
the chorus for a verse before rejoining it. Eventually the audience
is encouraged to join in the performance through singing and
clapping. Although the piano or organ player commences the

music and, to some degree, controls its movement, and although the vocal soloist temporarily breaks away from the group, the emphasis is on the communal production of music rather than on individual performances.

Finding a (Secular) Voice

Throughout his career Baldwin struggled with the tension between group identity and individual performance, which is analogous to other tensions in his work—public vs. private, bisexual, black, American self vs. self apart from societal categories, spokesman vs. artist. Despite its capacity for improvisation and spontaneity, gospel may have seemed too restrictive a form for the side of Baldwin that strove for unlimited individual expression. We see a fuller expression of this notion in Baldwin's first play, *The Amen Corner*, which emphasizes the story of a church performer who resists the doctrine of his mother, a preacher, in order to follow in the footsteps of his father, a jazz musician. The play both demonstrates the importance of the musical idiom to the black church and uses music as a metaphorical pathway out of that church into less restrictive secular musical forms, especially jazz and the blues. As LeRoi Jones writes, "Blues was a music that arose from the needs of a group, although it was assumed that each man had his *own* blues and that he would sing them"; but beginning in the early twentieth century, "The artisan, the professional blues singer, appeared; blues-singing no longer had to be merely a passionately felt avocation, it could now become a way of making a living" (82). Jones regards this professionalization with a healthy dose of skepticism, but for Baldwin it is akin to survival, in an intellectual and a spiritual as well as a physical sense.

The importance of gospel music to *The Amen Corner* is immediately evident: the play is nearly a musical, with a significant percentage of its lines comprised of gospel lyrics. But Baldwin dedicates the published version of the play to jazz, blues, and soul musicians: "For Nina, Ray, Miles, Bird and Billie" (vi). This dedication obviously refers to vocalist Nina Simone (sometimes called "The High Priestess of Soul"), Ray Charles, trumpet virtuoso Miles Davis, saxophone prodigy Charlie Parker, and Billie Holliday. Based on this dedication, despite the impact of religious music on Baldwin's conception of the play, he clearly meant it as an homage to jazz musicians. This is not to say that Baldwin repudiates gospel in *The Amen Corner*, but he was clearly in the process of making his violent break with the church when he composed the play; as Saadi Simawe puts it, "[T]he traditional quarrel between music and religion (or the musician and the preacher) is dramatically delineated" in Baldwin's play (23). The lure of the secular life is evident from the opening stage directions: the audience may be looking at a church interior with "hymnbooks and tambourines," but we also hear "snatches of someone's radio; and under everything, the piano, which David is playing in the church" (3). David stands astride his piano bench with one foot in the church and the other in the outer world. His duty is divided because although he is attracted to the outer world, where his musical gifts can flourish, it is clear that his piano-playing talent is key to the success of his mother's sermons. One of the church elders, Odessa, comments that another elder, Sister Price, cannot act as a substitute for David: "She just ain't got no *juices*, somehow" (20). David concurs: "I'm sure she's sanctified and all that, but she *still* can't play piano. Not for *me*, she can't. She just makes me want to get up and leave the service" (23). David wants to leave the service for many reasons, but these statements show how central musical performance is to black Christian worship and how some intangible combination of factors leads to its success or failure in this context. Yet David clearly rejects the notion that he is playing simply for external reasons, including the needs of the church; as he says to his mother late in the play, "I can't stay home. Maybe I can say something—one day—maybe I can say something in music that's never been said before" (120–21). He has clearly been called.

Sister Margaret, David's mother, acknowledges that he has "a *natural* gift for music," but she and her son each attribute it to different sources: Margaret says, "[T]he Lord give it to you, you didn't learn it in no school" (24). David believes that his talent originated with his father, Luke, a jazz musician who has

been gone for most of David's life. When Luke returns, music is
the thing that unites them. Luke says to David, "You play piano
like I dreamed you would" (58), and the boy replies: "I remembered how you used to play for me sometimes. That was why I
started playing the piano. I used to go to sleep dreaming about
the way we'd play together one day, me with my piano and you
with your trombone" (59). The father's and son's dreams of one
another are only partially fulfilled; Luke's death prevents them
from playing together and from his ever really hearing David
play outside of the church. The distance between them had been
caused by Margaret's enforcement of the separation of the secular and religious worlds; David tells his father, "Mama never
let us keep a phonograph. I just didn't never hear any of your
records—until here lately. You was right up there with the best,
Jellyroll Morton and Louis Armstrong and cats like that" (58).
David's defiance against his mother takes the form of bringing
a record player into their house, plugging it in, and playing his
father's music. Revealing her weakening power, she tells David:
"You ain't supposed to let your daddy come here and lead you
away from the Word. You's supposed to lead your daddy to the
Lord" (82).

David is, in fact, fed up with his obligation to produce music
only to inspire religious faith. He tells his father about a group
of young men who "come in the church and they heard me
playing piano and they kept coming back all the time. Mama
said it was the Holy Ghost drawing them in. But it wasn't" (61).
Luke rightly acknowledges that it was David's piano playing
that drew the men in, and David adds, "I didn't draw them
in. They drew me out. . . . things started happening inside me
which hadn't ever happened before. It was terrible. It was
wonderful" (61). This is Baldwin's first deep consideration of
the necessary anguish of the musician who uses his talent not
only to entertain others, but to define and express himself.
Part of Luke's role in the play is to inspire David to leave the
church to pursue a musical career, but also to warn him of
the potential loneliness and despair of the musician's life—
not unlike the subject of Hughes's "The Weary Blues," who
ends the poem in solitude with his song echoing in his head.

Luke says to David: "Music is a moment. But life's a long time. In that moment, when it's good, when you really swinging— then you joined to everything, to everybody, to skies and stars and every living thing.... Music's what you *got* to do, *if* you got to do it.... You know, the music don't come out of the air, baby. It comes out of the man who's blowing it" (64). Clearly music is a vocation in Baldwin's work, and he dedicates the play to other black musicians who evidently felt it was "what you *got* to do, *if* you got to do it."

The lives of the musicians he chooses for the dedication, though, tended toward the tragic. Bessie Smith died prematurely in a car wreck; Nina Simone suffered from bipolar disorder; Billie Holiday was addicted to drugs and alcohol and occasionally imprisoned before her death at the age of 44; and Charlie Parker, also addicted to heroin, died at the age of 34. The cost of musical fame proved immense to these artists, as it would for rock-music stars of the late twentieth century, but Baldwin's feeling is that one has to pay the price of the ticket. Charlie Parker thus resurfaces in Baldwin's most famous short story, "Sonny's Blues" (1957), which constitutes a possible continuation of David's story from *The Amen Corner*.

"Sonny's Blues" has received more critical attention than most of Baldwin's other work in terms of musical analysis. One of the most substantial essays on Baldwin and music, "The Black Musician: The Black Hero as Light Bearer," by Sherley Anne Williams, describes the musician in Baldwin's work as "an archetypal figure" who

is the hope of making it in America and the bitter mockery of never making it well enough to escape the danger of being Black, the living symbol of alienation from the past and hence from self and the rhythmical link with the mysterious ancestral past. That past and its pain and the transcendence of pain is always an implicit part of the musician's characterization in Baldwin. Music is the medium through which the musician achieves enough understanding and strength to deal with the past and present hurt. (147)

This is a succinct definition of Sonny, who has suffered in a way Luke in *The Amen Corner* prophesies that David will suffer. The narrator of "Sonny's Blues" tells us right away of his brother's arrest for possessing and using heroin, which seems an occupational hazard of the jazz musician. The narrator is concerned that Sonny and his friends "shake themselves to pieces pretty goddamn fast" (131). The echo of Charlie Parker's tragic life is clear, but Baldwin adds another allusion to the end of the story, when Sonny's brother buys him a scotch and milk, which was a drink that Parker used to order, partly because it was easier on his ulcer than straight liquor. But Baldwin takes no chances that the reader would overlook the parallel: at the center of the story is a conversation between the two brothers about Parker. When the narrator asks Sonny to name a jazz musician he admires, Sonny immediately responds, "Bird." When the narrator admits that he doesn't know who that is, Sonny fires back, "'Bird! Charlie Parker! Don't they teach you nothing in the goddamn army?... He's just one of the greatest jazz musicians alive.... Maybe *the* greatest,' he added, bitterly, 'that's probably why *you* never heard of him'" (121). The narrator resists Sonny's dream: "I simply couldn't see why on earth he'd want to spend his time hanging around nightclubs, clowning around on bandstands, while people pushed each other around a dance floor. It seemed—beneath him, somehow. I had never thought about it before, had never been forced to, but I suppose I had always put jazz musicians in a class with what Daddy called 'good-time people'" (120). The narrator is clearly a flawed character, whose chief flaw is his inability to listen. His mother gave him a piece of advice years earlier about his relationship to his brother Sonny: "You may not be able to stop nothing from happening. But you got to let him know you's *there*" (119). The narrator failed to listen carefully to this advice, and he neglects Sonny for years. Throughout the story, his unwillingness to listen to his younger brother is clear as he consistently interrupts him, even after asking him probing questions.

Moreover, the narrator merely hears the word *jazz* and imagines that it signifies a lack of seriousness, that it constitutes nothing more than cheap entertainment for "good-time people," and, more pointedly, that it will not be the key to success, which matters to him much more than anything like choosing a vocation based on passion (hence his own safe career as an algebra teacher). He has never listened to jazz, or, if he has, he has not understood it; Hayden Carruth writes, "Some people can hear jazz, and others, by far the greater number, cannot" (24). This sentiment is echoed in the epigraph to this chapter: the narrator admits his fault, and thus prepares himself to hear jazz, and to listen to his brother, Sonny, for the first time. What he hears is the blues (the "parent of all legitimate jazz," as Jones put it), his brother's unique blues, but also the depth of suffering it signifies, including his own unacknowledged suffering over the death of his infant daughter. Houston Baker defines the blues as "a synthesis... an amalgam that seems always to have been in motion in America—always becoming, shaping, transforming, displacing the peculiar experiences of Africans in the New World" (5). Perhaps the narrator's initial difficulty in hearing the blues is that he is unwilling to face suffering head on, whether it be personal, familial, or historical. This could be nothing more than self-preservation: he wants to avoid dealing with his daughter's death and with the death of his guitar-playing uncle, who was murdered by a gang of drunken white youths. He willfully avoids black vernacular music, and Sonny laughs at him when he sputters, "do you want to be a concert pianist, you want to play classical music and all that, or—or what?" (119–20). Sonny could be seen as Baldwin's new consciousness mocking the earlier self who believed that Beethoven or Bach, not Bessie Smith, was the key to his success.

The beginning of the narrator's transformation occurs when he hears a woman singing on the street in an "old fashioned revival meeting." Though he has heard this type of music countless times, he is fascinated by the reaction of the listeners and by his own reaction: "As the singing filled the air the watching, listening faces underwent a change, the eyes focusing on something within; the music seemed to soothe a poison out of them; and time seemed, nearly, to fall away from the sullen, belligerent, battered faces, as though they were fleeing back to their first condition, while dreaming of their last" (129). Sonny later comments on the profundity of his experience listening to the woman: "it struck me all of a sudden how much suffering she must have had to go through—to sing like that" (132). The narrator gradually begins to understand the connection between suffering and the blues, and in the lyrical final pages of the story, when he is finally able to hear Sonny through his music, he has an epiphany:

> Then Creole stepped forward to remind them that what they were playing was the blues. He hit something in all of them, he hit something in me, myself, and the music tightened and deepened, apprehension began to beat the air. Creole began to tell us what the blues were all about. They were not about anything very new. He and his boys up there were keeping it new, at the risk of ruin, destruction, madness, and death, in order to find new ways to make us listen. For, while the tale of how we suffer, and how we are delighted, and how we may triumph is never new, it always must be heard. (139)

Reviewing *Going to Meet the Man*, the story collection of which "Sonny's Blues" is the centerpiece, Joseph Featherstone writes, "The blues are an attempt to retain the memory of pain, to transcend catastrophe, not by taking thought—for that often only adds to the pain—but by an attitude, a nearly comic, nearly tragic lyricism" (152). This attitude is what allows the old story of the blues to sound so new when it is made personal, as it is so masterfully in this story.

Bringing It All Together

Over the course of his career as a writer, Baldwin explored music and musicians in his fiction. As Saadi Simawe points out, in many interviews "Baldwin describes his performance as a writer of fiction in terms of music, especially African American music" (17). Baldwin was clearly aware of his fictional musicians as alter egos when he named his 1985 poetry collection *Jimmy's Blues*.

Space limitations here prevent a thorough exploration of every intersection of music and narrative in Baldwin's work—whether it is Ida and Rufus (both musicians) in *Another Country;* the musician narrator of "This Morning, This Evening, So Soon," in the same collection as "Sonny's Blues"; or Leo in *Tell Me How Long the Train's Been Gone,* who worked as a singing waiter. But it is important to examine the fullest expression of the intersection of the blues, the tragic musician, and the African American experience in Baldwin's work—his final novel, *Just Above My Head.* This is a sprawling narrative comprised of Hall Montana's attempts to chronicle the life of his brother Arthur, a musician. Although it has been neglected or scorned by critics, along with virtually all of Baldwin's late writing, *Just Above My Head* has received some serious critical attention in terms of its treatment of music. A review by Eleanor Traylor, essays by Julie Nash and Warren Carson, and a book chapter by Lynn Orilla Scott all examine music in this novel from many angles. On one level, it is "Sonny's Blues" in the form of a massive novel: a "square" brother tells the story of his menaced musician brother. Yet Hall is self-aware and sympathetic toward his brother from the outset, and Arthur's demise is not so much the direct product of a dangerous lifestyle brought about through a career in music as it is a record of the way fame makes the lives of musical performers so much more precarious.

The famous vocalist alluded to repeatedly in this novel is Mahalia Jackson. Jackson's tombstone reads, "The World's Greatest Gospel Singer," which was also the title of her first album with Columbia Records in 1955, nearly two decades after her first recording. She was widely considered the most prominent gospel singer during her lifetime, and her career provides Baldwin with a model of phenomenal success in this musical genre, as Bessie Smith had in the blues, as Charlie Parker and Billie Holiday had in jazz, or as Ray Charles had in soul. All of these figures, like Baldwin, rose from humble or impoverished childhoods to relatively fantastic levels of fame and wealth. Jackson is significant in that she promoted and popularized the church songs that were the foundation of Baldwin's musical repertoire, though he may have seemingly been trying to escape their influence in works like *The Amen Corner*. The fact that his final musician character was a gospel singer proves that he could not.

Mahalia Jackson's favorite performer was none other than Bessie Smith, "whose vocal quality she greatly admired and admittedly sought to imitate" (Burnim 70). This connection between the "Empress of the Blues" and the "Queen of Gospel Music" is testimony to the fact that the secular/religious distinction between these genres is weak. The same could be said of another female vocalist described in royal terms: Aretha Franklin, the "Queen of Soul," whom Baldwin alludes to in *If Beale Street Could Talk*. Franklin also began her career as a gospel singer and built on it to achieve fame in the secular world of R & B and soul popular in the later 1960s and 1970s. Like Arthur Montana, Mahalia Jackson and Aretha Franklin can be seen as success stories who used the church and gospel music as stepping stones to public fame and popularity. Echoing the nicknames of both, Arthur is publicly promoted as "The Soul Emperor" (31). Unlike Baldwin, these singers managed to build on their religious origins without harboring any guilt or anger about the fact that they were singing their songs outside of a church context. Through Arthur, Baldwin was able to make a tiny peace offering to the church he had long scorned by developing a musician character not troubled by his religious origins. Though Baldwin never relented in his animosity toward the Christian church, he held no grudge against the church songs he used to sing.

Arthur Montana follows in the tradition of performers dying prematurely. In this, Baldwin was projecting his own anxieties about an early death, about the cost of fame, and about "peaking" in one's career too early. Arthur, Hall notes, died at "the untidy age of thirty-nine," and he was remembered in the British press as a "nearly forgotten Negro moaner and groaner" and as an "emotion-filled gospel singer" (13). Part of Hall's project is to rescue his brother from such dismissive labels and to humanize him, as Arthur had helped to humanize those whose lives he touched. In announcing his project, Hall seeks to work through the issue of his brother's authenticity: "I knew all your fucking little ways, man, and how you jived the people—but that's not really true, you didn't really jive the people, you sang, you sang, and if there was any jiving done, the people jived you, my brother because they didn't know that *they* were the song and the price of the song and the glory of the song: you sang" (15). Hall initially assumes that, as a performer, his brother has "jived" his audiences, or used them for his personal gain; but he reconsiders: Song is pure, and Arthur is not removed from his audience. They are his song. The difference between the person producing the music and the person hearing the music is at least partially reconciled here. Music has the opportunity to connect individuals, but there is a cost.

Hall suggests that the cost came when Arthur's audience turned against him, "when he branched out from gospel" (16). Hall and his mother retreat from the church, but they continue to sing and speak using its songs:

> She can sing to herself, without fear of being mocked, and find strength and solace in the song that says, *They didn't know who you were.* And she's not singing about Jesus, then, she's singing about her son. Maybe all gospel songs begin out of blasphemy and presumption—what the church would call blasphemy and presumption: out of entering God's suffering and challenging God Almighty to have or to give or to withhold mercy. There will be two of us at the mercy seat: *my Lord, and I!* (16)

Gospel, ironically, becomes a way for Hall and his mother to remove themselves from the church and to find a more honest relationship with God or with some spiritual force, much like David Leeming's assessment of Baldwin's need "to leave the church to save his soul" (31).

Despite his premature, tragic death, Arthur (unlike Sonny) does not act as though music has undone him. He is an unusual performer within Baldwin's work because he is both a pure musician, with "a voice that could go high enough to make you shiver and growl low enough to make you moan" (18)—a description with undertones of sexual ecstasy—and a cool performer who does not seem rattled by addressing the needs of his audiences.

He is comfortable singing a "takeoff on an old church song" (25) and with singing those old songs straight, without irony. He is deeply identified with his art: " 'When you sing,' he said, suddenly, 'you can't sing *outside* the song. You've got to *be* the song you sing. You've got to make a confession" (59). In "Sonny's Blues" the narrator must express a similar idea for his less-than-eloquent brother: "For, while the tale of how we suffer, and how we are delighted, and how we may triumph is never new, it always must be heard. There isn't any other tale to tell, it's the only light we've got in all this darkness" (139). In Arthur, Baldwin has created someone with Sonny's musical talent as well as with Sonny's brother's eloquence. This combination may explain why Arthur seems more in control of his life than either Sonny or his brother alone do.

The novel does not focus entirely on the fraternal relationship between Hall and Arthur; it also concentrates on Arthur's period of apprenticeship when he, along with the other members of his quartet The Trumpets of Zion, were learning together how to sing gospel, and also learning something about the blues. In a variation of the father-son relationship of *The Amen Corner*, the quartet has a mentor in Paul, Arthur's and Hall's father, who gives them a lesson in rhythm. He rehearses with them and drives them through a traditional song, as Creole did for Sonny in "Sonny's Blues"; he tells Arthur, "You almost made it that time, son. But don't be in a hurry when you play. If you don't let it take the time it takes, then you ain't got no time, you see what I mean? . . . You worry too much about the beat. But the beat comes out of the *time*—the space between one note and the next note. And you got to trust the time *you* hear—that's how you play your song" (87). Music becomes pure, individual expression: Arthur has a gift for it and Paul knows what the consequences are. He imagines that the other members of the quartet have no such gift, no such calling, and that their music is devoid of the passion that gives music its ability to move others:

[Arthur] sang, and there was something frightening about so deep and unreadable a passion in one so young. Arthur's phrasing was the key—unanswerable; his delivery of the song made you realize that he knew what the song was about.

Your reaction to this passion can destroy the singer. Paul knew this, and Arthur didn't. Paul marshaled the other boys around his menaced son, for he knew why *they* were singing. (The boys thought they knew, too.) He knew they would not sing long—something would get in the way. But if anything got in Arthur's way, Paul would be missing a son. (92)

Arthur's endangerment has something to do with the natural connection between his life and his art. He is able to salvage a song that the quartet is struggling with: "Arthur, alone, eyes closed, meaning every instant of it, beginning high, like a scream, then dropping low, like a whispered prayer, a prayer whispered in a dungeon, [*Savior!*] *don't you pass me by!*" (93). The song of Arthur's life is a cry for salvation, a salvation that comes through his art and through his connections to myriad lovers. Warren Carson argues that "Baldwin insists...that the song, whatever its genre—blues, gospel, or jazz—is inspired by an emotion, one emotion that eventually must reach the surface and free itself regardless of the consequences. Only by freeing the emotion and emptying that emotion through song is there any salvation for the soul" (220). This emotion is the difference, in Paul's estimation, between musicians who play to "make a living" and "real musicians" (96). The impulse behind real music, according to Paul, develops out of a primal scream: "Music don't begin like a song," he said. "Forget all that bullshit you hear. Music can get to *be* a song, but it starts with a cry. That's all. It might be the cry of a newborn baby, or the sound of a hog being slaughtered, or a man when they put the knife to his balls. And that sound is everywhere. People spend their whole lives trying to drown out that sound" (97). This cry, the essence of music, is a howl of either need or pain: furthermore, it is, according to Paul, what makes us human: "If you ever had to think about it—how we get from sound to music—Lord, I don't know—it seems to prove to me that love is in the world—without it—music, I mean— we'd all be running around, with our fangs dripping blood" (97). Music is, thus, the essence of humanity, and "real" musicians like Arthur not only express humanity themselves, but attempt to humanize their listeners.

This principle explains why Arthur is able to move between musical genres and touch many audiences, just like he is able to move between many lovers. The essence of both relationships is the same: the singer lives his song, painful though it may be, and converts it to a kind of pure art that he offers to his audience. Similarly, a lover risks vulnerability and emotional safety for the sake of his or her love. Music is love, in Paul's formula, and the musician and the lover are equally vulnerable; but to cease singing or to cease loving would be to withdraw from one's essential humanity, despite (or perhaps because of) the pain involved. As Hall suggests, gospel is just like the blues this way: "Niggers can sing gospel as no other people can because they aren't singing gospel—if you see what I mean. When a nigger quotes the Gospel, he is not quoting: he is telling you what happened to him today, and what is certainly going too happen to you tomorrow: it may be that it has already happened to you, and that you, poor soul, don't know it. In which case, *Lord have mercy!* Our suffering is our bridge to one another" (113). This type of observation is part of what leads Eleanor Traylor to describe this novel as "a gospel tale told in the blues mode" (217). To expound upon Hall's final thought, black suffering *expressed in gospel and blues music* is a unifying, connecting force.

A significant percentage of the novel, especially "Book Three: The Gospel Singer," is devoted to descriptions of the band touring through the South, rehearsing, achieving some level of notoriety, and going their separate ways. The connections between the band members are as intense as love affairs, and sometimes result in love affairs, but the passion and intensity of the music is what initially unites them. The ideal moments happen when two of the band members become as one, as when Arthur and Crunch "were moving together, here, now, in the song, to some new place; they had never sung together like this before, his voice in Crunch's sound, Crunch's sound filling his voice . . . as though Crunch were laughing and crying at the same time" (198). Yet the instances within the novel when gospel moves an individual listener are augmented by its ability to move large crowds, in secular as well as strictly religious settings. As Scott writes, "In *Just Above My Head* gospel music is represented as a protean discourse, in which meanings are derived from the historical experience of a people, reinterpreted by the particular experiences of individual performers, and mediated by the audiences' experiences and expectations" (144). Thus Arthur is called to sing at civil rights rallies as well as in churches and, later, in large concerts. Scott points out that "the novel also demonstrates how the popular success of black gospel, and the secular forms it has influenced, such as soul, has brought black music to new audiences who may have little understanding of its traditional roots and meanings and who experience it as spectators rather than participants" (145). This distinction may be why it is so imperative for Hall (and Baldwin) to tell the story of Arthur, for this popularization removes the singer from his origins and thus diminishes the importance of his personal story.

In one exchange with his brother, Arthur is able to articulate for the first time the importance of his musical and personal origins: "'It's strange to feel,' he said, 'that you come out of something, and something you can't name, you don't know what it is—something that has never happened anywhere, ever, in the world, before.' He grinned and clapped his hands. 'I don't know no *other* people learned to play honky-tonk, whorehouse piano in *church*! . . . And sing a sorrow song so tough, baby, that it leaves sorrow where sorrow is, and gets you where you going" (363). These succinct and poignant observations about gospel and the blues come immediately after he begins to resolve the dilemma of the difference between performer and listener that Sonny's brother expresses in the epigraph to this chapter. Arthur says, "I never had to listen to other people *listening* to [my music] before. So, I began to *hear* something because I was listening to them *listen*" (361–62). Hall points out, "really, you've been doing that—listening, I mean—ever since you started singing" (362). If Hall is right, this quality accounts for the self-possession that Arthur exudes more than Baldwin's other musician characters; it would follow that Arthur would be a survivor, too. Yet somehow he degenerates, quickly, following nurturing love affairs with Guy and Jimmy. The novel ends with Hall's dream in which Arthur repeats the question, "Shall we tell them? What's up the road?" Hall says, "The question torments me, like a song I once heard Arthur sing, and can't now, in my dream, for the life of me, remember" (559). Yet earlier in the novel, Arthur sings a duet, perhaps not coincidentally with a blues singer named Sonny, and Hall speculates just before the two finish their song, "Nor does [Arthur] know whether the road before him is open, or closed" (492). The future, in other words, is never certain, yet the song must be sung. At this moment in the novel, close to the end of Baldwin's career, a young gospel singer and an old blues singer harmonize. The question of what's up the road does not ultimately matter. What matters is the song, the long blues of the past merging with the personal, private, vanishing evocations of the present.

NOTES

1. For a commercially available recording of James Baldwin singing, see *A Lover's Question* by David Linx (rereleased by Les Disques Du Crépuscule in 1990).

WORKS CITED

Albertson, Chris. "Bessie's Life." In *Bessie Smith: Empress of the Blues.* New York: Schirmer Books (Macmillan), 1975. 7–28.

Baker, Houston A. *Blues, Ideology, and Afro-American Literature.* Chicago: University Press of Chicago, 1984.

Baldwin, James. *The Amen Corner.* New York: Dell, 1968.

———. *Going to Meet the Man.* New York: Vintage, 1965.

———. *Go Tell It on the Mountain.* New York: Dell, 1953.

———. *Just above My Head.* New York: Dell, 1979.

———. *Nobody Knows My Name.* New York: Dell, 1961.

———. "Sermons and Blues: Selected Poems of Langston Hughes." *New York Times Book Review* (March 29, 1959): BR6.

———. "The Uses of the Blues." *Playboy* 11 (January 1964): 131–32, 240–41.

Burnim, Mellonee V. "Religious Music." In *African American Music: An Introduction,* edited by Mellonee V. Burnim and Portia K. Maultsby. New York: Routledge, 2006. 51–77.

Byerman, Keith E. "Words and Music: Narrative Ambiguity in 'Sonny's Blues.'" In *Critical Essays on James Baldwin*, edited by Fred L. Standley and Nancy V. Burt. Boston: G. K. Hall, 1988. 198–204.

Carruth, Hayden. *Sitting In: Selected Writings on Jazz, Blues, and Related Topics.* Iowa City: University of Iowa Press, 1986.

Carson, Warren. "Manhood, Musicality, and Male Bonding in *Just Above My Head*." In *Re-Viewing James Baldwin: Things Not Seen*, edited by D. Quentin Miller. Philadelphia: Temple University Press, 2000. 215–32.

Featherstone, Joseph. "Blues for Mister Baldwin." In *Critical Essays on James Baldwin*, edited by Fred L. Standley and Nancy V. Burt. Boston: G. K. Hall, 1988. 152–55.

Jones, LeRoi. *Blues People.* New York: William Morrow, 1963.

Leeming, David. *James Baldwin.* New York: Knopf, 1994.

Miller, D. Quentin. *Re-viewing James Baldwin: Things Not Seen.* Philadelphia: Temple University Press, 2000.

Nash, Julie. "'A Terrifying Sacrament': James Baldwin's Use of Music in *Just Above My Head*." *Middle-Atlantic Writers Association Review* (December 1990): 107–11.

Scott, Lynn Orilla. *James Baldwin's Later Fiction: Witness to the Journey.* East Lansing: Michigan State University Press, 2002.

Simawe, Saadi A. "What Is in a Sound? The Metaphysics and Politics of Music in *The Amen Corner*." In *Re-viewing James Baldwin: Things Not Seen*, edited by D. Quentin Miller. Philadelphia: Temple University Press, 2000. 12–32.

Standley, Fred L., and Nancy V. Burt, eds. *Critical Essays on James Baldwin.* Boston: G. K. Hall, 1988.

Standley, Fred L., and Louis H. Pratt, eds. *Conversations with James Baldwin.* Jackson: University Press of Mississippi, 1989.

Traylor, Eleanor. "I Hear Music in the Air: James Baldwin's *Just Above My Head*." In *Critical Essays on James Baldwin*, edited by Fred L. Standley and Nancy V. Burt. Boston: G. K. Hall, 1988. 217–23.

Weatherby, W. J. *James Baldwin: Artist on Fire.* New York: Donald I. Fine, 1989.

Williams, Sherley Anne. "The Black Musician: The Black Hero as Light Bearer." In *James Baldwin*, edited by Keneth Kinnamon. Englewood Cliffs, N.J.: Prentice Hall, 1974. 147–54.

James Baldwin and Sexuality

Lieux de Mémoire and a Usable Past

Justin A. Joyce and Dwight A. McBride

The American idea of sexuality appears to be rooted in the American idea of masculinity.... But no other country has ever made so successful and glamorous a romance out of genocide and slavery; therefore, perhaps the word I am searching for is not idea but ideal.

The American ideal, then, of sexuality appears to be rooted in the American ideal of masculinity. This ideal has created cowboys and Indians, good guys and bad guys, punks and studs, tough guys and softies, butch and faggot, black and white. It is an ideal so paralytically infantile that it is virtually forbidden—as an unpatriotic act—that the American boy evolve into the complexity of manhood.

—James Baldwin, "Here Be Dragons" (1985)

The sexual question and the racial question have always been entwined, you know. If Americans can mature

on the level of racism, then they have
to mature on the level of sexuality.
—James Baldwin, "Go the Way Your
Blood Beats" (1984)

In the first epigraph above, culled from James Baldwin's essay "Here be Dragons," Baldwin's prophetic force comes through not only in his satirical description of an omitted American past, but also in his critical dismantling of a national mythology of masculinity. Baldwin provides more than just a trenchant criticism of the violence done in the name of the American ideal of masculinity, he analyzes the dichotomies that have had to be erected in order to preserve such a "flaccid" conception. His brief listing of the antithetical roles necessary to play out the drama of American masculinity captures the force and history of the ideal: cowboy ≠ Indian, good guys ≠ bad guys, punks ≠ studs, tough guys ≠ softies, butch ≠ faggot, and finally black ≠ white. Such formulas, for Baldwin, can only stifle growth; these limited positions and oppositional roles can only result in the continual infantilization of national character. In this brief sample of his writing, from rather late in his life and career, we glimpse the passionate urgency, stingingly insightful critique, and rhetorical deftness that secured Baldwin a seat in the pantheon of American letters.

Baldwin's words also tell us a great deal about the world in which his writings made such an impact. What is interesting here is the way Baldwin's conception of the American ideal of masculinity evinces a critical sensibility that only took hold much later. Cowboys, to take but the first example, are not the hired hands of large cattle corporations bringing herds of beef to the railheads, but rather are opposed—by the ironically simple "and"—to Indians. The diversity of racial and ethnic workers involved in the nineteenth-century cattle trade, to say nothing of the amalgam of distinctive tribal groups and cultures, are herein reduced to oppositional roles that evoke the racialized representations of Manifest Destiny and the raced and sexed iconography of an American film tradition. To be clear, the aim here is not to fault Baldwin's rhetorical use of this common trope, "cowboys and Indians." Rather, it is to point up the manner in which Baldwin consciously employed this reductive trope in order to comment on sexuality and gendered ideals. In other words, Baldwin mines an ideological construct to illuminate its dependence upon an antagonistic dichotomy and to elucidate its strategic deployment in the service of a nationalist mythology. In short, in both epigraphs, Baldwin speaks to the intersectionality of race, sex, class, and gender. Alternative conceptions of masculinity that would have congress under the rubric of "American," or different conceptions of race and sexuality that would equally cohere under the ideal of masculinity, seem impossible within the confines set up here. In other words, in 1985, at least for Baldwin and his audience, any departure from this ideal can be nothing other than deviant or freakish.[1]

This chapter attempts to contextualize James Baldwin's critical insights into sexuality. It is both descriptive and analytical; descriptive in its attempts to provide a genealogy of the heterosexist strain inherent in African Americanist discourse by reading it against the notion of black respectability; analytical in the reading of James Baldwin as a *lieu de mémoire*, ritualizing the limits and possibilities for sexuality within African American cultural critique. The notion of *lieux de mémoire* (sites of memory) is employed to trace the ritual of Baldwin's life and work as "sensational" sites for both policing and citation in an attempt to trace Baldwin as originally dismissed, then misremembered in dominant critical genealogies of African American letters, and only recently rediscovered and remembered for the challenges he poses to the ideologies of both race and sexuality.

In his 1994 essay, "The Black Writer's Use of Memory," Melvin Dixon extends Pierre Nora's concept of *lieux de mémoire* to analyze the metaphorical importance of the trope of Africa in African American literature. For Nora, the self-referential nature of history calls for a distinction between history and memory, whereby memory becomes something more self-evident, more "sacred" than history. *Lieux de mémoire* can be places, events, or documents. Noting that something, someplace, someone becomes a *lieu de memoire* "only if the imagination invests it with symbolic importance" (19), Nora stresses the importance of ritual in the creation of *lieux de mémoire* and suggests that such sites have the potential to transform traditional historiography:

> Reflecting on *lieux de mémoire* transforms historical criticism into critical history—and not only in its methods; it allows history a secondary, purely transferential existence, even a kind of reawakening. Like war, the history of *lieux de mémoire* is an art of implementation, practiced in the fragile happiness derived from relating to rehabilitated objects and from the involvement of the historian in his or her subject. It is a history that, in the last analysis, rests upon what it mobilizes....(24)

Dixon extends Nora's conception of *lieux de mémoire* to consider the rhetorical importance of Africa as place, and the metaphorical trope of Africa, in African American culture. "What is useful in Nora's argument," notes Dixon, "is his broad recognition of how *lieux de mémoire* may contribute to the process of cultural recovery" (56). Pointing to the way street names in New York evoke memories of an unknown Africa or signify the past of a prominent figure like Malcolm X, Dixon stresses how these names have been used as a source of "re-membering," to delineate not just streets or places but deliberately wrought connections of symbolic, indeed ritual significance: "Not only do these names celebrate and commemorate great figures in black culture, they provoke our active participation in that history. What was important yesterday becomes a landmark today. Invoking memory of that time or that person is the only way to orient oneself today" (59).

In his discussion of *lieux de mémoire* and their significance to African American culture, Dixon pushes Nora's conception to include literary figures and characters within select novels. Using Dixon's expanded understanding of *lieux de mémoire*, this chapter traces the importance of James Baldwin within African Americanist discourse since World War I to illuminate the challenges his work poses to the confines of traditional race-centered discourse and to suggest the symbolic importance of a recent return to his work. Emphasis will be placed upon *Giovanni's Room*, a text whose reception and scholarly history strongly illustrates the ritualistic quality of James Baldwin and his work as sites for mobilizing discourses of sexuality in African Americanist critique.

Returning to the epigraphs, the omissions[2] within Baldwin's nonetheless powerful criticism speak more to the limitations of dominant discourse than to limitations in Baldwin's own imagination. For surely it has been this imagination, the presence and prescience of Baldwin's searing voice, that has helped us to arrive at a critical moment in which it is commonplace to note that when we are speaking of sexuality we are always already speaking about gender, race, and class. This chapter, then, can also be linked finally to Baldwin's own call to "do your first works over," which he explains means "to reexamine everything": "Go back to where you started, or as far back as you can, examine all of it, travel your road again and tell the truth about it. Sing or shout or testify or keep it to yourself: but *know whence you came*" (*Price of the Ticket* xix).

Respectability and Echoes of Sexuality in the Discourse of the New Negro

To locate James Baldwin within African American cultural critique and to situate the significance of the challenge he posed to that heritage, we must begin a genealogy of the disavowal of black queers in representations of the African American community by moving briefly beyond Baldwin to consider the generation of writers that preceded him (Langston Hughes, Alain Locke, and Claude McKay). When we think back to the time of the New Negro or the Harlem Renaissance—a period in which, for the first time, black men and women (writers, artists, and scholars), only a generation or two out of slavery, had the space in which to begin imagining, thinking, and theorizing about the possibilities, character and nature, political function, and so on of black art—one can even now glimpse the awesome, overwhelming, and wildly liberating sense of mission they had to confront. It comes through most clearly in their proclamations, speculations, and theorizations about "Negro art" and the "Negro artist." They were convinced that the day of the New Negro had arrived. And this was a story of progress if there ever was one—ugly, fraught, complicated, back-breaking, yes. But a story of progress nonetheless. A story that, if it was not to be centered in our academic narratives about modernity, would certainly be a ghost in its machinery with which these narratives would some day have to reckon.

But now we're getting ahead of ourselves. So, first the question: What is it that caused this "New Negro" in his particular version of modernity as progress, specifically as racial progress, to cling fervently to an admixture of moral and racial respectability as his entrée to the modern, his calling card to humanity, his salvation from the dark ages of oppression? Black antiracist strategy at the turn of the century viewed adherence to a cultural code of moral/racial respectability[3] as the best means to resist white racism and for the Negro to progress as an equal partner in the project of modernity. It is important to note—though perhaps it goes without saying—that blacks developed such reasoning under the perception of the white hegemonic eyes, whose gaze was fixed firmly upon them. Indeed, it is not to overstate the case to say that white racism—and its pursuant logics—was a key factor in the production of this particular brand of racial/moral respectability. And once we begin to recognize this particular narrative that characterizes blacks' relationship to modernity as progress, which tells the story of an unflagging commitment to respectability, then we come a long way toward appreciating the echoes, the elliptical rhetoric, and the intensity of intra-racial critique that characterizes a good deal of African American literary criticism at the turn of the century.

To demonstrate the limitations imposed upon African American critique by the notion of respectability, let us turn to two essays by Alain Locke, called by some the "Dean of the Harlem Renaissance." The first is "Self Criticism: The Third Dimension," which appeared in *The Phylon Quarterly* in 1950. The second is "The New Negro," the opening essay in the 1925 volume of the same title, which Locke edited. The prescriptive power of the politics of respectability is so evident in the transition from the Locke of 1925 to the Locke of 1950 that we shall begin by quoting at some length from "Self Criticism":

> The Negro intellectual is still largely in psychological bondage not only ... 'to the laws and customs of the local (Southern) culture,' but to the fear of breaking the tabus [*sic*] of Puritanism, Philistinism and falsely conceived conventions of "race respectability." Consciously and subconsciously, these repressions work great artistic harm, especially the fear of being accused of group disloyalty and "misrepresentation" in portraying the full gamut of Negro type, character and thinking. We are still in the throes of counter-stereotypes.
>
> The releasing formula is to realize that in all human things we are basically and inevitably human, and that even the special racial complexities and overtones are only interesting variants. Why, then, this protective silence about the ambivalences of the Negro upper classes, about the dilemmas of intra-group prejudice and rivalry, about the dramatic inner paradoxes of mixed heritage ... or the tragic breach between the Negro elite and the Negro masses, or the conflict between integration and vested-interest separatism in the present-day life of the Negro? These, *among others*, are the great themes, but they *moulder in closed closets like family skeletons* rather than shine brightly as the Aladdin's lamps that they really are. (393–94, emphasis added)

The Alain Locke who authored this essay was more open-eyed about the Negro Renaissance and what it was actually able to accomplish than his earlier self, who edited and authored the introduction to *The New Negro*. The Locke of 1925 spoke urgently of the New Negro's perceptibility in terms such as a "changeling," "a metamorphosis," and "the promise and warrant of a new leadership" (3–5). The Locke of 1950, however, strikes a notably different tone from the Locke of twenty five years before, beginning "Self Criticism" by describing the Harlem Renaissance in a somewhat less laudatory register, with such phrases as "the so-called Negro Renaissance," "a certain lingering immaturity," and "the admitted shortcomings of our literary and artistic output in the Nineteen-twenties, thirties, and forties" (391). While Locke's solemnity here is evident, it would be wrong to say that Locke had entirely abandoned the ideas he had espoused in 1925 about the Negro Renaissance and its possibilities. He had, however, come face to face with the formidable foes of American racism and black racial/moral respectability and their incredibly deforming properties and potentials as they concern the work of the writer and artist.

Whatever the differences in tone between the two essays, one striking similarity lies in the clear references and nonreferences to sexuality that haunt the racial text—with its commitments to and at times defiance of (in Locke's case) black moral/racial respectability. As we listen to Locke's sometimes excited stridency, we can hear the echoes of the silent brother in his quiet critique of the hegemony of dominant antiracist discourses and strategies. In one of many diasporic moments in the 1925 essay, Locke's comments about the diversity (and we are suggesting that term in all its complexity for Locke) of Harlem (and by extension of the black community) reads thus:

> It has attracted the African, the West Indian, the Negro American; has brought together the Negro of the North and the Negro of the South; the man from the city and the man from the town and village; the peasant, the student, the business man, the professional man, artist, poet, musician, adventurer and worker, preacher and criminal, exploiter and social outcast. Each group has come with its own special motives and for its own special ends, but their greatest experience has been the finding of one another. (6)

There are many things to say about this passage, but we shall focus on the list here. Locke is rhetorically a man of lists and metaphor. Both are always fruitful places to linger in his work. He gives us cultural diversity, regional diversity, and class diversity. All the occupations he lists up to preacher are reputable. There is no shame in being a peasant or a worker, and the rest of these are mostly prestige occupations. It is at preacher, however, the symbolic purveyor of morality and religion, that the list takes a decided turn to the "criminal, exploiter and social outcast." Black same-gender-loving folk in such a list—certainly any who were open about their sexuality in 1925—would have belonged to the last listed category of "social outcast." Still, Locke's tone retains a ring of the "can't we all just get along" motif to it. This changes by the time we get to his lists in the 1950 essay, where he writes of "the ambivalences..., the dilemmas..., the dramatic inner paradoxes..., the tragic breach..., or the conflict..." (394). His tone is far more critical.

In the 1950 essay, he is not celebrating diversity and the solace of the "finding of one another." Rather he is deeply concerned with the ways in which "consciously and subconsciously, these repressions [associated with "race respectability"] work great artistic harm" (393). He decries the "protective silence" about the long list of items discussed earlier in this section. "These," he reminds us, "among others, are the great themes, but they moulder in closed closets like family skeletons rather than shine brightly as the Aladdin's lamps that they really are" (394). The reference to "closed closets," though not a term likely used in the way it is in our post-Stonewall era, may be read as prescient by Locke. In this context, these "closed closets" certainly retain the connotation of secrecy, especially when compared in a simile with "family skeletons," which might certainly be read as encompassing the silenced sexuality of so many of the writers of the Harlem Renaissance, including Locke himself. Indeed, in the sentence just quoted, it is the elliptical nature of the phrase that immediately follows his list and precedes this reference to closed closets that is most telling: "These, among others, are the great themes...." That little dependant clause, which names the thing or things that he could not name, is the space in which Locke enacts the very tyranny he is wrestling against in this essay and which he was hopeful in the earlier essay that the Negro Renaissance might help to defeat.

Locke in 1925 was not alone in hopeful predictions about the potential of the Negro Renaissance to dislodge the oppressions of black moral/racial respectability. Forecasting predictions of his own in a 1926 essay "The Negro Artist and the Racial Mountain," Langston Hughes places his hope for the future of black art in the African American majority—particularly the "low-down folks," as he referred to the remaining 90 percent, declaring, "And they are the majority—may the Lord be praised!" (1537). Hughes opines that "perhaps these common people will give the world its truly great Negro artist, the one who is not afraid to be himself" (1538). Hughes's thinking was that "whereas the better-class Negro would tell the artist what to do, the people at least let him alone when he does appear.... We younger Negro artists who create now intend to express our own individual dark-skinned selves without fear or shame" (1538–40).

Hughes takes a romantic view that he might find some sense of salvation or refuge from respectability and its artistic and social limitations in the "low-down folks." Perhaps the most popular male writer of the Harlem Renaissance, Hughes' own enigmatic sexuality prompted some of his close friends to describe him as "asexual." He knew all too well the restrictions on the Negro artist of which Locke speaks. The closing paragraph of Locke's 1950 essay is so remarkable in further demonstrating Locke's understanding of the restrictions of respectability that we quote it in its entirety:

> To break such tabus [sic] is *the crucial artistic question of the moment*, the wrath of Negro Rotarians, preachers, college presidents and journalists [a respectable list if ever there was one] notwithstanding. It is this inner tyranny that must next be conquered.... I am far from suggesting that even a considerable part of this revelation will be morally risqué or socially explosive; some of it will be, of course. But I do sense a strange and widely diffused feeling that many of these situations are Masonic secrets—things to be talked about, but not written or officially disclosed. Maybe, now that a few Negro authors have demonstrated the possibility of financial independence and success as writers, *some of our younger talents can shake free of the white-collar servitudes of job dependency on the one hand and conventional "race loyalty" on the other.* If so, we may confidently anticipate an era of fuller and more objective presentation by Negro authors of their versions of contemporary living in general and Negro life and experience. (394, emphasis added)

Locke's closing description of "race loyalty," sadly, resonates more today than it ought. Similar rhetoric could well be used to describe the homophobia and heterosexism that animates much of race politics and African Americanist critical discourse today. Nevertheless, it is important to note here the hopeful plea within Locke's reexamination of the Harlem Renaissance. Even in his seeming dismissal of the New Negro era—which he describes at one point as an adolescent, "gawky and pimply" (391)—Locke recalls this *lieu de mémoire* in order to invoke again the liberating sense of this earlier time. In his listing of the omissions of history, history becomes a site of critical intervention. He speaks of a moment from whence he has come, mobilizing again the ritualized sites of a cultural memory in his call for a break from "inner tyranny," positing his hopes in the work of "younger talents" better situated to shake off the mantle of "race loyalty," proclaiming that the breaking of taboos is "the crucial artistic question" of the moment. Put another way, the time had come for new talent to expand the description of sexuality and to push African American art to challenge the strictures of respectability. The time, recall, is 1950; the talent is James Baldwin.

James Baldwin, *Lieu de Mémoire*

In our treatment of Baldwin to follow, we want to build on the previous examination of Locke as an important figure who might serve as a model in our search for a usable past for black queer studies. In so doing, we hope to bring together a set of concerns about the related state of African American studies, the state of Baldwin scholarship, the complicated relationship Baldwin exhibits to identity politics, and how that complexity presages the need for a critical sensibility evident in black queer studies.[4] In a narrative for the tradition of queer African American literature, Baldwin represents a kind of transitional figure from that earlier generation of writers as the first "openly gay" black writer. That is, he was the first to talk publicly about his homosexuality and purposefully to make use of it in his fiction. In an interview from the latter years of his life (captured in Karen Thorsen's 1989 documentary, *James Baldwin: The Price of the Ticket*), when asked to reflect upon why he chose so early on to write *Giovanni's Room*, given that he was already dealing with the burden of being a black writer in America, Baldwin's response is instructive: "Well, one could say almost that I did not have an awful lot of choice. *Giovanni's Room* comes out of something that tormented and frightened me—the question of my own sexuality. It also simplified my life in another way because it meant that I *had no secrets*, nobody could blackmail me. You know...you didn't tell me, I told you [emphasis added]." This is not the same, of course, as saying that Baldwin embraced gay sexuality as associated with the gay liberation movement, to which he had a rather complicated relationship.[5] Still his public "outing" of himself is significant not only to the development of this particularized tradition of queer African American fiction, but also as posing a challenge to dominant, respectable, sanitized narratives of the African American literary tradition and what it can include.

Baldwin was no more content to be simply a black writer, a gay writer, or an activist than he was to write exclusively in the genre of the novel, drama, poetry, or the essay. And the topoi of his work and the landscape of his critical and creative imagination are broad, to say the very least. Scholarship, however, has often tended to relegate Baldwin to one or the other of these identities; it has been slow to move our thinking—not only of Baldwin, but of African American studies generally—in a direction that speaks to the intricate social positions African Americans occupy. Neither Baldwin's life nor his work is easily given over to such an approach. Again in Thorsen's 1989 documentary of Baldwin's life, there are at least two moments that demonstrate the discursive polarity whereby Baldwin was identified either racially or sexually. The first is a statement made by Amiri Baraka, and the second is a statement made by Baldwin himself culled from television interview footage. These less literally textual examples elucidate how in our more casual or less scripted moments, our subconscious understanding of the realities of race discourse is laid bare even more clearly.

Baraka's regard for Baldwin is well documented by the film. He talks about how Baldwin was "in the tradition" and how his early writings, specifically *Notes of a Native Son*, really impacted him and spoke to a whole generation. In an attempt to describe or to account for Baldwin's homosexuality, however, Baraka falters in his efforts to unite the racially significant image of Baldwin that he clings to with the homosexual Baldwin. Baraka states the following: "Jimmy Baldwin was neither in the closet about his homosexuality, nor was he running around proclaiming homosexuality. I mean, he was what he was. And you either had to buy that or, you know, *mea culpa*, go somewhere else." The poles of the rhetorical continuum that Baraka sets up here for his understanding of homosexuality are very telling. To Baraka's mind, one can either be in the closet or "running around proclaiming homosexuality" (the images of the effete gay man and the gay activist collide here, it would seem). What makes Baldwin acceptable to enter the pantheon of race men for Baraka is the fact that his sexual identity is unlocatable. It is neither here nor there, or perhaps it is everywhere at once, leaving the entire question an undecided and undecidable one—and, if Baldwin is undecided about his sexual identity, the one identity to which he seems firmly committed is his racial identity. The rhetorical ambiguity around his sexual identity, according to Baraka, is what makes it possible for Baldwin to be a race man—a category Hazel Carby complicates in her book *Race Men*—who was "in the tradition."

Baldwin himself, it seems, was well aware of the dangers—indeed, the "price of the ticket"—of trying to synthesize his racial and sexual identities. He understood that his efficacy as race man was—in part at least—dependent upon his limiting his public activism to racial politics. The frame of the documentary certainly confirms this in the way it represents Baldwin's own response to his sexuality. Baldwin states:

> I think the trick is to say yes to life. . . . It is only we of the twentieth century who are so obsessed with the particular details of anybody's sex life. I don't think those details make a difference. And I will never be able to deny a certain power that I

have had to deal with, which has dealt with me, which is called love; and love comes in very strange packages. I've loved a few men; I've loved a few women; and a few people have loved me. That's...I suppose that's all that's saved my life.

It may be of interest to note that while he is making this statement, the camera pans down to Baldwin's hands, which are fidgeting with the cigarette and cigarette holder. This move on the part of the camera undercuts the veracity of Baldwin's statement here and suggests that Baldwin himself may not quite believe all of what he is saying.[6]

If Baldwin's statement above raises the complications of speaking from a racial/sexual identity location, the following excerpt from a 1973 television interview on the *Dick Cavett Show*—featured in Thorsen's documentary—illustrates this point all the more clearly:

I don't know what most white people in this country feel, but I can only conclude what they feel from the state of their institutions. I don't know if white Christians hate Negroes or not, but I know that we have a Christian church which is white and a Christian church which is black.... I don't know if the board of education hates black people, but I know the textbooks they give my children to read and the schools that we go to. Now, this is the evidence! You want me to make an act of faith risking myself, my wife, my woman, my sister, my children on some idealism which you assure me exists in America which I have never seen.

This passage is conspicuous for the manner in which Baldwin assumes the voice of representative "race man." In the very last sentence, when Baldwin affects the position of race man, part of the performance includes the masking of his specificity, his sexuality, his difference. And in black antiracist discourse, when all difference is concealed, what emerges is the heterosexual black man "risking [himself], [his] wife, [his] woman and [his] children." The image of the black man as protector, progenitor, and defender of the race is what Baldwin assumes here. The truth of this rhetorical transformation is that in order to be a representative race man, one must be both heterosexual and male.[7] Further, these moments indicate the ways that James Baldwin's life performed as a *lieu de mémoire*, a site for the ritualized policing of race and sexuality by denying the intersectionality of these identificatory modes. Again, it is not our intention here to fault Baldwin for this move, but to say that even with his own recognition of the politics of his circumstances, he does find ways to mount a counterdiscourse (usually through his fiction) to such exclusive racial-identity constructions. A prominent example of this counter-discourse is, of course, *Giovanni's Room*.

Baldwin makes plain a logic in 1956 that has come to be a received part of public discourse about homosexuality in America today. That is, one of the reasons that people fear queer sexuality so violently is that it threatens an ideology in America older and stronger even than baseball or apple pie—it threatens the idea of "home." This is what Baldwin understands and presages so well in *Giovanni's Room* through the representation of the complexity of David's character, drawn as he is at the crossroads of nationality (Americanness), sexuality (or homosexuality or at least bisexuality), and home (or place and social responsibility/respectability). In order that the themes of this work might be (to use an ugly word for a moment) "universalized," Baldwin knew enough about how race worked, and continues to work, in America to know that it was impossible to use black characters. In a letter (dated January 1954) to William Cole (the editor who first brought Baldwin and *Go Tell It on the Mountain* to the attention of Knopf), Baldwin himself wrote the following words about *Giovanni's Room* shortly after he had begun working on it:[8]

> It's a great departure for me; and it makes me rather nervous. It's not about Negroes first of all; its locale is the American colony in Paris. What is really delicate about it is that since I want to convey something about the kinds of American loneliness, I must use the most ordinary type of American I can find—the good, white Protestant is the kind of image I want to use. This is precisely the type of American about whose setting I know the least. Whether this will be enough to create a

real human being, only time will tell. It's a love story—short, and wouldn't you know it, tragic. Our American boy comes to Europe, finds something, loses it, and in his acceptance of his loss becomes, to my mind, heroic.

Here we see, among other things, that only whiteness is sufficient to represent large, broad, "universal" concerns. To Baldwin's mind, black characters—in their always overdrawn specificity—could only represent in the 1950s popular imagination the problems specific to blacks, and are therefore easily dismissed as irrelevant beyond those confines. Marlon Ross puts the entire business of the whiteness of the characters in *Giovanni's Room* somewhat differently, though along similar lines of thought, when he writes: "If the characters had been black, the novel would have been read as being 'about' blackness, whatever else it happened actually to be about. The whiteness of the characters seems to make invisible the question of how race or color has, in fact, shaped the characters—at least as far as most readers have dealt with the novel" (25).

Giovanni's Room is not a novel about gay sexuality as much as it is a novel about the social and discursive forces that make gay sexuality into a "problem." Even in this context, however, Baldwin does not sacrifice the complexity of the forces involved in this process. Everywhere in *Giovanni's Room,* for example, national identity is sexualized. Consider the following scene from David's visit to the American Express Office in Paris and how he describes the Americans:

At home, I could have distinguished patterns, habits, accents of speech—with no effort whatever: *now* everybody sounded, unless I listened hard, as though they had just arrived from Nebraska. *At home* I could have seen the clothes they were wearing, but *here* I only saw bags, cameras, belts, and hats, all clearly from the same department store. *At home* I would have had a sense of the individual womanhood of the woman I faced; here the most ferociously accomplished seemed to be involved in some ice-cold or sun-dried travesty of sex, and even grandmothers seemed to have no traffic with the flesh.

> And what distinguished the men was that they seemed inca-
> pable of age; they smelled of soap, which seemed indeed to be
> their preservative against the dangers and exigencies of any
> more intimate odor; the boy he had been shone, somehow,
> unsoiled, untouched, unchanged, thorough the eyes of the
> man of sixty, booking passage with a smiling wife, to Rome.
> (118, emphasis added)

David sees these Americans abroad in the new light of the for-
eigner's eye. The language he invokes to characterize them is
not dissimilar in tone to the language Giovanni will later use to
describe David in the heat of their final argument in the novel.
Especially noteworthy here is the claim that Americans preserve
a kind of innocence that has "no traffic with the flesh."

Part of David's dilemma throughout the novel is that he
views sexual identity as being in need of domestication so that it
can be turned into "home" (witness his despair about "wandering" [84], his "sorrow," "shame," "panic," and "great bitterness"
about the "beast Giovanni had awakened in him" [110–11]). This
sense of home, fixity, stability—represented by America and his
father in the novel—comes through most clearly in his father's
letter to David where we learn of his (surely tongue-in-cheek)
nickname, Butch. The father writes:

> Dear Butch...aren't you ever coming home? Don't think I'm
> only being selfish but it's true I'd like to see you. I think you
> have been away long enough, God knows I don't know what
> you're doing over there, and you don't write enough for me
> even to guess. But my guess is you're going to be sorry one
> of these fine days that you stayed over there, looking at your
> navel, and let the world pass you by. There's nothing over
> there for you. You're as American as pork and beans, though
> maybe you don't want to think so anymore. (119–20)

To David's father's mind, if David is not being a man of action (and
acting in accordance with a rather predetermined heteronormative script, at that), then he is wasting time, wandering. Wandering
is an important theme in *Giovanni's Room*. Wandering, or lack of
focus, are associated with wayward sexualities (Hella in Spain,

David with Giovanni) and with foreign spaces, places not explicitly associated with America, with "home." It is dangerous. Gay sexuality in the novel points up desire's ability to be unfocused. This lack of focus is ultimately one of the biggest threats to heterosexuality (in a world where heterosexuality = focus). Hearth, home, nation, and heteronormative pairings are all impossible without the sexual focus they presuppose in the form of monogamous, heterosexual coupling.

David's desire for Hella itself represents his desire for the idea of "home." Consider the scene when they are reunited at the train station in Paris:

> I had hoped that when I saw her something instantaneous, definitive, would have happened in me, something to make me know where I should be and where I was. But nothing happened....
> Then I took her in my arms and something happened then. I was terribly glad to see her. It really seemed with I Iella in the circle of my arms, that my arms were home and I was welcoming her back there. She fitted in my arms as she always had, and the shock of holding her caused me to feel that my arms had been empty since she had been away. (158–59)

If home = heterosexuality = nationhood, then what David recognizes in Hella is his desire to fulfill the heteronormative narrative laid out for him as his American birthright. Indeed, the lure of it is so strong in this moment that it has the force—even if only for the moment—of erasing any and all of David's prior wayward sexual exploits. He feels as if his "arms had been empty since she had been away." Again, this suggests that a rather complicated relationship between home, nation, and sexuality (not sorted out completely here) is represented in the text and bears further consideration.

From the time we begin to hear David's story, he is, to the logic of his mind, already in trouble—an American in Paris, exiled, unfocused, wandering. David is plagued, not simply by some nebulous ideology about gay sexuality, but by the complex set of responses that arise when the young American man comes up against the overwhelming weight of what is expected of him in the world. This is the drama that drives David's psychological angst in the narrative. Giovanni names it in the final argument between the two of them:

> [David] "All this love you talk about—isn't it just that you want to be made to feel strong? You want to go out and be the big laborer and bring home the money, and you want me to stay here and wash the dishes and cook the food and clean this miserable closet of a room and kiss you when you come in through that door and lie with you at night and be your little *girl*...that's all you mean when you say you love me. You say I want to kill *you*. What do you think you've been doing to me?"
>
> "I am not trying to make you a little girl. If I wanted a little girl, I would be *with* a little girl."
>
> "Why aren't you? Isn't it just that you're afraid? And you take *me* because you haven't got the guts to go after a woman, which is what you *really* want?"
>
> He was pale. "You are the one who keeps talking about *what* I want. But I have only been talking about *who* I want."
> (188–89)

The last word is Giovanni's here. David is still trying to explain his feelings, his sexuality, in terms of a heteronormative cultural narrative. This is why he is consumed by the "what" (ideological forces). Whereas, Giovanni—unhampered by such concerns—is focused on the "who" (David) and not on what it means.

This exchange should remind us of an earlier moment in the same argument between Giovanni and David, when Giovanni first ruminates on why David is leaving him:

> "You do not," cried Giovanni, sitting up, "love anyone! You have never loved anyone, I am sure you never will! You love your purity, you love your mirror—you are just like a little virgin, you walk around with your hands in front of you as though you had some precious metal, gold, silver, rubies, maybe diamonds down there between your legs! You will

never let anybody touch it—man or woman. You want to be clean. You think you came here covered with soap and you think you will go out covered with soap—and you do not want to stink, not even for five minutes, in the meantime.... You want to leave Giovanni because he makes you stink. You want to despise Giovanni because he is not afraid of the stink of love. You want to kill him in the name of all your lying little moralities." (186–87)

The weighted contrast between Giovanni, who "is not afraid of the stink of love," and David, who is obsessed with being pure and clean (rendered as a desire that is, by association, very American and complicated by nationality) reveals a characteristic topos of Baldwin's work and art. He did not care for purity. Rather he wallowed in the dirt of the unclean places of the psyche, the cluttered rooms where life—for him—really happened. While the price exacted from Giovanni for the choice to live freely in defiance of social order is high, it seems to receive Baldwin's ultimate approbation. While, on the other hand, David, though he lives, is the one who represents a more profound death—indeed, an emotional death with which he must continue to live.

As a novel with no African American characters, written by an African American, gay writer, *Giovanni's Room* itself challenges dominant understandings of what constitutes African American literature, the work that proceeds under the rubric of African American literary criticism, and the forms of analysis that would come to have congress under the institutional formation of African American studies. Given the novel's unusual status, it seems somewhat prophetic in its call for a criticism, a way of thinking, a critical sensibility that would not arrive on the scene until many years after its publication in 1956. A further broadening of Baldwin's analytical description of the intersections of race and sexuality can be seen within his next novel, *Another Country.*

First published in 1962, *Another Country* builds on the critiques of Baldwin's previous novels. Whereas *Go Tell It on the*

Mountain (1953) explicitly treats moral/religious respectability and *Giovanni's Room* examines the social, cultural, and political significance of homosexuality or bisexuality, *Another Country* examines the further broadening of the matrices of desire and identification which here also include the strictures of interracial intimacy. Formally, the novel contains *lieux de mémoire*, structured as it is around Rufus's regretful remembrance of his relationship with Leona and around the other characters' mobilization of the memory of Rufus and his tragic suicide. The novel's central characters' remembering of Rufus constitutes the absent center around which they attempt to rebuild their lives. Beyond this structural device, *Another Country* also evinces Baldwin's expansion of his particular critique of racial and sexual normativity within his cultural moment.

At the heart of *Another Country's* challenge to then-dominant notions of race and sexuality is, as has been widely noted, its explicit treatment of interracial pairings. The novel candidly explores the social, political, and cultural dynamics that render such relationships threatening. Particularly explicit in this regard is the frank description of the violence that appears inevitably linked with desire between Rufus and Leona:

> Rufus opened his eye for a moment and watched her face, which was transfigured with agony and gleamed in the darkness like alabaster. Tears hung in the corners of her eyes and the hair at her brow was wet. Her breath came with moaning and short cries, with words he couldn't understand, and in spite of himself he began moving faster and thrusting deeper. He wanted her to remember him the longest day she lived. And shortly, nothing could have stopped him, not the white God himself nor a lynch mob arriving on wings. Under his breath he cursed the milk-white bitch and groaned and rode his weapon between her thighs. She began to cry. *I told you,* he moaned, *I'd give you something to cry about,* and, at once he felt himself strangling, about to explode or die. A moan and a curse tore through him while he beat her with all the strength he had and felt the venom shoot out of him, enough for a hundred black-white babies. (21–22, emphasis in original)

There is much to say about this climactic moment, particularly
the foreshadowing of the disastrous consequences that the full
consummation of this relationship will have on the lives of both
Leona and Rufus, but for the moment let us confine our discussion
to the violence inherent within this sex scene. Linking sexuality
and masculinity under the rubric of violence, Baldwin represents
Rufus, it seems, as unable to completely give himself over to his
desire for Leona without enacting a viciously violent fantasy, without, in short, playing the role of the black rapist ravaging the white
woman. His passion entirely predicated on seeing Leona as white,
Rufus sees her gleaming as "alabaster" just before he imagines
the forces that may be employed to stop him—"the white God
himself" or a "lynch mob." This is not an entirely unconscious
role-playing here either, for "in spite of himself," in spite of his
recognition of the dangers he glimpses in the feeling of "stran-
gling " and "exploding," Rufus continues to "ride his weapon" as
he curses and beats Leona with a violence that will only grow
worse after this act. Such explicit imagery of violence within the
genital description "weapon" can only be paired here, for Baldwin,
with the "venom" needed to make mixed-race children. Coming
in 1962, just five years prior to the Supreme Court's ruling holding that antimiscegenation statutes are unconstitutional,[9] *Another
Country*'s unabashed treatment of interracial sexuality worked
to problematize a particularly pressing social and political issue.
Another Country also stands as a significant *lieu de mémoire* within
Baldwin's oeuvre, evincing further his confrontation with the
politics of respectability and his continuing specification of the
multiple intersections of race and sexuality.

   The critical legacy of Baldwin's work has been relatively sparse
when viewed in proportion to his voluminous contribution to
African American letters, and critical discussions of his work continue often to coalesce around the poles of either race *or* sexuality. The reception of *Giovanni's Room* in the context of Baldwin's
corpus, for example, indicates the disciplinary proscriptions that
would continue to separate discussions of race and sexuality.
Dismissed by many upon its initial publication, *Giovanni's Room*
was widely regarded as a detour, a distraction, from Baldwin's
previous successes with *Go Tell it on the Mountain* and *Notes of*

a Native Son, both texts more ostensibly engaged with racial issues. Similarly indicative is Eldridge Cleaver's much-discussed homophobic dismissal of Baldwin's work in his 1968 *Soul on Ice.* Even recent work, like Kemp William's otherwise enlightening formal analysis "The Metaphorical Construction of Sexuality in *Giovanni's Room*" is unable to consider the intersectionality of race within the novel's depiction of sexuality.[10] We note this not to fault Williams, but to point up the disciplinary strictures of more traditional literary analysis, which seem unable to reconcile Baldwin's early and continued challenge to rethink the relationship of these axes of social identification.

That is not to say that Baldwin "the man" has not been of great interest, nor that he has not appeared or shown up often in epigraphic and aphoristic ways. Baldwin's words have been used in the work of film directors ranging from Marlon Riggs to Spike Lee, alluded to and cited in popular black gay fiction of the likes of James Earl Hardy's *B-Boy Blues,* and quoted by notable African American cultural critics and race men of the likes of Henry Louis Gates, Jr., and Cornel West. Still, what has gone missing is sustained, critical engagement with Baldwin's content, in the thoroughly active way that criticism has continued to engage a Richard Wright, for example. This is a point that echoes with more than a little déjà vu, since a similar claim was forwarded by Trudier Harris in her groundbreaking study *Black Women in the Fiction of James Baldwin* (1985):

> On occasion I was surprised to discover that a writer of Baldwin's reputation evoked such vague memories from individuals in the scholarly community, most of whom maintained that they had read one or more of his fictional works. When I began a thorough examination of Baldwin scholarship, however, some of that reaction became clearer. Baldwin seems to be read at times for the sensationalism readers anticipate in his work, but his treatment in scholarly circles is not commensurate to that claim to sensationalism or to his more solidly justified literary reputation. It was discouraging, therefore, to think that one of America's best-known writers, and certainly one of its best-known black writers, has not

attained a more substantial place in the scholarship on Afro-American writers. (3–4)

It is interesting to observe that in 1985 Harris could still note with authority her supposition that many read Baldwin for the "sensationalism" he and his work represented. Implicitly, Harris starts to recognize that Baldwin was read in part because of his exceptionalism, aberrance, and difference from other black writers. Baldwin provided a generation of American and African American readers with characters who were racialized, sexualized, and class inflected in complex ways, with *lieux de mémoire* to be mobilized in the rituals of identification and desire. Given the advent of cultural studies in the academy—with its focus on interdisciplinarity (or transdisciplinarity) critical theory and an ever-broadening notion of "culture"—it finally became possible to engage a prophetic Baldwin in all of the complexity he represents to critical inquiry by considering the various roles he has occupied. This is largely because the trend in scholarship itself—prior to cultural studies—was ostensibly to identify a particular theme, a category, or a political ideology at work in a text or across an oeuvre in order to fix that variable as part of the process of examining the work in question. Neither Baldwin's life nor his work is easily given over to such an approach. Ideas, even in the realm of his imaginative representations, are rarely static for him. Rather, they are drawn to reflect the complex experience of these ideas in our lives.

We say all of this here simply to illustrate the critical challenge Baldwin's works posed to traditional modes of analysis. His fiction worked to show that it is possible to think critically about African Americans and African American culture without simply essentializing the category of racial blackness; appealing to outmoded and problematic notions of an authentic blackness; or fixing, reifying, or separating race, gender, and sexuality in the name of their political serviceability to racial blackness. With the advent of cultural studies, it seems finally possible to understand Baldwin's vision of and for humanity in its complexity, to mobilize the *lieux de mémoire* from his life, works, and legacy to locate him not as exclusively gay, black, expatriate, activist, or the like, but as an intricately negotiated amalgam of all of those things, which had to be constantly tailored to fit the circumstances in which he was compelled to articulate himself.

NOTES

1. It seems important to note here that "Here Be Dragons" was first published in *Playboy*—a publication committed to the dissemination of normative gender and sexuality—under the title "Freaks and the American Ideal of Manhood" (1985).

2. One must note the absence of any treatment of femininity in Baldwin's account of historical and rhetorical violence done in the name of American masculinity.

3. Evelyn Brooks Higginbotham characterizes black respectability in the following manner:

> Respectability demanded that every individual in the black community assume responsibility for behavioral self-regulation and self-improvement along moral, educational, and economic lines. The goal was to distance oneself as far as possible from images perpetuated by racist stereotypes.... There could be no laxity as far as sexual conduct, cleanliness, temperance, hard work, and politeness were concerned. There could be no transgression of society's norms. From the public spaces of trains and streets to the private spaces of their individual homes, the behavior of blacks was perceived as ever visible to the white gaze. (196)

For more on the politics of black respectability, see Evelyn Brooks Higginbotham's *Righteous Discontent: The Women's Movement in the Black Baptist Church, 1880–1920*, particularly chapter 7.

4. Indeed, we are in a moment now when this critical sensibility called black queer studies is self-consciously in search of a usable past to define and clarify the significance of its arrival onto the scene in its current incarnation. This is evidenced by a proliferation of recent work produced at the margins of race and sexuality. It's most self-conscious manifestations to date, perhaps, come in the form of the extraordinary "Black Queer Studies in the Millennium Conference" organized by E. Patrick Johnson and Mae G. Henderson at the University of North Carolina, Chapel Hill, in

April 2000; a volume of essays resulting from that event, *Black Queer Studies: A Critical Anthology,* coedited by Johnson and Henderson; and a special issue of the journal *Callaloo,* coedited by Jennifer Brody and Dwight A. McBride, titled "Plum Nelly: New Essays in Black Queer Studies," launched at that same historic conference. After the "Black Nations/Queer Nations" conference held in New York City in 1995, the University of North Carolina conference represents the single most significant gathering of this kind to take place in the country, though more recently the "Race, Sex, Power" conference on black and Latino sexualities that took place in April 2008 at the University of Illinois, Chicago, has extended this discussion beyond cultural studies to include the social sciences and the health sciences as well. Though the conference announcement and listing of participants is no longer available at the time of this writing, excellent overviews of the University of North Carolina conference can be found in either Bryant Keith Alexander's "Reflections, Riffs and Remembrances: The Black Queer Studies in the Millennium Conference (2000)" and Vincent Woodard's "Just as Quare as They Want to Be: A Review of the Black Queer Studies in the Millennium Conference."

5. As but one example, Baldwin's comments about self-identifying as gay from a 1984 interview by Richard Goldstein, "Go the Way Your Blood Beats" are telling:

> The word "gay" has always rubbed me the wrong way. I never understood exactly what is meant by it. I don't want to sound distant or patronizing because I don't really feel that. I simply feel it's a world that has very little to do with me, with where I did my growing up. I was never at home in it....I didn't have a word for it. The only one I had was "homosexual" and that didn't quite cover whatever it was I was beginning to feel. (174)

This interview can be found in Quincy Troupe's edited volume *James Baldwin: The Legacy.*

6. Judging by "Preservation of Innocence," the 1949 essay that he wrote and published in *Zero,* Baldwin knows just how profoundly important sexuality is to discussions of race. But the desire registered here for sexuality not to make a difference is important to recognize. When we understand this statement as spoken in a

prophetic, or aspirational, mode, it imagines a world in which the details of a person's sex life can "matter" as part of a person's humanity but not "matter" in terms that usurp their authority or legitimacy to represent the race.

7. Black women, in this regard, would appear, in the confines of race discourse, to be ever the passive players. They are rhetorically useful in that they lend legitimacy to the black male's responsibility for their care and protection, but they cannot speak any more than the gay or lesbian brother or sister can. The gendered portion of this critique has long been argued by black feminist critics since at least the early 1970s with the likes of Toni Cade Bambara up to the more recent works of Hazel Carby, Valerie Smith, E. Frances White, Farah Griffin, and many others.

8. Read by Cole in Karen Thorsen's 1989 film *James Baldwin: The Price of the Ticket*. Unfortunately, Baldwin's estate has barred publication of his letters so Cole's reading here is the fullest quotation available, though mention the content of this letter is made in two biographies of Baldwin by David Leeming and Joseph Campbell. For more on the barred publication of Baldwin's letters, see Campbell's,"Notes on a Native Son."

9. *Loving v. Virginia*, 388 U.S. 1 (1967).

10. An important exception is Douglas Field's essay, "Passing as a Cold War Novel: Anxiety and Assimilation in James Baldwin's *Giovanni's Room*," which argues that the novel, published two years after *Brown v. Board of Education* (1954), reflects anxieties that African American culture would miscegenate white American culture and also that, as a work of homosexual fiction, the novel taps into concerns that homosexuality could go unnoticed. Field argues that the novel probes and critiques rigid postwar identity categories—focusing on the intersections of race and sexuality.

WORKS CITED

Alexander, Bryant Keith. "Reflections, Riffs and Remembrances: The Black Queer Studies in the Millennium Conference (2000)." *Callaloo* 23.4. (Autumn 2000): 1285–1305.

Baldwin, James. *Giovanni's Room*. 1956. New York: Dell, 1988.

———. "Here Be Dragons." In *The Price of the Ticket: Collected Nonfiction, 1948–1985*. New York: St. Martin's/Marek, 1985. 677–90.

———. "Preservation of Innocence." *Out/Look* 2.2 (Fall 1989): 40–45. Originally published in *Zero* 2 (Summer 1949): 14–22. Reprinted in *James Baldwin: Collected Essays*, edited by Toni Morrison. New York: Library of America, 1998. 594–600.

Brody, Jennifer Devere and Dwight A. McBride. Eds. "Plum Nelly: New Essays in Queer Black Studies," a special issue of *Callaloo: A Journal of African and African-American Arts and Letters.* 23. 1. (Winter 2000).

Campbell, James. "Notes on a Native Son." *The Guardian.* (February 12, 2005) p. 4.

———. *Talking at the Gates: A Life of James Baldwin: With a New Afterword.* Berkeley, CA: University of California Press, 2002.

Carby, Hazel. *Race Men.* Cambridge, Mass.: Harvard University Press, 1998.

Dixon, Melvin. "The Black Writer's Use of Memory." In *A Melvin Dixon Critical Reader,* edited by Justin A. Joyce and Dwight A. McBride. Jackson: University of Mississippi Press, 2006. 55–70.

Field, Douglas. "Passing as a Cold War Novel: Anxiety and Assimilation in James Baldwin's *Giovanni's Room.*" In *American Cold War Culture,* edited by Douglas Field. Edinburgh: Edinburgh University Press, 2005. 88–105.

Goldstein, Richard. "'Go the Way Your Blood Beats': An Interview with James Baldwin" (1984*).* In *James Baldwin: The Legacy,* edited by Quincy Troupe. New York: Touchstone/Simon & Schuster, 1989. 173–85.

Griffin, Farah. "Black Feminist and DuBois: Respectability, Protection, and Beyond." *Annals of the American Academy of Political & Social Science* 568 (March 2000): 28–40.

Harris, Trudier. *Black Women in the Fiction of James Baldwin.* Knoxville: University of Tennessee Press, 1985.

Higginbotham, Evelyn Brooks. *Righteous Discontent: The Women's Movement in the Black Baptist Church, 1880–1920.* Cambridge, Mass.: Harvard University Press, 1993.

Hughes, Langston. "The Negro Artist and the Racial Mountain." 1926. Reprinted in *The Heath Anthology of American Literature.* Vol. D., edited by Paul Lauter. New York: Houghton Mifflin, 2006. 1537–40.

Johnson, E. Patrick and Mae G. Henderson. Eds. *Black Queer Studies: A Critical Anthology.* Durham, NC: Duke University Press, 2005.

Leeming, David. *James Baldwin: A Biography.* New York: Henry Holt and Company, 1994.

Locke, Alain. "The New Negro." In *The New Negro: Voices of the Harlem Renaissance,* edited by Alain Locke. 1925. New York: Touchstone, 1997. 3–16.

———. "Self Criticism: The Third Dimension." *Phylon* 11.4 (1950): 391–94.

Nora, Pierre. "Between Memory and History: *Les Lieux de Mémoire.*" In "Memory and Counter-Memory." Special issue, *Representations* 26 (Spring 1989): 7–24.

The Dick Cavett Show. Season 6, Episode 3. (September 5, 1973).

Thorsen, Karen, director. *James Baldwin: The Price of the Ticket.* Nobody Knows Productions, 1989.

Troupe, Quincy. Ed. *James Baldwin: The Legacy.* New York: Simon & Schuster Inc., 1989.

Ross, Marlon. "White Fantasies of Desire: Baldwin and the Racial Identities of Sexuality." In *James Baldwin Now,* edited by Dwight A. McBride. New York: New York University Press, 1999. 13–55.

Williams, Kemp. "The Metaphorical Construction of Sexuality in Giovanni's Room." *Literature and Homosexuality.* Ed. Michael J. (ed and introd). Meyer. Amsterdam, Netherlands: Rodopi, iii, 2000. 23–33.

Woodard, Vincent. "Just as Quare as They Want to Be: A Review of the Black Queer Studies in the Millennium Conference." *Callaloo* 23.4. (Autumn, 2000): 1278–84.

Challenging the American Conscience, Re-Imagining American Identity

James Baldwin and the Civil Rights Movement

Lynn Orilla Scott

James Baldwin's writing and his role as a public intellectual from 1957 through the early 1970s must be understood within the context of the racial struggle at the center of American life. Baldwin's fifteen-year engagement with the black freedom struggle as it evolved from civil rights to Black Power raises some key questions: What was the relationship between his role as a movement "spokesman" and his vocation as a (literary) writer? How did Baldwin represent the movement in his writing and how did that experience impact his writing over time? I put the word *spokesman* in quotation marks to acknowledge that Baldwin disavowed the term, preferring to call himself a "witness," so as not to presume to speak for others.[1] However, the term *spokesman* accurately describes Baldwin's role by 1963 as a highly visible black intellectual whose opinions were widely sought out and publicized. The extent of Baldwin's involvement has not been widely acknowledged in studies of the civil rights movement, as Carol Polsgrove notes in *Divided Minds: Intellectuals and the Civil Rights Movement* (2001). Polsgrove sets out to rectify this situation, although she stops short of tracing Baldwin's political engagement after the early 1960s. In addition to Polsgrove, the best published sources for Baldwin's civil rights participation are the biographies, especially David Leeming's, but the subject has yet to receive full and focused attention.

Baldwin's extensive writing, interviews, and recorded conversations on the movement and more broadly on American racism from 1957 through the early 1970s reflect several consistent themes. From the beginning, Baldwin deeply admired the role black youth played in challenging the racial status quo. His sensitivity to the physical and emotional price they paid for that role kept his admiration from becoming sentimental. From the beginning of the sit-in movement, Baldwin wrote about the generational divide within the civil rights struggle and the ambiguous relationship of black leadership to the black masses. At the same time he maintained ties with both the mainstream leaders and groups and the more radical ones that emerged. Baldwin often stood in the gap, interpreting disparate voices to disparate communities. As early as 1961, Baldwin would bring an international perspective to the American civil rights movement, putting it in the context of the third-world liberation movements that were exploding myths of white supremacy. He addressed civil rights issues as a moralist delivering a sharp critique of the failure of (white) liberalism to address racism, which scholars continue to find relevant.[2] While the tone of Baldwin's jeremiad against "criminal" white "innocence" would become harsher and even more despairing as time went on, his work always pointed toward a utopian re-visioning of American identity. Most importantly, however, Baldwin explored the sexual aspect of racism. He would argue, as Marlon B. Ross has phrased it, that "sexual knowledge and exposure are crucial to racial understanding and progress" (19). The internalization of America's racial history in the private lives of individuals, and the connections between American national, racial, and sexual identities is Baldwin's great theme. It is a theme that preceded his involvement in the civil rights movement, but is reinforced by his experiences in the movement and informs his representation of the civil rights struggle in *The Fire Next Time* (1963), *Blues for Mister Charlie* (1964), "Going to Meet the Man" (1965), *Tell Me How Long the Train's Been Gone* (1968), and *No Name in the Street* (1972).

Early Trips South

After living in France for nine years, Baldwin decided to return to the United States in 1957. There were multiple reasons for this decision, not the least of which was his desire to witness the emerging civil rights movement (Leeming 120, 133). However, by the time Baldwin wrote *No Name in the Street* (1972), he would trace this decision to a specific moment in fall of 1956 when he was covering the first International Conference of Black Writers and Artists, at the Sorbonne, in Paris for *Encounter*. On the way to lunch with Richard Wright and other black writers from the conference, Baldwin writes that they were faced with newspaper images of "fifteen-year-old Dorothy Counts being reviled and spat upon by the mob as she was making her way to school in Charlotte, North Carolina" (50). In fact, this recollection is historically inaccurate, because Dorothy Counts would not be reviled and spat upon for another year, not long before Baldwin arrived in Charlotte to cover the desegregation struggle. However inaccurate in detail, Baldwin's retrospective narrative of this important turning point in his life does serve two key purposes of *No Name in the Street* which are to account for his personal involvement in the movement and to assess the state of race relations following the assassinations of Malcolm X, Medgar Evers and Martin Luther King. First, by implicitly contrasting himself with Richard Wright and other black intellectuals, Baldwin defends his decision to become involved in the civil rights struggle, a decision for which he had been frequently chastised by reviewers of his work after the mid-sixties, who saw his political involvement as damaging to his art. Unlike Wright, Baldwin would become an engaged black intellectual who would "no longer sit around in Paris discussing the Algerian and the black American problem," but respond to the moral challenge presented by the civil rights movement; "everybody else was paying their dues, and it was time I went home and paid mine"

(50). Second, the image of Dorothy Counts helps Baldwin frame the trajectory of the movement from civil rights to Black Power. On his desk "the photograph of Angela Davis has replaced the photograph of Dorothy Counts" (52). Baldwin had written an impassioned defense of Angela Davis for the *New York Review of Books* (January 7, 1971) after her picture appeared on the cover of *Newsweek* in handcuffs (October 26, 1970). For Baldwin the treatment of Dorothy Counts and Angela Davis were of a piece, and they summed up the failure of the American will to change the condition of black Americans.

For his first trip south, in 1957, Baldwin arranged financial backing from *Harper's* and the *Partisan Review*. He would visit Charlotte, Atlanta, Birmingham, Montgomery, Nashville, Little Rock, and Tuskegee, and would meet Martin Luther King Jr., among other leaders. He went south in September, the same month in which President Eisenhower intervened in the Little Rock crisis using the 101st Airborne Division to enforce the Supreme Court's decision on school integration. He would arrive in Montgomery, Alabama, only nine months after the successful conclusion of the bus boycott, which had catapulted a twenty-seven-year-old Martin Luther King into national leadership. The newly heightened black consciousness and determination in the South was being matched by a growing, violent white backlash, and Baldwin approached the trip with a great deal of trepidation. The South was the "old country," the home of his ancestors, the place where they had been enslaved and brutalized, and the place from which they had escaped. Moreover, a black man like James Baldwin—a northerner, an intellectual, a homosexual, a man of slight stature—could make a good target for racist whites looking for "outside agitators," especially for blacks who didn't know their place. However, the South was also the location of a black, blues culture of resistance; for Baldwin, it was a home that was not yet habitable, and this double sense of the South would underlay much of his representation of it.[3]

The two essays from this period, written to fulfill his contracts with *Harper's* and the *Partisan Review,* were republished as "A Fly in the Buttermilk" (1958) and "A Letter from the South: Nobody Knows My Name" (1959).[4] The first, based on Baldwin's

interviews with the unnamed participants in a school integration struggle, shows his concern with the effect of the struggle
on the private lives of individuals and the psychological price
being paid by those asserting their right to a quality education
in the mainstream of American life. The fifteen-year-old boy
whom Baldwin interviews minimizes the appalling treatment
he has received as the only black student allowed to "integrate"
his high school. Baldwin wonders, "What was all this doing
to him really?" He describes the boy as "disquietingly impas-
sive.... Pride and silence were his weapons" (166). For Baldwin
these were familiar responses to white racism that he explored
at length in his autobiographical novels, first in the character of
John Grimes in *Go Tell It on the Mountain* (1953) and again, fifteen
years later, in Leo Proudhammer, the protagonist of *Tell Me How
Long the Train's Been Gone*. Baldwin is remarkably sensitive to
the plight of the white school principal as well, a man who tells
Baldwin that "he'd never dreamed of a mingling of the races."
Baldwin describes him as "gentle and honorable," a "victim of
his heritage" (167–68). Segregation, writes Baldwin, "allowed
white people ... to create ... only the Negro they wished to
see." Now, they will "be forced to reexamine a way of life and
to speculate, in a personal way, on the general injustice" (169).
Already speculating on the "price of the ticket," Baldwin did not
yet imagine how expensive it would be or the degree of white
intransigence.

 "A Letter from the South" also addresses the integration struggle, but frames it within Baldwin's larger argument about the
sexual component of racism. The "criminally frivolous dispute"
about education being carried on in "bad faith" by "completely
uneducated people" is really a dispute about power and sex (185).
This is a particularly rich early essay, in which Baldwin situates
himself symbolically in relationship to the denial of America's
interracial history. The South is the place of his "inescapable identity." He meditates on the reasons for his outsider status from
both the southern black and white communities and figures the
dilemma of the northern Negro as the dilemma of the American.
The landscape of the South "seems designed for violence," a
place of tabooed desire, "private, unspeakable longings" (189).

In addition to articulating central Baldwin themes, the essay is remarkably prescient in its description of the role southern governors would continue to play in trying to maintain segregation in the South. (The essay was written before Governor Ross Barnett's effort to block James Meredith from the University of Mississippi and before Governor George Wallace's stand at the schoolhouse door in Alabama). Baldwin predicts how the role of southern governors would stiffen resistance and how that resistance would spread to northern cities. The essay is insightful on the political structure of South, which, as Baldwin says, is "not monolithic." It also provides a critique of the small black middle class in the "wholly segregated" city of Atlanta, which plays an untenable and potentially self-defeating role in "a very complex and shaky social structure" (190).

Over twenty years later, Baldwin would return to the subject of Atlanta's racial and class structure in his article, "The Evidence of Things Not Seen" (1981), and in his last book, by the same title (1985). Baldwin had gone to Atlanta to report on the unsolved case of the city's thirty missing and murdered poor black children and later to cover the trial of the man who was arrested for them, Wayne Williams. By the early 1980s Atlanta had a black-led city administration and police force that were coming under increasing criticism for their failure to solve the murders. In his essay, Baldwin quotes "A Letter from the South," and claims that the racial structure and the trap in which black leadership found itself was essentially unchanged (312). He reiterated this in his book and argued that the "fable" of racial progress was being sustained in part by the rise of black political rule, which Baldwin describes as "a concession masking the face of power which remains white" (26).[5] The murders of the poor, mostly male, black children threatened to expose the illusion of racial progress. As early as "A Fly in the Buttermilk," Baldwin would comment on the potentially negative consequences of integration on black schools and institutions. In "The Evidence of Things Not Seen" he refers to the "hammer of integration" as the effects of "the choices we had made" during the civil rights movement that had further marginalized poor blacks. "The terror in Atlanta begins to alter, or to reveal, the relationship among black people" (314). But if "integration" was a "hammer," it was also an illusion, much like the civil rights movement, that America had transformed into a "propaganda medal" for itself (*Evidence of Things Not Seen* 24). Atlanta, whose long-time appelation was "The City Too Busy to Hate," was in reality still a racially divided city with a very large impoverished population of blacks and whites who seemed to Baldwin to have no interaction with each other ("Evidence of Things Not Seen" 142). In his book he states: "Others may see American progress in economic, racial, and social affairs—I do not. I pray to be proven wrong, but I see the opposite, with murderous implications, and not only in North America" (56). By the late 1960s Baldwin's denial of American "progress" would provoke many of his former liberal admirers to call him bitter and out of touch. Yet there was plenty of "evidence" to support his view: The economic gap between white and black Atlantans had widened considerably since the civil rights movement; black teens faced dramatically increased unemployment, poverty, and ghettoization; and 30–40 percent of the population lived below the national poverty level (Headley 26).

Baldwin's second trip south, in the spring of 1960, occurred at the height of the sit-in movement that had begun on February 1, when four black students at the Agricultural and Technical College of North Carolina tried to order a cup of coffee at a segregated lunch counter. During 1960 and 1961, approximately 70,000 people participated in sit-ins, wade-ins, kneel-ins, and read-ins at public institutions all over the South (Anderson 46). A month before Baldwin's arrival, the Student Non-Violent Coordinating Committee (SNCC) was formed, a group he would join and maintain ties with, as he did with the Congress of Racial Equality (CORE). The two essays that came from this trip, "They Can't Turn Back" (*Mademoiselle*, August 1960) and "The Dangerous Road Before Martin Luther King" (*Harper's*, February 1961), would not be collected until the publication of *The Price of the Ticket* in 1985. "They Can't Turn Back" is an illuminating description of the desegregation struggle occurring in Tallahasee, led by Florida A&M University (FAMU) students. Baldwin arrived about two months after a large sit-in demonstration in which the students had been attacked by members of the White Citizens' Council with baseball bats and then gassed and arrested by the police. No one had shown up to defend the students, which Baldwin said was typical of the response students were meeting throughout the South. These events had also "created great divisions in the Negro world" (218), especially a generational division. Baldwin points to the unhappy situation of the Negro college president, who must choose between supporting the students or preserving his job which depends on a system that "has always been used by the southern states as a means of controlling Negroes" (219) and Baldwin is concerned with the demoralization that occurs when youth can't emulate their elders (221). The essay captures the intraracial as well as the interracial dimensions of the struggle and affirms the emergence of a new black consciousness among the youth. The students no longer accept "the legend of the Negro's inferiority" upon which southern life had been constructed. "The point of view of the subjugated is finally and inexorably being expressed" (216). Yet, Baldwin is, as always, acutely aware of the price, the difficult choices the students are making, "the abnormal self-containment of such young people" (224), and "the depth of official hostility and community apathy" (225). The situation of the movement is precarious, the outcome uncertain. Baldwin wonders "what kind of page" in history this will be, "recording our salvation or our doom" (227).

Baldwin had received Martin Luther King's permission to write a profile of him for *Harper's,* and King would write to thank Baldwin for the essay "The Dangerous Road Before Martin Luther King" and for the collection *Nobody Knows My Name,* saying, "Your honesty and courage in telling the truth to white Americans, even if it hurts is most impressive" (quoted in Polsgrove 140). The essay combines a biographical sketch of King, whom Baldwin finds remarkably "unscarred" by racism, with a cautionary tale about the dilemmas faced by Negro leaders, beginning with a description of Montgomery race relations in the wake of the bus boycott three years earlier, when he had first met King. Baldwin has no doubt that King is a new kind of Negro leader, one who is willing to say the same thing to whites that he says to Negroes (246); yet with the rise of the student sit-in movement, King is "now in the center of an extremely complex cross fire" (252). Not only do whites find King dangerous, but "many Negroes also find King dangerous, but cannot say so" (258). Baldwin further develops the theme of the difficulties of black leadership that he had alluded to in the earlier essay "They Can't Turn Back," situating the pressure King is under in the unlucky situation of the black bourgeoisie "trapped as they are, in a no-man's land between black humiliation and white power" (260). King was caught in the gap between the official Negro leaders and "the young people who have begun what is nothing less than a moral revolution" (261). Baldwin is not uncritical of King, suggesting he had lost some moral credit among the youth for bowing to political pressure to distance Bayard Rustin and James Lawson from the Southern Christian Leadership Conference. Yet, overall the essay greatly admires King, who has changed the terms of the struggle by carrying "the battle into the individual heart" (262). Baldwin ends the essay by placing the southern struggle against segregation in an international context of liberation movements that are exploding the myth of white supremacy and thus creating new identities for both Negroes and whites.

Baldwin's Dual Role

By the summer of 1961, following the publication of *Nobody Knows My Name*, Baldwin emerged as a spokesperson for the civil rights movement. His magnificent verbal skill, his passion, his magnetic personality, his intellect, and most of all his sense of responsibility and commitment to the cause of Negro freedom made him sought after by civil rights organizations and the media for interviews, debates, and speaking engagements on the so-called Negro Problem, which Baldwin deftly redefined as the "white problem." Baldwin published interviews, letters, and speeches in a wide range of popular and specialized periodicals, from *Mademoiselle* to *Muhammad Speaks*. The journal *Freedomways: A Quarterly Review of the Negro Freedom Movement* published several of his short pieces between 1963 and 1979.[6] Pacifica Archives has a number of sound recordings of his speeches and interviews. Baldwin's life became a whirlwind of public engagements for many years. Negotiating his role as writer/artist with his role as spokesperson/activist became increasingly difficult. On one level it was a problem of time. Baldwin's celebrity status—and his inability to say no to various requests—meant that he had to leave the United States to find the time and ease to write. Baldwin became a "transatlantic commuter." Much of the writing in the 1960s took place in Turkey as well as France.

On another level Baldwin, and later his critics, saw the dual role as a problem of conflicting responsibilities. Art and protest were not entirely compatible. At least this was Baldwin's apparent theme in his famous and controversial 1949 essay, "Everybody's Protest Novel," which compared Richard Wright's *Native Son* with Harriet Beecher Stowe's *Uncle Tom's Cabin.* Both novels, he charged, reduced the human being to their social category and thus failed as art. Yet his criticism was not primarily aesthetic: he argued that these novels that were intended as social protest failed as effective protest, because they created Negro characters who weren't fully human; thus the novels actually reified the stereotypes of black life that underlay racism. From early on Baldwin had conflated a certain aesthetic ideal, the intricately developed character of the Jamesian realistic novel, with the moral/political goal of liberating the nation from white myths about blacks. Such a conflation is consistent with Baldwin's own interest in representing the impact of history on the inner life of individuals and especially in creating characters who were not just victims, but agents operating within the constraints of a deforming context. Yet "Everybody's Protest Novel," while useful as a young author's artistic manifesto, does oversimplify the complex relationship between aesthetic ideals and social purposes. The essay would not have resonance for the Black Arts movement, which emerged in the mid-1960s, whose search for an aesthetic of liberation would be influenced less by the realistic tradition of Henry James and more by the forms of African American music. Baldwin, himself, would increasingly look to sources in African American music and culture to shape his art. Ironically, however, by the mid-1960s, "Everybody's Protest

Novel" became the staging ground for Baldwin's most vociferous critics, who would claim that he had given up on art and was writing propaganda. Much of this criticism, I have argued elsewhere, was politically driven by white liberals who believed Baldwin had abandoned his "integrationist" politics for Black Power and who actually paid little attention to Baldwin's art.[7]

Baldwin continued to be preoccupied with the conflicting responsibilities of art and protest. In a 1961 radio broadcast, he took part in a panel discussion, "The Negro in American Culture," with Lorraine Hansberry, Langston Hughes, and others. Moderator Nat Hentoff begins the discussion by quoting a review by Baldwin, stating that Langston Hughes was "not the first American Negro to find the war between his social and artistic responsibilities all but irreconcilable" (205), and asking if this claim is true for Baldwin as well. The ensuing discussion is very revealing not only of Baldwin's experience of this conflict, but of its lack of resonance for both Langston Hughes and Lorraine Hansberry, who saw no inherent conflict specific to the Negro writer between art and social criticism.[8] For Baldwin, however, at the center of this war between artistic and social responsibility is the problem of anger. He says, "to be a Negro in this country and to be relatively conscious, is to be in a rage almost all the time. So that the first problem is how to control that rage so that it won't destroy you." The rage is due not only to what happens to Negroes in America, but to the "criminal indifference...and ignorance of most white people in this country." The "great temptation" for the artist, then, is "to simplify the issues under the illusion that if you simplify them enough, people will recognize them" (205). In an argument similar to "Everybody's Protest Novel," he goes on to say that an artist who creates characters who "are people" that have a "universal appeal" has gone further "not only artistically, but socially" (205). The second problem for the Negro writer is guilt. The writer must "[step] out of a social situation in order to deal with it," but at the same time he feels he should be "on the firing line, tearing down the slums and doing all these obviously needed thing...." (205–6). Throughout the conversation Baldwin uses phrases like "remake the world," "moral revolution," and "unify the country" to describe the role of the Negro writer. While he describes a conflict between art and protest caused by anger and guilt, his language tightly binds his artistic and social vision in a moral, even messianic, discourse.

In another radio broadcast also from 1961, "Black Muslims vs. The Sit-Ins," Baldwin debated with Malcolm X about the importance of the nonviolent student movement.[9] The debate occurred two months after "The Dangerous Road Before Martin Luther King" appeared in *Harper's*, where Baldwin had called attention to the divisions between the young activists and the older civil rights leadership. Now Baldwin would defend the students from a very different challenge. The debate is a preview for a number of arguments in *The Fire Next Time* (1963). Baldwin deftly negotiates the conflicting discourses of racial integration vs. Black Nationalism and nonviolence vs. self-defense. Malcolm X begins with an appeal to racial pride, characterizing the sit-ins as "a passive thing" that prevent blacks from standing up and fighting like men and "integration" (which he saw as abandoning one's racial identity) as an unworthy goal. Malcolm accuses all the mainstream civil rights organizations of "waiting" for rights to be granted. The black man in America, he notes, is the only one who is encouraged to be nonviolent or is accused of being racist or extremist if he advocates standing up for himself. Whites, he says, obviously, "idolize fighters," especially freedom fighters; until whites practice nonviolence, it is "insane" for blacks to adopt such a strategy. Baldwin's response is to defend the sit-in movement as a powerful challenge to white power while implicitly acknowledging some of Malcolm's criticism of the established civil rights organizations. Baldwin also acknowledges "a certain clarity" in the Black Muslim message for its accurate description of the Negro condition, when "the country has lied about the Negro situation for so long." As he would say in *The Fire Next Time*, "I, in any case, certainly refuse to be put in the position of denying the truth of Malcolm's statements simply because I disagree with his conclusions, or in order to pacify the liberal conscience" (59).

However, in the debate Baldwin would make his fundamental disagreements with the Black Muslims clear by redefining the terms *integration, race, manhood,* and *violence.* "Integration" is a false issue, claims Baldwin, because, whether one likes it or not, the American Negro was integrated in the womb; one can't deny history. As for the Black Muslim appeal to "race," Baldwin sees it as part of their "theology"; for him, "all theologies are suspect." There is something "insidious in the whole question of race." Baldwin wants to be part of "a world where there are no blacks and whites" and where you don't need to invent a history to feel superior to others. As for "violence," the real problem is that violence is likely to occur with devastating consequences. Baldwin (correctly) predicts that "Birmingham will probably blow up and will stretch to Boston"—but, he wonders, "what will happen then?" Most importantly, Baldwin rejects Malcolm's appropriation of the American revolutionary tradition and its link between masculinity and violence. "Patrick Henry is not one of my heroes," says Baldwin. "Because white men have committed crimes doesn't mean black men should do the same things.... A warrior isn't necessarily a man.... It is very difficult to be a man.... The standards have to be revised."[10] Although Baldwin was regarded as "moderate" and Malcolm as "radical," it is worth noting that Baldwin's call for a reconstruction of American identity and a redefinition of "manhood" situates the "radical" Malcolm X's ideas as the more traditionally American of the two. In *The Fire Next Time*, Baldwin would argue that the Black Muslim's theology was just a reaction, a mirror image of the beliefs of white racists. Less understood, perhaps, is that Baldwin's appeal to white America in *The Fire Next Time* was more complicated and more difficult than a call for simple inclusion or for America to live up to its purported values of freedom and democracy. Baldwin argued that "the American Negro is a unique creation" (84) and that changing his situation necessarily implies "the most radical and far-reaching changes in the American political and social structure" (85). Thus, the American Negro is strategically positioned to redeem America, but only via a radically altered American identity.

Within a few years the views of Malcolm X and Baldwin would seem less disparate. Malcolm would break from the

Nation of Islam and write Martin Luther King, calling for a United Front of all Negro Factions. Malcolm would tell Kenneth B. Clark, the noted black psychologist, that he had "assumed the difficult role of publicly projecting extreme positions" so that other black leaders, like Baldwin, "would be heard" (Clark 11). For his part, Baldwin, who had described his encounter with Elijah Muhammad in *The Fire Next Time,* hoping to stir up the white conscience, would find that white "innocence" and paternalism continued to be intractable obstacles to change. By the later 1960s, Baldwin would frame the solution to the race problem less in terms of a redeemed national identity and more in terms of the international struggles against colonialism, much like Malcolm X and his political descendants the Black Panthers did. His later fiction would focus less on the American interracial experience than on the resources of black culture and black consciousness as strategies for resistance to ongoing racial oppression. As for his rejection of Patrick Henry, whose battle cry was "give me liberty or give me death," Baldwin would explore the challenge and the hazards of a revolutionary black masculinity in his characters Richard Henry in *Blues for Mister Charlie* and Black Christopher in *Tell Me How Long the Train's Been Gone.*

Kenneth Clark had arranged a meeting between Baldwin, King, and Malcolm X on February 23, 1965; two days earlier, Malcolm X would be murdered. Baldwin, deeply distressed by the murder, compared it to the assassination of Medgar Evers; the killers, white and black, were "by-products of the plague—the 'white problem' in America" (Leeming 246). Less than five years after the assassination, Baldwin would spend several months in California working for Columbia Pictures on a screenplay of Malcolm X's life. Conflicts over the script and who would play the part of Malcolm led to Baldwin severing his ties with Columbia. He eventually published the script in 1972 as *One Day When I Was Lost: A Scenario Based on Alex Haley's* The Autobiography of Malcolm X. Baldwin's Malcolm would be both admirable and complex, a man whose past continued to inform his present, a man still changing.

The Fire Next Time

The problem of rage and guilt that Baldwin discussed in "The Negro in American Culture" finds its most eloquent expression in *The Fire Next Time* (1963), Baldwin's post-Christian version of an Old Testament jeremiad. Baldwin makes rage speak in a way that could be heard and admired by many Americans. Published as a monograph near the end of January 1963, *The Fire Next Time* is comprised of two essays: "My Dungeon Shook: Letter to My Nephew on the One Hundredth Anniversary of the Emancipation," initially published in *The Progressive* (December 1962), and "Down at the Cross: Letter from a Region of My Mind," initially published in *The New Yorker* (November 1962). Begun in early 1962 in Switzerland and finished in Istanbul, these two essays were conceived and written on four different continents and rooted in the escalating American racial crisis.

"My Dungeon Shook," written in the form of a letter to his fifteen-year-old nephew, was inspired by the miseducation of African students in an elementary school in Dakar whom Baldwin witnessed reciting the phrase, "Our ancestors, who came from Gaul..." (Leeming 212). Baldwin had toured several African cities in July 1962 on commission for *The New Yorker*. David Leeming said that "Africa had cemented his belief that to be of African descent in the West was 'to be the flesh of white people—endlessly mortified'" (211). Baldwin's experience in the civil rights movement is part of the context as well. He had kept in touch with members of the SNCC, whom he had met during his second trip into the American South. The essay has a dual audience: the message to his nephew is by extension a message to young black activists and the message to whites is shaped by the disappointing liberal response that urged civil rights leaders to go slow and criticized them for provoking violence. "My Dungeon Shook" introduces all the themes of the longer essay: the danger for blacks in believing the white world's judgment of them; the criminal white innocence that denies the reality of black suffering; the role that blacks must play in re-educating whites and re-creating America; and a clarification of the true meaning of two badly misunderstood terms associated with the civil rights struggle, *integration* and *acceptance*. Integration is not about "the impertinent assumption" that whites must accept blacks, but the necessity for blacks to accept whites: "[I]f the word *integration* means anything, this is what it means: that we, with love, shall force our brothers to see themselves as they are, to cease fleeing from reality and begin to change it. For this is your home, my friend, do not be driven from it; great men have done great things here, and will again, and we can make America what America must become" (10). In "My Dungeon Shook," Baldwin places his white readers in the position of an uninformed, eavesdropping audience, overhearing a private black conversation: "I know your countrymen do not agree with me about this, and I hear them saying, 'You exaggerate'" (8). The epistolary form is a rhetorical strategy that Baldwin employs to reverse white liberal paternalism and perform the very work that he encourages his nephew to do—educate whites.

The longer essay, "Down at the Cross," part autobiography, part social commentary, and part sermon, is the most famous of the two essays that comprise *The Fire Next Time*. The opening section, which examines Baldwin's adolescent experience in a black holiness church and his subsequent rejection of its theology and hypocrisy (if not its music and its drama), contains some of Baldwin's most powerful writing. His critique of the Black Muslims, discussed earlier, parallels the critique of his own church experience and pushes the essay forward to its call for an interracial solution to the racial crisis, based on a recognition that "the black and the white, deeply need each other here if we are really to become a nation—if we are really, that is, to achieve our identity, our maturity, as men and women" (97).

The Fire Next Time quickly became a bestseller and was almost universally well reviewed. In *The New York Review of Books*, F. W. Dupee wrote that "much of it is unexceptionably first-rate." Baldwin's style was "the ideal prose of an ideal literary community, some aristocratic France of one's dreams." Yet, Dupee's admiration was qualified by what he saw as a disturbing tendency to "[replace] criticism with prophecy." Dupee wanted Baldwin to put his assertions to a "pragmatic test." Questioning the "social utility" of prophecy or exhortation, especially generalizations that characterized "the behavior of entire populations," Dupee was concerned that in its "madder moments" *The Fire Next Time* would "inflame anti-Negro extremists" and confuse Negroes. Dupee was not alone in his skepticism. In a *New York Post* essay, Langston Hughes also questioned Baldwin's political judgment and lack of solutions to the race problem: "Maybe Baldwin can just cry, 'Fire,' and not have the least idea how to put it out," Hughes wrote (Rampersad 375). However, others who read *The Fire Next Time,* like Harlem leader Anna Arnold Hedgeman, found in Baldwin someone who could articulate black anger to whites. She wrote, "we were glad that at last the public media had put into print every word of the beautifully written and true story of the angry, impatient, disgusted and cynical mood of the Negro" (quoted in Boyd 42). Dupee overestimated the inflammatory power of the essay and underestimated its power to transform thinking on what had been called the "Negro problem." Dupee's and Hughes' reservations, however, are an early taste of what would become much harsher criticism of Baldwin's work by 1965. To some extent, their comments reflect Baldwin's own concerns, articulated in "The Negro in American Culture," that the temptation for the Negro artist, enraged over white ignorance, was "to simplify the issues" so that people would recognize them.

The Fire Next Time employs provocation to cure the disease of racism. It is the literary equivalent of the strategy of "nonviolent direct action" that Martin Luther King was using in Birmingham to end racial segregation. Its closest literary relative is another epistolary masterpiece published less than three months later, King's "Letter from a Birmingham Jail" (April 1963), written in response to eight white clergyman who called the demonstrations in Birmingham "untimely and unwise" and implicitly blamed King for the violence. Although different in tone and persona, "Down at the Cross" and "Letter from a Birmingham Jail" each address a white liberal audience, who, fearful of white backlash, are telling movement leaders to go slow, to "wait." The two texts contain a set of strikingly parallel passages. The first occurs midway through "Down at the Cross," where Baldwin states that the segregation Negro soldiers faced after World War II was a turning point in black consciousness. Directly addressing his reader, Baldwin writes, "you must put yourself in the skin of...," and then presents a long list of injustices that Negro soldiers faced. He ends by stating, "imagine yourself being told to 'wait'" (54–55). The famous 316-word sentence of King's letter also addresses the reader in the second person, uses parallel structures to produce a long list of injustices (although King's are more focused on women and children), and ends with the understated main clause, "then you will understand why we find it difficult to wait." Both King and Baldwin write powerful polemics aimed at transforming white consciousness. Both draw on the Judeo-Christian value of love and on the political ideals of American democracy. While King positions himself squarely within the Christian church, speaking with Olympian restraint of his disappointment in the eight white clergyman and by extension all southern white moderates, Baldwin positions himself outside the church, speaking as an apostate, a secular Jeremiah, angry at a "criminal" white "innocence." In his letter King uses the metaphor of a surgeon lancing a boil to describe the strategy of nonviolent direct action. The demonstrators are "merely bring[ing] to the surface the hidden tension that is already alive. Like a boil that can never be cured so long as it is covered up but must be opened with all its ugliness to the natural medicines of air and light injustice must be exposed ... to the light of human conscience and the air of national opinion, before it can be cured." A month later in an interview for *Mademoiselle* magazine, titled "Disturber of the Peace," Baldwin would use King's metaphor. The interviewer asks Baldwin if he worries that he may be only "reinforc[ing] feelings of guilt and fear in white people." Baldwin replies: "I think that what I feel about guilt is that it is like a festering sore that must be worked upon until it's opened and the pus can run out" (175).

On the Public Stage

During the first few months of 1963, Baldwin went on two fundraising trips for CORE, making dozens of appearances in New Orleans, Durham, Greensboro, and other southern cities, speaking in churches and schools. In Jackson, Mississippi, he would meet both Medgar Evers and James Meredith. Jane Howard created a striking photo documentary of the southern trip for the May 23, 1963, issue of *Life* magazine. At the height of the Birmingham campaign, in April 1963, Baldwin made a second trip for CORE, speaking at universities from California to Connecticut. On May 17 Baldwin's portrait appeared on the cover of *Time* magazine. The issue described the ongoing violence in Birmingham, illustrated by the infamous pictures of Bull Connor's police manhandling a Negro woman and the blast of fire hoses knocking down a Negro boy, and it contained a two-page article on Baldwin. The introduction described Baldwin as "effeminate" and "fragile . . . filled with frets and fears," someone who "is not, by any stretch of the imagination a Negro leader," and who "often loses his audience with overblown arguments" (26). Nevertheless, the article includes a picture of Baldwin speaking before a huge crowd of students at the University of California, quotes extensively from *The Fire Next Time* and other Baldwin essays, predicting "if he can make himself heard . . . everybody will know his name" (27). Carol Polsgrove, who has carefully documented Baldwin's public interaction during this period, states that Baldwin

> had become—by virtue of his frankness, eloquence, and reputation—a spokesman for the movement. He was speaking out publicly on events as they happened: releasing statements, appearing at press conferences, making speeches, giving interviews, going on television. He spoke for political organizations when they asked him to help raise funds or spirits; but he spoke on his own, too. Unfettered by strategic political considerations, he spoke as he pleased, frankly, honestly, directly from the heart of his own convictions. (185)

One result of Baldwin's increasing visibility was an invitation to meet with Attorney General Robert Kennedy. Baldwin had sent Kennedy a telegram taking him to task for "allowing the Birmingham situation to occur" (Leeming 222). Following a brief, and apparently cordial breakfast meeting, Robert Kennedy asked Baldwin to assemble a group of Negroes to meet with him the next day in New York City. Baldwin brought over a dozen people from varied backgrounds, including Clarence Jones (King's legal council as well as Baldwin's), Harry Belafonte, Lena Horne, Lorraine Hansberry, Kenneth Clark, CORE activist Jerome Smith, Bob Mills (Baldwin's literary agent), his brother David, and his friend Rip Torn (a white actor who would play Lyle Britten in *Blues for Mister Charlie*). Burke Marshall, the assistant attorney general, who had helped negotiate what *Time* referred to as a "pallid peace" in Birmingham was also present. The meeting, which generated front-page *New York Times* coverage for three consecutive days, has been described in a number of historical and biographical sources, all characterizing it as a disaster.[11] Kenneth Clark described it as "one of the most violent, emotional verbal assaults that [he] had ever witnessed. It was a searing, emotional interaction and confrontation" that went on for about three hours in which Kennedy became increasingly tense and silent (Stein 121).

CORE activist Jerome Smith's "genuine emotion set the tone of the meeting." When Kennedy and Marshall tried to get him to temper his protest, all the members of Baldwin's group sided with Smith (Clark 14–15). Jerome Smith had endured a series of beatings in trying to integrate bus facilities in Mississippi and was one of the Freedom Riders who had been imprisoned in Parchment Penitentiary following the federal government's compromise with Mississippi authorities.[12] He had come to New York for medical treatment for his injuries (Clark 14). When Kennedy expressed his fear that Negroes were turning to Black Muslims, Jerome Smith responded that the real trouble wouldn't be the Muslims, but people like himself giving up on nonviolence: "You have no idea what trouble is...because I'm close to the moment where I'm ready to take up a gun" (quoted in Branch, *Parting the Waters*, 810). To underline Jerome's commitment to nonviolence,

Baldwin asked him if he would take up arms to defend America; when he vehemently responded, "never," Kennedy was shocked at his lack of patriotism. Emphasizing how he felt pleading before the attorney general for rights he should already have had as an American citizen, Smith said that "sitting there with Kennedy made him want to vomit" (Branch, *Parting the Waters*, 811). Kennedy heard the remark "as a gratuitous expression of personal contempt" (Schlesinger 962). When Kennedy tried to compare the situation of his Irish immigrant ancestors to blacks, Baldwin told him, "Generations before your family came as immigrants, my ancestors came to this country in chains, as slaves. We are still required to supplicate and beg you for justice and decency" (Clark 15). Baldwin's group tried to communicate a sense of urgency to Kennedy; they wanted the administration to exert its moral authority through a public gesture, like having the president escort a Negro child integrating a southern school. Kennedy thought such a gesture would be phony; he wanted "practical" advice regarding political action, money, and legislation. In a later interview, Baldwin said, "Bobby didn't understand what we were trying to tell him. . . . And our apprehension of his misunderstanding made it very tense, and finally very ugly" (Stein 119). Kennedy thought the Negroes didn't know anything about what the administration was trying to do and that they were naive about politics (Schlesinger 963). Finally, Lorraine Hansberry ended the meeting by leading a walk-out.

Following this abrasive encounter, Baldwin quickly became subject to increased FBI interest. The FBI had started a file on Baldwin in 1960 after he signed a petition circulated by the Fair Play for Cuba Committee, but within days following the meeting with the attorney general, the FBI would write a lengthy report on Baldwin, place a wiretap on Clarence Jones's phone (which would give the FBI information on King's private life), and investigate others at the meeting. Baldwin would be placed on the "Security Index," the list of people considered dangerous to national security, and be followed and harassed for years to come. Baldwin's public statements criticizing the FBI and in particular its director, J. Edgar Hoover, for its lack of action in Birmingham and Selma were of particular interest to the bureau as was Baldwin's sexuality. Hoover would refer to him in a memo as a "known pervert." The file would grow to well over a thousand pages; the investigation of Baldwin wouldn't end until 1974.[13] Baldwin never saw his FBI file, but he had no doubt he was under surveillance. Following the assassinations of so many public figures associated with civil rights, he "often spoke of fearing for his own life" (Leeming 226).

Nevertheless, the seemingly disastrous meeting with Robert Kennedy may well have furthered the cause of civil rights. Kenneth Clark, who at the time thought they had made no impact and found Kennedy "an extraordinarily insensitive person," came to believe their judgment of him had been too harsh (Stein 121–22). Indeed, there is evidence that their message to the administration was heard. Taylor Branch describes a conversation in which Vice President Lyndon Johnson tells John Kennedy's speech writer, Theodore Sorenson, "So the only big problem is saying to the Baldwins and to the Kings and to the rest of them, 'We give you a moral commitment. The government is behind you'" (*Pillar of Fire* 94–95). Johnson's own speech that Memorial Day at Gettysburg would treat civil rights as a moral issue. Then, on June 11, after nationalizing the Alabama state guard to enforce the desegregation of the University of Alabama, President Kennedy would call for civil rights legislation in a televised address, saying that the country faced "a moral crisis. . . . A great change is at hand, and our task, our obligation, is to make that revolution, that change, peaceful and constructive for all" (quoted in Schlesinger 965).

The day after Kennedy's speech, Medgar Evers, field secretary for the National Association for the Advancement of Colored People (NAACP) in Mississippi, was shot dead in front of his home. Baldwin had met Medgar Evers that January. In one of his more frightening experiences in the South, Baldwin had traveled with Evers on back-country Mississippi roads, investigating the murder of a black man by a white storekeeper. Baldwin heard of Evers's murder while in Puerto Rico, working on his play *Blues for Mister Charlie* (*No Name in the Street* 153). The news would spur Baldwin to complete the play, which was loosely based on the

Emmett Till case, but also based on the case he helped Medgar Evers investigate.

Baldwin's Literature of the Civil Rights Movement

Blues for Mister Charlie, completed in October 1963, was conceived five years earlier in conversation with Elia Kazan, but it was shaped by more immediate events: Baldwin's work on behalf of CORE and SNCC; the meeting with Robert Kennedy; the murder of Medgar Evers; the March on Washington; the bombing of the Sixteenth Street Baptist Church, which killed four girls; and his participation in the voter registration drive in Selma. These are the contexts for Baldwin's drama of the civil rights movement at the crossroads. The play takes an historical turning point and moves it into the present. Nine years earlier the murder of fourteen-year-old Emmett Till for allegedly whistling at a white woman, and the failure of Mississippi to convict the murderers, had been a catalyst for the civil right's movement. Similarly, the murder of Baldwin's character, Richard Henry, and the failure to convict his murderer represents the catalyst for a new phase in the movement, as the call for militancy and self-defense began to replace that of nonviolent protest. Unlike the historical Emmett Till, Richard Henry is an adult, whose decision to vulgarly taunt the "manhood" of Lyle Britten, a known white racist and murderer, makes Richard less a victim than a conscious radical who refuses to live like his father, Meridian Henry, a preacher and leader of the local civil rights struggle. If Richard's angry, provocative behavior appears suicidal, it is not without impact. As the play opens, the young black civil rights workers are questioning the strategy of nonviolence. In Act I, Meridian tells his white friend, Parnell, "Maybe I was wrong not to let the people arm" (55). At the end of the play, Meridian says, "You know, for us, it all began with the Bible and the gun. Maybe it will end with the Bible and the gun." Meridian has put Richard's gun "in the pulpit. Under the Bible. Like the pilgrims of old" (158). Baldwin thus links the ongoing black freedom struggle to the country's revolutionary history, one that doesn't preclude the violence of self-defense. The play opened at the ANTA Theater on Broadway on April 23, 1964. It was produced by The Actors Studio Theatre, then under the direction of Lee Strasberg, and directed by Burgess Meredith. The contentiousness of the production is legend. Baldwin, who attended almost all of the rehearsals, found himself in conflict with the studio over issues of language, casting, direction, and the price of the tickets, which Baldwin wanted to keep low to insure a black as well as a white audience. The play did attract racially mixed audiences: blacks tended to be very appreciative, while whites were sometimes shocked and angry (Leeming 238). The reviews were as divided and as emotionally charged as the play itself. Howard Taubman in the *New York Times* reviewed it favorably, and most reviews praised the acting, but some were upset by what was perceived as antiwhite sentiment. In an especially vitriolic review for *The New Republic*, titled "Everybody's Protest Play," Robert Brustein not only accused the play of "perpetuating stereotypes" and of "moral and intellectual deficiency," but claimed that Baldwin "the complex man of sensibility has been totally absorbed by the simplistic man of power" (36–37). On the other hand, Tom Driver defended Baldwin's presentation of the struggle as "racial," not simply as economic or constitutional. He argued that the representation of southern white people is more accurate than in any other play and describes the form as Brechtian, neither comic nor tragic, but a call to action. Although *Blues for Mister Charlie* did attract sizable audiences, it ran into financial difficulties because of the low ticket prices and large cast, almost closing after a month. A number of Baldwin's friends and celebrities signed a petition to save the play; financial help came from two Rockefeller sisters. The play closed in New York on August 29, 1964.

Blues for Mister Charlie takes place in "Plaguetown, U.S.A." "[T]he plague is race" and "our concept of Christianity," says Baldwin in his prefatory "Notes for Blues" (7). Racial division is symbolized by the stage set, dominated by a church and a court room, which is divided into "black town" and "white town." The down-stage pulpit (a witness stand in Act III) is placed at an angle, so the congregation (and later the courtroom) and the audience are addressed simultaneously. The play's title refers to the white man's blues, the expression "Mister Charlie" being a slang term for an oppressive white boss. In "Notes for Blues" Baldwin describes his purpose as exposing the mentality of the racist in order to liberate his children. Aware that "no man is a villain in his own eyes" (6), he was concerned with representing "a valid portrait of the murderer" (6). The murderer, Lyle Britten, is a type, but not a stereotype; he represents Baldwin's understanding of the complexity of American racism, the roots of which are economic, but the sustaining force of which is psychological and cultural. Lyle's "manhood" is based on his whiteness, which is fundamentally connected to his sense of honor, family, and tribe. The idea that "white identity" is based on a denial and subsequent projection onto blacks of tabooed fears and desires is revealed in Lyle's attraction to black women, whom he treats like whores, "poontang," and in his marriage to Jo, a white woman who has maintained her virginity until marriage. Lyle is a poor white man, who feels lucky to have found a respectable, "clean," white woman to marry him and bear his child. He is supported by a southern white community that is virulently racist and threatened by the challenge that the movement is making to their way of life. Jo says, "I'm scared—like I don't know what's going to happen next. How come the colored people hate us so much, all of a sudden? We *give* them everything they've got!" (70). That Lyle must murder Richard—who calls him a "no-good, ball-less peckerwood" (101), mocks his poverty, insults his wife, brags about his own sexual superiority, and knocks him down—is a foregone conclusion, as is Lyle's acquittal by the all-white jury. What is not a foregone conclusion is how Parnell, the white southern liberal who is friends with both Lyle and Meridian, will react. It is Parnell who is "Mister Charlie." As Meridian says in Act 1, "there's no hope if Mister Charlie can't change" (59). Parnell, regarded as a race traitor by other whites and a spineless "friend" by the blacks, fails to get a confession out of Lyle and doesn't counter Jo's lie on the witness stand. By the end of the play, however, Parnell breaks with Lyle and asks to join the black protest march, leaving open the possibility that "Mister Charlie" can still change.

Thus, the play is not just about the conflict between black and white as some reviews assumed, but about the divisions within each group. It continues the depiction of the generational divide within the movement that Baldwin began exploring in "They Can't Turn Back" and "The Dangerous Road Before Martin Luther King." Meridian Henry represents the old-style leadership, based on Christian morality, nonviolence, and allegiances with whites. His son, Richard, sees his father as "whipped." Meridian's failure to protect his son makes him reconsider his position and radicalizes him. Meridian's struggle, expressed in the long funeral monologue for his son, is also Baldwin's struggle: "Now, when the children come, my Lord, and ask which road to follow, my tongue stammers and my heart fails. . . . can I ask the children forever to sustain the cruelty inflicted on them by those who have been their masters?" (105). The play asks: How can the black man be a father, a leader, and a man? It effectively captures the movement at mid-decade, the increasing militancy of a black community no longer cowed by fear, the intransigence of the southern white racist, and the ambivalence of the white liberal, unsure of his allegiance.

A number of the play's critics were bothered by Baldwin's emphasis on the sexual aspects of racism, rather than on its economic or political dimensions, even charging that he was perpetuating the very stereotypes of the black male that he criticized. A flawed character like Richard Henry shows, however, the power of the myth of black sexuality and the extent to which it has corrupted black men as well as white men and defined the struggle between them. Furthermore, Baldwin believed that the solution to the "white problem" would entail not only legislation and economic programs, but a change in the individual conscience, which required challenging the way sexual taboos had kept racial inequalities in place. Baldwin's exploration of the sexual aspect of racism precedes his involvement in the civil rights movement and is arguably the central theme of all of his work, but his experience in the movement reinforced his idea that underlying white racism is the myth of a desirable and dangerous black sexuality. Baldwin saw this myth as having its roots in the economy of the slave system, in the violation of black women by white slave masters, whose motivation was not simply lust, but greed, since the offspring became the master's property. As Baldwin pointed out, "Blacks were not the only stallions on the slave-breeding farms!" (*No Name in the Street* 62). A guilty projection and fear of retaliation lead to the literal and figurative castration of the black man, who became viewed as a sexual threat to white women.

The sexual aspect of racism is an important topic of *No Name in the Street* (1972), where Baldwin reflects back on his early trips south covering the movement and reveals more of his personal experience than he had in earlier essays. One experience in particular convinced Baldwin that the sexual dynamics of the old slave system were still operating. Recalling his shock at being groped by a very powerful white man, one whose phone call could "prevent or provoke a lynching," Baldwin says, "We were both, abruptly, in history's ass-pocket. It was very frightening—not the gesture itself, but the abjectness of it, and the assumption of a swift and a grim complicity: as my identity was defined by his power, so was my humanity to be placed at the service of his fantasies" (61). The incident made Baldwin realize the sexual price blacks were still expected to pay for white protection. The riddle of southern history that had shaped the present must be understood in terms of the "disasters which had overtaken the private life" (55). Exposing these disasters, especially the hidden relationship between sexuality and public conduct, becomes an important part of Baldwin's representation of civil rights movement by the 1960s. As the conflict between Richard Henry and Lyle Britten shows, the challenge blacks presented to whites by stepping out of their "place" was not just economic and institutional, but libidinal.

Baldwin would again explore the sexual roots of virulent white racism in the short story, "Going to Meet the Man" (1965). The story offers an explanation for the violent white backlash to the movement in the South through the character of Jesse, a forty-two-year-old deputy sheriff. Jesse refers to the sheriff as "Big Jim C.," so the story was likely inspired by Baldwin's participation in SNCC's 1963 voting rights drive in Selma, where he was harassed by Sheriff Jim Clark's police (Leeming 228–29). (Baldwin also took part in the famous march from Selma to Montgomery in 1965.) The problem of Jesse's impotence, which opens the story, follows his unsuccessful attempt to subdue a "nigger" protester by beating him in jail. The protester, who won't stop singing songs of resistance, tells him, "you going to call our women by their right names yet" (202). Beating the "nigger" gives Jesse a feeling "close to a very peculiar, particular joy" (202) and stirs something in his memory that he can't articulate. Jesse, who believes he is "fighting to save the civilized world," is also aware that the segregationist cause is no longer viewed as honorable. "They were soldiers fighting a war, but their relationship to each other was that of accomplices in a crime. They all had to keep their mouths shut" (207). Jesse faces the imminent loss of community and identity. The formation of Jesse's white identity is revealed in a long flashback in which Jesse remembers his terror as a young child in being taken by his parents to a public lynching of a black man. Described in gruesome detail, the lynching is first seen through the eyes of an innocent child, who wonders what the man did to deserve his fate. Then the event takes on the quality of a ritual of initiation. The burned, still-living body is castrated, and Jesse experiences a sexual charge, bonding with his father and community. "At that moment Jesse loved his father more than he had ever loved him. He felt that his father had carried him through a mighty test, had revealed to him a great secret which would be the key to his life forever" (217). Jesse's memory of the lynching brings the story full circle; thinking of "the boy in the cell" and "the man in the fire," Jesse overcomes his impotence and makes love to his wife. It's important to recognize that "Going To Meet the Man" not only portrays blacks as sexual scapegoats in the development of white male identity, but strongly suggests that repressed homoerotic desire underlies the myth of black sexuality in the construction of a racist white identity.

Although a character like Jesse appears again briefly as Officer Bell, a white policeman, in Baldwin's later novel *If Beale Street Could Talk* (1974), Baldwin would turn his attention to representing primarily black characters and communities in his fiction after 1965. Baldwin recognized that the movement had brought the issue of sexuality in American race relations to the fore, not just in the construction of white identity, but in the construction of black identity as well. In *Tell Me How Long the Train's Been Gone*, for the first time, Baldwin would treat the subject of black homosexuality explicitly and, in doing so, implicitly challenge the homophobia of the emerging Black Power movement.[14] Much of this novel, written between 1965 and 1967, was composed in Istanbul, where Baldwin would retreat to escape the demands of his public life in the United States. While the difficulty Baldwin was having balancing his commitment to the black freedom struggle and finding the time and privacy he needed to write was not a new problem, it was an increasingly urgent one, and it becomes the subject of this novel. The novel also addresses the relationship between the artist and the revolutionary and holds out the possibility of a transformative political theater, thus looking back at Baldwin's goal for *Blues for Mister Charlie*.

The autobiographical main character, "double-minded" Leo Proudhammer, is a middle-aged actor, a bisexual, and a celebrity spokesperson for the movement. As an artist who lives an unconventional life, Leo knows that he is disapproved of by other "luminaries" within the movement, yet he continues to share a public platform with them because their differences are less important than their common responsibility (*Train* 83–85).[15] Most importantly, Leo does not want to "fail" the younger generation, who have become increasingly militant and regard Leo skeptically as "a fat cat" (366). Leo's heart attack at the beginning of the novel symbolizes a personal crisis, resulting from the larger racial crisis and the growing division within the civil rights movement. Forcing him off the public stage, the heart attack provides Leo the respite necessary for self-reflection. He discovers that he has hidden behind the mask of his public life, becoming a stranger to himself. His pride, once so necessary for survival, is also an "affliction." He is "imprisoned in the stronghold [he] had built" (32). Leo's memories structure the novel in a series of flashbacks. His divided racial and political loyalties are symbolized by his sexual partners—Barbara, a southern white woman who has been a friend and sometimes lover since his youth, and Black Christopher, a young black militant with whom Leo has recently fallen in love. This love triangle with its incestuous overtones (Christopher is figured as the "child" of Leo and Barbara, who are described as the "incestuous brother and sister" [336]) symbolizes the long-denied interracial American family and Baldwin's revised oedipal story of the hidden connections between race and sex in American myth. *Tell Me How Long the Train's Been Gone* has been Baldwin's most underrated novel. The initial reviews tagged it as angry Black Power propaganda of little artistic merit. In fact, the novel offers a complex view of racial and sexual politics of the later 1960s. It challenges the liberal idea that the success of a black individual is evidence of racial progress, and it challenges the radical idea of the black revolutionary as an always heterosexual male buoyed up by "pride." Christopher wants to take up arms, but Leo want him to live. The open-ended novel offers no solutions, ending as it started with Leo "standing in the wings . . . waiting for [his] cue" (370).

    Two months after *Tell Me How Long the Train's Been Gone* was released, Martin Luther King Jr. was assassinated. King's death changed Baldwin's dialogue with white America. In a long conversation with Margaret Mead, published as *A Rap on Race* (1971), Baldwin would tell Margaret Mead that he had given up on the dream that the movement would "bring about some kind of revolution in the American conscience, which is after all, where everything in some sense has to begin" (10). In *No Name in the Street*, he describes his early role in the movement as "the Great Black Hope of the Great White Father," ruefully suggesting his naivete (95). By the 1970s, he would refer to the civil rights movement as "the latest slave rebellion" to suggest the continuity of the struggle of blacks for freedom throughout American history. Even more than the "success" story, the "freedom" story is essential to the American mythos, and we learn at an early age to view our national history within the narrative of an ever-expanding arc of freedom. Baldwin's refusal to tell the story of the movement or his own story in accord with that narrative resulted in his marginalization from public discourse after the

1960s. Edward Said paid a moving tribute to Baldwin in his 1994 book, *Representations of the Intellectual*. He describes Baldwin as "being relegated to the role of a witness who testifies to a horror otherwise unrecorded" (xvii). Baldwin emphasized the price paid by those who risked their lives to bring about change, the worsening conditions of black life in American ghettos, the government repression of activists, and the continuation of white "innocence." Always a "disturber of the peace," Baldwin continued to look for ways to speak truth to power and be heard.

NOTES

1. See, for example, Baldwin's 1984 interview with Julius Lester, "James Baldwin: Reflections of a Maverick," reprinted in Standley and Pratt's *Conversations with James Baldwin:* "I have never seen myself as a spokesman. I am a witness.... A spokesman assumes that he is speaking for others. I never assumed...that I could" (226).

2. See for example Rebecca Aanerud's article "Now More Than Ever: James Baldwin and the Critique of White Liberalism."

3. In *Just Above My Head*, Baldwin's last novel, which focuses on the experience of a black gospel singer, Arthur Montana, the South is a black cultural homeland (the key to Arthur's musical development), a homoerotic space (where Arthur and Jimmy consummate their love), and a still dangerously racist environment (where their friend Peanut is presumably murdered during the civil rights movement).

4. All references to Baldwin's shorter essays are from the collection *The Price of the Ticket*, unless otherwise indicated.

5. Criminologist Bernard Headley confirms this portrait of Atlanta in his book *The Atlanta Youth Murders and the Politics of Race*. He says that while the rise of black rule in Atlanta had raised the expectations of the city's black poor, "the type of power arrangement into which an educated black elite had entered did not allow for a reordering of existing priorities.... The priorities over which a black political class was to preside revolved around making Atlanta a safe, attractive place for capital, where a small business elite could continue to accumulate super profits while dominating the producing classes, black and white" (15).

6. Baldwin's writing in *Freedomways* includes: "What Price Freedom," 4.2 (Spring 1964): 191–95, a speech given at the Conference on Food and Freedom" in November 1963 in Washington, D.C.; "Anti-Semitism and Black Power," 7.1 (Winter 1977): 75–77, an explanation of "Black Power" and a sharp criticism of anti-Semitic articles published in *The Liberator*, a black journal of which Baldwin had been on the advisory board; "The War Crimes Tribunal," 7.3 (Summer 1967): 242–44, Baldwin's explanation of his membership on Lord Bertrand Russell's tribunal investigating U.S. government's acts of aggression in Vietnam; and "A Letter to Americans," 8.2 (Spring 1968): 112–16, which both *The London Times* and the *New York Times* had refused to print. Baldwin had read the letter to a capacity crowd at Carnegie Hall on the occasion of the DuBois Centennial Celebration, where he made his last appearance with King. The letter is a defense of Stokley Carmichael, whose passport was revoked after being accused of inciting a riot and it indicts the government's efforts to silence dissent.

7. One of the central arguments of my book, *James Baldwin's Later Fiction: Witness to the Journey*. See especially the reception of *Tell Me How Long The Train's Been Gone*, described on pages 21–24.

8. The text of the broadcast was reprinted as "The Negro in American Culture," in *Cross Currents* (Summer 1961). In addition to Baldwin, Hansberry, and Hughes, Alfred Kazin and Emile Capouya also participated in the discussion. Hansberry says she "can't imagine a contemporary writer any place in the world today who isn't in conflict with his world" (206). It simply comes with the territory. Hughes embraces the term propaganda writer: "I am, of course, as everyone knows, primarily a-I guess you might even say a propaganda writer; my main material is the race problem-and I have found it most exciting and interesting and intriguing to deal with it in writing, and I haven't found the problem of being a Negro in any sense a hindrance to putting words on paper. It may be a hindrance sometimes to selling them..." (207).

9. A recording of this debate of April 25, 1961, is available from Pacifica Archives (http://www.pacificaradioarchives.org/). Baldwin refers to a couple of public debates with Malcolm X in *No Name in the Street* (94–96). Two days before this debate, on April 23, Baldwin was part of a radio discussion moderated by Eric Goldman that included Malcolm X, the black conservative journalist George

S. Schuyler, and historian and author of *The Black Muslims in America* C. Eric Lincoln. It was this debate that most likely led to the invitation from Hon. Elijah Muhammad that resulted in the dinner at Muslim headquarters in Chicago, which Baldwin wrote about in *The Fire Next Time.*

10. Baldwin first criticizes the American "tough guy" ideal of masculinity in "Preservation of Innocence" (1949), published the same year as "Everybody's Protest Novel." The essay argues that the American ideal of masculinity has demeaned homosexuals and women and is at the heart of American immaturity, or "innocence."

11. In addition to the Baldwin biographies, I consulted Carol Polsgrove, Taylor Branch, Arthur Schlesinger, Kenneth B. Clark, and Jean Stein.

12. Robert Kennedy reached an agreement with Senator James Eastland from Mississippi not to use federal troops to enforce the Supreme Court's decision against segregation in interstate travel—if the Freedom Riders were protected from mob violence. As a result, when they arrived in Jackson, the Freedom Riders were immediately arrested and taken to Parchment Penitentiary.

13. The best source on Baldwin's FBI file is James Campbell's article "I Heard It Through the Grapevine."

14. Just how effective Baldwin was at countering the homophobia of 1960s' black nationalism or to what extent he was compromised on questions of sexuality by his alliance with the Black Panthers is a question of debate. In "Looking for Jimmy Baldwin: Sex, Privacy, and Black Nationalist Fervor," Douglas Field argues "that Baldwin's move away from the subject of homosexuality came directly out of the criticism that he received by African American writers such as Eldridge Cleaver; this in turn led to Baldwin's increasing anxiety over his role as both an artist and a spokesman" (466).

15. Polsgrove states that several mainstream civil rights leaders, including Whitney Young of the National Urban League, Roy Wilkins of the NAACP, and even Martin Luther King, were not eager to appear in public with him (182–83). Baldwin, who had organized support among the expatriate community in Paris for the march on Washington in 1963, returned to the United States to take part in it. He was not asked to speak. His friend June Shagaloff of the NAACP, who attended with him, did not think being on the program had

occurred to Baldwin (Polsgrove 189). But David Leeming says that "he was disappointed that he had not been asked to participate in any meaningful way" (228). Baldwin certainly knew that his reputation as a homosexual made many mainstream civil rights leaders uncomfortable with his role. However, organizers of the march were probably at least as concerned with what might have been the political content of Baldwin's speech. SNCC leader, John L. Lewis, was persuaded to alter his speech which initially had been critical of the federal government. The speech he was not allowed to give called the "administration's civil rights bill . . . too little, and too late. There's not one thing in the bill that will protect our people from police brutality" (Lewis 27).

WORKS CITED

Aanerud, Rebecca. "Now More Than Ever: James Baldwin and the Critique of White Liberalism." In *James Baldwin Now*, edited by Dwight A. McBride. New York: New York University Press, 1999. 56–74.

Anderson, Terry H. *The Movement and the Sixties: Protest in America from Greensboro to Wounded Knee.* New York: Oxford University Press, 1995.

Baldwin, James and Malcolm X. "Black Muslims vs. the Sit-Ins." Radio broadcast on WBAI New York (April 25, 1961). Pacifica Radio Archive, archive no. BB5322. Los Angeles.

———. *Blues for Mister Charlie.* New York: 1964. New York: Dell, 1969.

———. "Disturber of the Peace: James Baldwin." *Mademoiselle* (May 1963): 174–75, 199–207.

———. "The Evidence of Things Not Seen." *Playboy* (December 1981): 141–42, 308–16.

———. *The Evidence of Things Not Seen.* New York: Holt, Rinehart & Winston, 1985.

———. *The Fire Next Time.* 1963. New York: Random House, Vintage International edition, 1993.

———. *Going to Meet the Man.* 1965. New York: Laurel-Dell, 1976.

———. *If Beale Street Could Talk.* New York: Dial Press, 1974.

———. *Just Above My Head.* 1979. New York: Laurel-Dell, 1990.

———. *No Name in the Street.* 1972. New York: Delta-Dell, 1973.

————. *One Day When I Was Lost: A Scenario Based on Alex Haley's* The Autobiography of Malcolm X. New York: Dell, 1972.

————. "The Preservation of Innocence. *Zero* 1 (Spring 1949): 14–22.

————. *The Price of the Ticket: Collected Nonfiction, 1948–1985.* New York: St. Martin's/Marek, 1985.

————. Margaret Mead. *A Rap on Race.* Philadelphia: J. B. Lippincott, 1971.

————. *Tell Me How Long the Train's Been Gone.* 1968. New York: Dell, 1969.

————, et al. "The Negro in American Culture" *Cross Currents* 11.3 (1961): 205–24.

Boyd, Herb. *Baldwin's Harlem: A Biography of James Baldwin.* New York: Atria Books, 2008.

Branch, Taylor. *Parting the Waters: America in the King Years, 1954–63.* New York: Simon & Schuster, 1988.

————. *Pillar of Fire: America in the King Years, 1963–65.* New York: Simon & Schuster, 1998.

Brustein, Robert. "Everybody's Protest Play" (review of *Blues for Mister Charlie). The New Republic* (May 16, 1964): 35–37.

Campbell, James. "I Heard It Through the Grapevine." *Granta* 73 (Spring 2001). 151–81. Reprinted in *Syncopations: Beats, New Yorkers, and Writers in the Dark,* by James Campbell. Berkeley: University of California Press, 2008. 73–102.

————. *Talking at the Gates: A Life of James Baldwin.* New York: Viking Penguin, 1991.

Clark, Kenneth B. *King, Malcolm, Baldwin: Three Interviews: With New Introduction.* Middletown, Conn.: Wesleyan University Press, 1985.

Driver, Tom. "Blues for Mister Charlie: The Review That Was Too True to Be Published." *Negro Digest* 13 (September 1964): 34–40.

Dupee, F. W. "James Baldwin and the 'Man'" *The New York Review of Books* 1.1 (February 1, 1963). http://www.nybooks.com/articles/13755

Field, Douglas. "Looking For Jimmy Baldwin: Sex, Privacy, and Black Nationalist Fervor." *Callaloo* 27.2 (2004): 457–80.

Headley, Bernard. *The Atlanta Youth Murders and the Politics of Race.* Carbondale: Southern Illinois University Press, 1998.

King, Martin Luther, Jr. "Letter from a Birmingham Jail" (April 16, 1963). © Estate of Martin Luther King Jr. http://www.stanford. edu/group/King/frequentdocs/birmingham.pdf

Leeming, David. *James Baldwin: A Biography.* New York: Alfred A. Knopf, 1994.

Lewis, John. "Wake Up America." *Takin'It To the Streets: A Sixties Reader.* Eds. Alexander Bloom and Wini Breines. 2nd edition. New York: Oxford University Press, 2003. 27–29.

Polsgrove, Carol. *Divided Minds: Intellectuals and the Civil Rights Movement.* New York: W. W. Norton, 2001.

"Races: Freedom-Now." *Time.* 17 May 1963: 23–27.

Rampersad, Arnold. *The Life of Langston Hughes.* Vol. 2, *1941–1967: I Dream a World.* New York: Oxford University Press, 1988.

Ross, Marlon B. "White Fantasies of Desire: Baldwin and the Racial Identities of Sexuality." In *James Baldwin Now,* edited by Dwight A. McBride. New York: New York University Press, 1999. 13–55.

Said, Edward. *Representations of the Intellectual.* New York: Vintage Books, 1994.

Schlesinger, Arthur M., Jr. *A Thousand Days: John F. Kennedy in the White House.* Boston: Houghton Mifflin, 1965.

Scott, Lynn Orilla. *James Baldwin's Later Fiction: Witness to the Journey.* East Lansing: Michigan State University Press, 2002.

Standley, Fred L., and Louis H. Pratt, eds. *Conversations with James Baldwin.* Jackson. University of Mississippi Press, 1989.

Stein, Jean, and George Plimpton. *American Journey: The Times of Robert Kennedy.* New York: Harcourt Brace Jovanovich, 1970.

"In the Same Boat"

James Baldwin and the Other Atlantic

Magdalena J. Zaborowska

> What time will bring Americans is at last their own identity. It is on this dangerous voyage and in the same boat that the American Negro will make peace with himself and the voiceless many thousands gone before him.
>
> —James Baldwin, "Encounter on the Seine: Black Meets Brown" (1950)

James Baldwin's essay "Encounter on the Seine: Black Meets Brown" (1950) frames the uneasy face-off between "American Negroes" and Africans in post–World War II Western Europe against the background of a transatlantic geopolitical context and this writer's lifelong exploration of Americanness. From Harlem and lower-class black families who migrated South-to-North in his first novel, *Go Tell It on the Mountain* (1953), through explorations of belonging and freedom within and without the nation in the essay collections *Notes of a Native Son* (1955), *Nobody Knows My Name* (1961), and the *Fire Next Time* (1963), to probing intersections of gender, race, and sexuality in his transnational novels, *Giovanni's Room* (1956), *Another Country* (1962), and *Just Above My Head* (1979), Baldwin wrote about Americans of all hues caught up in search for identity. This chapter's epigraph, from "Encounter on the Seine," bespeaks the racialized dimension of this quest, while also casting whites and blacks as fellow travelers on the same "dangerous voyage," literally in the "same boat."

Sketched broadly against the historical and cultural backdrop of the Cold War and the breakup of colonial empires in "Encounter on the Seine," Baldwin's "dangerous voyage" reappears at the center of a short story resounding with autobiographical themes that he wrote a decade later, "This Morning, This Evening, So Soon" (1959–60). Published at the end of his first stint abroad, in France, where he lived from 1948 to 1957, this story illustrates poignantly Baldwin's significant, if seldom noted by critics, preoccupation with themes of migration and elements of immigrant narrative.[1] A pivotal moment in this text invites a reexamination of this writer's frequent use of the motifs of departure, passage, arrival, acculturation, and the ways in which he shows them embroiled with representations and articulations of racialized identities.

On approaching New York Harbor on one of his return trips, the nameless protagonist of "This Morning, This Evening, So Soon"—an African American singer and actor who has made his career in France—observes his fellow passengers undergoing a replay of a clichéd immigrant landing. While the enjoyment of the whites around him is apparent, he experiences an acute sense of alienation, displacement, and longing that makes him question his sanity:

I watched . . . [New York] come closer and I listened to the people around me, to their excitement and their pleasure. There was no doubt that it was real. I watched their shining faces and wondered if I were mad. For a moment I longed, with all my heart, to be able to feel whatever they were feeling, if only to know what such a feeling was like. As the boat moved slowly into the harbor, they were being moved into safety. It was only I who was being floated into danger. I turned my head, looking for Europe, but all that stretched behind me was the sky, thick with gulls. . . . A big, sandy-haired man

held his daughter on his shoulders, showing her the Statue of
Liberty. ("This Morning" 162)

Encapsulated in this brief, allegorical moment when the boat
approaches land, there are two larger, divergent narratives about
transatlantic crossings and arrivals. First, we witness the black
narrator's realization that the terrors of his African ancestors'
Middle Passage and their brutal fate as slaves in the New World
are indelibly imprinted on his identity and forever marginalize
him vis-à-vis his compatriots. Second, he relates the whites' fes-
tive arrival in "America," complete with the clichéd view of the
Statue of Liberty.

In the "mad" narrator's eyes, their joyous homecoming attests
to their immigrant ancestors' naturalization and subsequent
upward social mobility in the "land of the free." The white arrivals are "being moved into safety," whereas the black narrator is
"being floated into danger." They move so on parallel journeys,
as it were, while a the same time being separated from each other
by W. E. B. Du Bois's "color line"—that key "problem" of the
twentieth century. Arising from worldwide racism that affects
all spheres of social life, this problem shapes how people think
of themselves and how they see others. But rather than merely
delineating the well-known historical, spatial, and narrative differences between the epidermally charged stories of black and
white national origins, Baldwin's story insists on something that
is less widely acknowledged, namely that the two narratives are
inextricably intertwined—a fact that is recognized only by his
complexly located and racially marked narrator.

Like the voyage "in the same boat" in "Encounter on the
Seine," Baldwin's transatlantic journey in "This Morning, This
Evening, So Soon" can be read as a theorization of a multidimensional model of narrative and spatially contingent national
identity that was radical for its time and is important to reassessing our complex cultural and political moment in American literary studies today. The unnamed protagonist-narrator of "This
Morning, This Evening, So Soon" is perhaps the most *American* of
all the passengers on the boat because his insider-outsider-native-
other viewpoint reflects most fully the geographic and national

hybridity of the country that has persistently denied him the status of a fully fledged citizen: American, African, and European.[2] His deliberately dislocated account allows several stories to enter into dialogue, however contentious, and enables a layered reading of Baldwin's text from our millennial-juncture vantage point.

Between the turbulent mid–twentieth century, when Baldwin wrote, and our present moment in the twenty-fist, when we have witnessed the election of the first African American and immigrant U.S. President in Barack Obama, we have learned to link the literal and the literary, to read the history of race relations in dialogue with its literary representations and other cultural productions. We have no trouble seeing connections between the historical accounts of Africans carried on slave ships across the Black Atlantic, the regional artifacts and narratives created by the survivors and descendants of the Middle Passage, the brutalization of Rodney King in 1991, and the recent racist events in Jenna, Louisiana. These "black" stories of suffering intertwine in troubling ways with "white" artifacts, historical accounts, and literary representations of the Europeans who came to the New World on immigrant ships, and whose ascendancy in the racialized national hierarchy of identities we can link as much to the actions of the policemen who brutalized King as to the motivations of students from Jenna and other campuses who hung nooses on trees to manifest their views on race in 2007.

My purpose in this chapter about strange literary boat-fellows in Baldwin's works is threefold. First, I show how this writer employs motifs of (white European) immigrant narrative to tell stories of black and white characters burdened by legacies of transatlantic slavery and thrown together "in the same boat" in the tragic processes of racist nation-building. Second, I demonstrate how we can read Baldwin's deployments of literary and literal "color lines," or the metaphorical and material social spaces that have been designed to segregate peoples and stories according to their skin color, as constructing alternative dialogic connections between literary traditions, such as African diasporic and European immigrant, the traditions that until very recently have been construed as having little to say to each other. Last, I contend that Baldwin's works not only reveal the workings of

the black-on-white dichotomy at the heart of the grand narrative
of American national identity, but that they also offer a dynamic,
migratory, and heterotopic model of a richly hued and multidimensional American identity.

Apart from drawing attention to Baldwin's daring employ-
ment of immigrant narrative, my larger goal in these pages is
to show that his works are indispensable to remapping how we
"do" American literatures in the twenty-first century, at a time
when we have become invested more than ever in reevaluating
these literatures' transnational contexts. Aware of the continued tension between consent and descent, or what in the 1980s
Werner Sollors termed "achieved rather than ascribed [American]
identity" (Beyond Ethnicity 36), we can do well to look back at
Baldwin's works from the 1950s and realize that they performed
then what the critic Lisa Lowe described more recently as the
"interventions into dominant forms, whether these forms are
the institution of citizenship, that traditional novel, the national
historical narrative, or the transnational assembly line" (175). At
the time when texts by foreign-born Americans were not considered literature and immigration studies was only emerging as an
academic field, Baldwin's works probed cross-racial immigrant
passages as embroiled with the issues of national belonging, narrative production, and social constructions and performances of
racialized identities.

The first part of what follows introduces the key concepts of
this chapter, immigration and heterotopia, against the background of Baldwin's auto-thematic musings on the place of a
mid–twentieth-century black writer in American literature.
The second part focuses on European immigrant narrative elements in Baldwin's essays "The Price of the Ticket," "Notes
on the House of Bondage," and "Many Thousands Gone,"
and reads their ideas in conversation with a late nineteenth-
century visual example, in which allegorical representations
of the Middle Passage and the Europe–to–"America"–via–Ellis
Island crossing meet in the same frame of newly racialized
and gendered national vision. By glimpsing the ways in which
"color lines" were drawn across the national imagination in the

century preceding Baldwin's, this second part ushers in the last section, which stages a cross-disciplinary dialogue between Baldwin and the immigration historian Oscar Handlin. The conclusion touches upon C. L. R. James's "undesirable alien" heterotopia in Cold War United States sketched in *Mariners, Renegades, and Castaways* (1953), the work that is in conversation with Baldwin's visions of American national literature as a perpetually adrift, shape-shifting ship of conflicting selves.

Black Heterotopias

James Baldwin's first trip across the Atlantic took place on Armistice Day in 1948, when he sailed from New York Harbor to Paris. This journey, like the one that led him to Turkey in 1961,[3] where he spent time on and off for a decade, had lasting impact on his works and marked his understanding of his position as an American writer. John Winthrop, Olaudah Equiano, Herman Melville, Anzia Yezierska, C. L. R. James, Robert Hayden, and Toni Morrison—to mention a few of Baldwin's fellow literary transatlantic travelers—all show us that boats, ships, and attendant metaphors of mobility, departure, journey, passage, and arrival have featured prominently in narratives depicting various formations of national identity. From within the late twentieth-century Old World, the philosopher Michel Foucault emphasizes the symbolic importance of the transatlantic vessel to Western civilizations, for which a ship or boat has been "[a] floating piece of space, a place without a place, that exists by itself, that is closed in on itself and at the same time is given over to the infinity of the sea and that, from port to port, from tack to tack, from brothel to brothel, it goes as far as the colonies in search of the most precious treasures they conceal" (Foucault 27).

Foucault's metaphorical boat is an example of *heterotopia*, a concept that designates places that exist as "counter-sites" in every society—that is, as "effectively enacted utopia[s] in which . . . all the other real sites that can be found within the culture, are simultaneously represented, contested, and inverted" (24). Examples of heterotopic places in Western cultures include cemeteries, museums, and libraries, but a ship is a "heterotopia par excellence." Foucault links the material and the metaphorical properties of the ship, arguing that, given its ability to move through time and space and carry a self-contained society that can be seen as reflecting a whole culture (as in Herman Melville's novel *Moby Dick*), it has been the "great instrument of economic development," but also the "greatest reserve of the imagination" (25–27). This temporal-spatial theoretical model can be fruitfully applied to the moment of landing described in Baldwin's "This Morning, This Evening, So Soon." A black heterotopia of sorts that it becomes in Baldwin's short story, it helps to elucidate his emphasis on spatial and kinesthetic qualities of narratives about forced or voluntary migrations that shape the genre and plot of his text.[4]

But Baldwin, whose story appeared over thirty years before Foucault's "Of Other Spaces and Others" (1986), does not merely anticipate the Western discourses on social space and racialized identity. Rather, his contribution makes both the theories and our ability to apply them to diverse "precious treasures [that American literature] conceals" in centuries past and present possible and compelling. The moment of landing in Baldwin's "This Morning, This Evening, So Soon" can be thus read as an occasion for a rereading of Foucault's concept of heterotopia through the black American writer's earlier, more provocative vision of racialized national identity. In this story, Baldwin offers an immigrant and black intervention into, and a fascinating dialogue with, classic literary examples of heterotopic narratives of white Americanness by such canonical writers as Melville, Twain, Poe, and Hemingway. Yet while his educated, successful African American, cosmopolitan protagonist serves as a vehicle that helps Baldwin to acknowledge the domestic literary and Western cultural legacies that he shares with these "best books" writers, Baldwin ultimately questions these legacies by revealing the myth of exclusionary American national origins at their core.[5]

In all his works, Baldwin's complex notions of African Americanness and U.S. national identity are contingent on the interplays of race, location, and mobility and reflect and refract multinational and multigenre landscapes of mid- and late-twentieth-century American literature. Echoing Baldwin's views on the task of the writer, his fellow traveler from Trinidad C. L. R. James argues for the "inseparability of great literature and of social life" in *Mariners, Renegades, and Castaways* (1953), a book on Herman Melville's *Moby Dick*, composed while he was imprisoned on Ellis Island as an "undesirable alien."[6] Completed soon after the publication of Baldwin's essays on his experience in France, "Encounter on the Seine," "Stranger in the Village," and "Many Thousands Gone," James's text engages many similar ideas on literature, history, and discourses of displacement, passage, and location that preoccupied African diaspora intellectuals at the time. Halfway through, James asks about Melville's novel: "How could a book from the world in 1850 contain so much of the world in 1950s?" (69). Let us pose a similar question about Baldwin's literary legacy today. More specifically for my purposes: How does Baldwin help us to approach and construe as more heterotopic the sites that have been critically inseparable from social life—the creative and disciplinary sites known as American and African American literary histories?

Reading Baldwin as not just a writer but also as a literary critic attempting to answer this question makes one painfully aware that mixing narratives of dispersal, not to mention identities of the authors and identity politics of their subjects, is risky business. But then so is studying literature in its complex historic and cultural contexts, as Paul Gilroy emphasizes in "It ain't where you're from, it's where you're at" (1991) and David Roediger echoes in his introduction to *Black on White* (1998). Cornel West reminds us that "black people forged ways of life and ways of struggle under circumstances not of their own choosing." Echoing Baldwin's earlier statements, he also acknowledges that the "specificity of black culture...lies in both the *African* and *American* character of black people's attempts to sustain their mental sanity and spiritual health, social life and political struggle" (79). Our "wider [literary] landscape," claims Toni Morrison, can nevertheless open up "space for discovery...without the mandate for conquest" (3). Tracing the shadowy presence of the Africanist persona in canonical texts, Morrison calls for an interrogation of not just national literary history, but also the very terms of the debate in which these texts feature as primary sources.

In a similar vein, my key terms—*immigration* and *heterotopia*— invoke both the problematic and multidirectional, as well as material and metaphorical, quality of individual and group movements, *and* the reductive ways in which we have come to view and define these movements and their literary representations. For example, when Anzia Yezierska proclaims in an interview that "you can't be an immigrant twice" (Yezierska, *Children of Loneliness* 261), it may seem curious to some readers that Yezierska, an early-twentieth-century, lower-class, East European, Jewish, woman writer, would persistently employ the one-way, Old World-to-New clichéd model of transatlantic crossing. While all her stories reveal the darker side of immigrant life in the Promised Land—hunger, poverty, sexism, xenophobia, and exploitation—they nevertheless embrace the American Dream by means of their, often unexpected and unrealistic, happy endings. A more nuanced reading reveals, however, that the portrayals of Yezierka's plucky heroines, as much as her narrative choices, could have been shaped by the powerful forces of the publishing market and the need to protest the omnipresent racialization and gendering of East European ethnics like her. Caught up in that double bind, not to mention wanting for money and food as an aspiring writer from the ghetto, she may have simplified complex stories and trajectories, including her own, but felt justified in doing so to make her mark as an immigrant author and a Jewish woman.

Richard Wright in the 1940s and Gwendolyn Brooks, Ann Petry, James Baldwin, and other black writers in the 1950s, 1960s, and 1970s would face oddly similar dilemmas of meeting or rejecting racialized expectations of publishers, reviewers, and readers. By that time, light-skinned European immigrants who came through Ellis Island, and their upwardly mobile descendants, were rapidly becoming white. The terms of the discourse on national identity and its echoes in literature reflected the starkness of the black/white dichotomy and its essentialist tenets. In the essay that never fails to rile up scholarly controversy, "Everybody's Protest Novel" (1949), Baldwin reflects on this phenomenon as a reader of American literature and as a writer, while looking back at Harriet Beecher Stowe's *Uncle Tom's Cabin* (1851) as a literary historic textbook on race relations. In a statement that echoes interestingly the nineteenth-century European realists, such as Stendhal or Flaubert, he cautions his readers that novels reflect their authors' identities and make lucid the social relationships of power: "the oppressor and the oppressed are bound together within the same society; they accept the same criteria, they share the same beliefs, they both alike depend on the same reality" (32).

In the same essay, rather than merely criticizing Wright's famous *Native Son* (1940) for accepting some of the racial essentialism of Beecher Stowe's novel, Baldwin cautions against viewing American literature according to identity "categorization alone" (33). He clarifies this approach in his literary manifesto, the essay published in 1962 in the *New York Times*, "As Much Truth as One Can Bear," in which he positions himself as a black writer within American literary history. He reminds his readers that they live in a "country in which words are mostly used to cover the sleeper, not to wake him up" (11), and speaking thus implicitly against U.S. isolationism and explicitly against segregated literary criticism, he calls for acknowledging the international and racialized roots of American literary production. The crossbreeding of languages, identities, and ideologies that comprises this production makes literary canons obsolete because, by the mid–twentieth century, at the height of the Cold War, "the [Atlantic] ocean...had shrunk to the size of a swimming pool" ("As Much Truth as One Can Bear" 38).

Coming from a child of displaced southerners, this pronouncement has international and *intra*national, regional connotations, and in uncanny ways anticipates our own transnational moment. For American blacks, the passage to the "Promised Land," another loaded immigrant term, has been often deployed to describe their migration from the South to the North. In the 1959 essay, "Nobody Knows My Name: A Letter from the South," Baldwin claims that "Negroes in the North are right when they refer to the South as the Old Country" and compares his first trip to the American South to that of an "Italian emigrant who finds himself in Italy, near the village where his father first saw the light of day" (184). The migration of Baldwin's ancestors must therefore be seen as one among the many population movements that have shaped U.S. history and culture and, at the same time, be contextualized as part of the global migrations that have shaped the transatlantic world. Amy Kaplan's recognition of "immigration as a multidirectional movement" in the 2003 American Studies Association Presidential Address is an indication that we are moving in that direction (12). Baldwin's much earlier writings on this theme help us to acknowledge the heterotopic, if complexly contested, authorship of this idea in the works of diverse and multiply located writers, whom until recently we have been reluctant to see as traveling in the same boat of national literature. As he contends in "As Much Truth as One Can Bear": "Writers are extremely important people in a country, whether or not the country knows it" (38).

Passing: From the Boat to the House of Bondage

In the essay "Notes for a Hypothetical Novel" (1960), Baldwin articulates racialized identities as key to understanding various cultural scripts of Americanness and foreshadows some of his literary and critical impact on his artistic followers: "The country's image of the Negro...has never failed to reflect...the state of the mind of the country" (238). His articulation of the African American "shadow...athwart our national life" in another essay "Many Thousands Gone" (1951) precedes by some four decades Toni Morrison's acclaimed discussion of the "Africanist persona" and the tropes of immigration and slavery in national letters in *Playing in the Dark: Whiteness and the Literary Imagination* (1992). Unlike Morrison, Baldwin stresses that the "shadow" proliferates in all American minds, no matter the hue of the epidermis of their owners: "The Negro in America...is far more than that. He is a series of shadows, self-created, intertwining, which now we helplessly battle. One may say that the *Negro in America does not really exist* except in the darkness of *our* minds" ("Many Thousands Gone" 66).

Baldwin's work has been in the avant-garde of mining this darkness and has inspired numerous writers, artists, and critics—Cornel West, Henry Louis Gates, Jr., Quincy Troupe, Maya Angelou, Audre Lorde, Isaac Julien, William Styron, Norman Mailer, Calvin Levels, Randall Kenan, Melvin Dixon, Susan Lori Parks, John Edgar Wideman, and many others. While it is widely known that his attainments owe something to his admiration for and well-publicized disagreements with Richard Wright and Langston Hughes, as well as his readings of Henry James, Charles Dickens, and Fyodor Dostoyevsky, he evolved a category of artistic achievement that must be recognized as his own. His place in American literature has been confirmed with the recent publication of two volumes of his writings, collected essays and early novels, by the the Library of America.

But while Baldwin's prominence in American letters has been quietly affirmed, the importance of Baldwin's works for charting discussions on immigration in the context of national (and nationalist) literature's embroilment with race has not been studied at all. I cannot provide an exhaustive review of the new exciting literature on this topic, but would like to highlight Lisa Lowe's *Immigrant Acts* (1996), which stresses that, in the production of nationalist discourse, "immigration has been historically a *locus* of racialization and a primary site for the policing of political, cultural, and economic membership in the U.S. nation-state" (174). Whereas Lowe's work emphasizes narrative aspects of racialized immigration and provides an interesting context for rereading what Baldwin has to say on the subject, Mae M. Ngai's more recent *Impossible Subjects: Illegal Aliens and the Making of Modern America* (2004) highlights the historic and legal importance of the "iconic immigrant [who] serves exceptionalist political culture" (5) and whose presence has spurred various state industries "produc[ing] new categories of racial difference" (7). Decades before these works, Baldwin's writings explore the various iconographies resulting from, and material historic consequences of, state-made and state-mandated racial difference.

An aspiring young writer driven away from his homeland by racism and homophobia, James Baldwin chose to live most of his literary career abroad. Although his first journey to Europe in 1948 seems a simple enough, albeit ironic, inversion of the Europe-to-America immigrant crossing, he sees it as a much more complex rite of passage. In the well-known and much-quoted essay, "The Discovery of What It Means to Be an American" (1959), he explains his move from the New to the Old World as one that, by making him into a writer, also made him embrace and wrestle with the mixed blessings of his Americanness. Once in Europe, he in fact had to recognize what he thought he had fled from, the ties of national and cultural identity between himself and white Americans: "It became terribly clear in Europe . . . that we knew more about each other than any European ever could . . . that, no matter where our fathers had been born, or what they endured, the fact that Europe had formed us both, was part of our identity and part of our inheritance" (172).

Yet this inheritance feels more like baggage—if not a ball and chain—than cultural capital. While working on his first novel, *Go Tell It on the Mountain*, immersed in the icy whiteness of a Swiss mountain village, where he traveled with his lover, the painter Lucien Happersberger, Baldwin is also "the stranger" amidst Western culture. His only link to his African American roots is a music record—Bessie Smith singing the blues against the backdrop of the towering Alps:

> I had never listened to Bessie Smith in America (in the same way, that, for years, I would not touch watermelon), but in Europe she helped to reconcile me to being a "nigger." I do not think that I could have made this reconciliation here. Once I was able to accept my role—as distinguished, I must say, from my "place"—in the extraordinary drama which is America, I was released from the illusion that I hated America. ("The Discovery of What It Means to Be an American" 172)

This release from hatred of his country means in fact a release from self-hatred as America's outcast dark child. Keenly aware of his African ancestry, Baldwin also acknowledges and reconciles to the idea of his hybridity as the Fanonian "bastard of the West" ("Autobiographical Notes" 6).

Baldwin's reappropriation and deconstruction of his role as a "nigger"—the ironic and brutal legacy of his mixed birthright encapsulated in a word—has to be negotiated through his art: "I want to be an honest man and a good writer," he states in "Autobiographical Notes," which open his first collection of essays, *Notes of a Native Son* (1961). He writes in the same essay: "I love America more than any other country in the world, and, exactly for this reason, I insist on the right to criticize her perpetually" (6). Baldwin's paradoxical patriotism—or a specific brand of "African Americanism" that falls right in between the exclusionary binary of "exceptionalism" and "transatlanticism/cosmopolitanism" (Stevens 9)—arises from a deep commitment to dissent and a prophetic desire to improve his country by critiquing the place wherein he was thrust by accidents of geography and genetics. Baldwin's "extraordinary drama which is America" thus gains a dimension of an immigrant passion play staged at the clash points of multiple transatlantic crossings by various populations that ended up stuck rather than liberated in the New World. He seems to echo Anzia Yezierska's working-class, Polish-Jewish immigrant heroine, who, disillusioned with the unattainable American Dream, asks rhetorically: "But from America where can you go?" ("How I Found America" 119).

As if recalling yet another rhetorical question, J. Hector St. John de Crèvecoeur's famous interrogation in the century of migrations—"What is an American, that new man?"—Baldwin sums up the main elements of the concluding part of white immigrant narrative in his late essay, "The Price of the Ticket" (1985): "They come through Ellis Island, where Giorgio becomes Joe, Pappavasiliu becomes Palmer, Evangelos becomes Evans, Goldsmith becomes Smith or Gold, and Avakian becomes King. So, with a painless change of name, and in the twinkling of an eye, one becomes a white American" (*PT* xix). This part of the immigrant story concerns arrival, renaming, and passing through the famous immigration station in New York Harbor that has become an architectural symbol for European newcomers and a vital icon in the mythology of national origins. Ellis Island—that palatial structure and island/ship/floating prelude to Manhattan—is the symbolic entry, a gateway of immigrant passage into American nationhood. It is also Emma Lazarus's "golden door," guarded by her "New Colossus," the Statue of Liberty, and the place where Old World national identities are shed, bodies inspected and evaluated, accepted or rejected, minds interrogated, new names given and old ones lost in translation. The glorious story of the nation's immigrant origins celebrated at the Ellis Island Museum of Immigration today and eulogized in documentaries and publications ends with the passage and throwing open of the "door to America." In the culture hooked on happy endings, the aftermath of the entry into the New World obscures the hardship of the process of getting there, reasons for flight from home, not to mention lives of the "other half" that never attained the American Dream. Traditional immigrant narratives mythologize the achievements of the few successes, like the industrial magnate Andrew Carnegie, who has entered the national pantheon of culture heroes, and corporate giant Lee Iacocca, who has aided the creation of the museum to celebrate his immigrant origins. Less known are the black-and-white, gritty images of undocumented aliens, pages of anti-immigrant legislation, corps of social workers and crowded schools for immigrant children, anti-Chinese posters, and volumes by governmental commissions itemizing the eugenic evils of foreign ethnic infusion.

In a radical move to look for that repressed, "other" passage underlying the immigrants' induction into American whiteness, Baldwin's "The Price of the Ticket" (1985) places the results of the European crossing in the context of the journey of no return that was forced on his African ancestors. He writes about the Irish newcomers: "Later, in the midnight hour, the missing identity aches. One can neither access nor overcome the storm of the middle passage. One is mysteriously shipwrecked forever, in the Great New World" (*Price of the Ticket* xix). To Baldwin, the African and European "middle passages" seem to interact, as the freshly minted Americans find themselves not enriched by a new identity, but rather stripped of the only one they had ever had upon arrival; they are "ship-wrecked" in the "Great New World." Baldwin dispels the utopia of immigrant progress by revealing the reality of grueling, and often tragic, stories of post-passage and by bringing what has been mythologized as a narrative of exclusionary national origins into confrontation with the tragic story of African enslavement, Middle Passage, and survival in diaspora. He thus performs a doubly ironic and "sacrilegious" move, given the reliance of both models—white immigrant and African diasporic—on the Judaic rhetoric of exodus, passage, and arrival in the Promised Land.

By intertwining these two narratives of passage and arrival, then, Baldwin obliterates their mutually exclusionary and competitive positioning vis-à-vis each other on the opposite ends of the national spectrum marked by epidermally based identity politics. At the same time as he never loses sight of the dramatically disparate consequences of the arrival and "Americanization" for whites and blacks, he shows that their loss of self and home can be shared across racial and class differences: "The Irish middle passage, for but one example, was as foul as my own, and as dishonorable on the part of those responsible for it. But the Irish became white when they got here and began rising in the world, whereas I became black and began sinking" (*PT* xx). Baldwin not only braids together the stories of the Irish and African crossings that "made the American people," to quote somewhat perversely from Oscar Handlin's immigrant classic, *The Uprooted*, but goes on to proclaim that there were comparable causes and costs of the journey for the European newcomers and the Africans as they encountered the New World. In the greater space of transatlantic negotiations of Americanness, the prices of the white and black "tickets" are part and parcel of the same painful transaction that brought European whites and African blacks to very different places in national and social hierarchy. In Baldwin's accounting on the economy of race within the constructions of national identity:

> The price that white American paid for his ticket was to become white—: and, in the main, nothing more than that, or, as he was to insist, nothing less. This incredibly limited not to say dimwitted ambition has choked many a human being to death here: and this, I contend, is because the white

American has never accepted the real reasons for his journey. I know very well that my ancestors had no desire to come to this place: but neither did the ancestors of the people who became white and who require of my captivity a song. They require of me a song less to celebrate my captivity than to justify their own. (*PT* xx)

Baldwin is opening up an uneasy space for dialogue between the two narratives of racialized passage by asserting that the Irish immigrants did not desire America any more than Africans in bondage did, that the Irish suffered a loss of name much like the slaves—again, in a somewhat structurally similar process of passage between worlds but with dramatically different consequences upon arrival and subsequent racialization. Although not free from awkwardness and risk, this radical maneuver enables him to chip at the "myth of America to which we [all] cling so desperately" ("The Discovery of What It Means to Be an American" 173). The necessity for the black story/song to "justify [the white captivity]" arises from the fact that the national myth covers up the political reality of what Baldwin in a later essay terms the "house of bondage." This edifice, he wrote in 1980, "accomplished for what we will call the classic white American...the destruction of his moral sense, except in relation to whites...it also destroyed his sense of reality and, therefore, his sense of white people had to be as compulsively one-dimensional as his vision of blacks. The result is that white Americans have been one another's jailers for generations" ("Notes on the House of Bondage" 672–73).

Baldwin's ideas on the Irish immigrant–African slave-descendant dialogue, as well as on the American racialized "house of bondage," can be framed with the aid of an interesting visual example of nineteenth-century migrant propaganda. T. H. Maguire's lithographs "Outward Bound" and "Homeward Bound" (1854)[7] highlight a broader and complex historical background for the kinds of troubled and intertwined passages and their narrative representations that I have discussed in the previous section of this essay.

Figure 6.1   Outward Bound, The Quay of Dublin, *engraved by T. H. Maguire,
1854 (color litho (see 189921), by J. Nicol (19th century) (after) © Collection of the
New-York Historical Society, USA / The Bridgeman Art Library.*

Figure 6.2   Homeward Bound, The Quay of New York, *engraved by
T. H. Maguire, 1854 (color litho) (see 189006) by J. Nicol (19th century) (after)
© Collection of the New-York Historical Society, USA / The Bridgeman Art
Library.*

Maguire's lithographs depict an Irishman, or a racialized Celt, as Mathew Fry Jacobson would refer to him, given that in the nineteenth century the Irish were seen as "black" (13–91). In the two images, the Celt appears before and after his journey to the New World. In the "before" image, he is looking at a poster advertising fares to New York—the outer world. He seems considerably stockier, darker-skinned, and bedraggled, if not "barbarian," than in the picture that depicts him after his immigrant stint in America. The latter image shows a slimmer, taller, lighter-skinned, well-dressed man who is contemplating passage fares to Dublin. These two visual representations of a male immigrant narrative of economic success bracket an important, implied sequence of events that those looking at the pictures can easily reconstruct in their minds as a well-known, all-American story. In this traditional narrative, a poor European crosses from the Old World to the New, where he takes advantage of economic opportunity and access to democracy and undergoes a transformation into a "new man." In the "after" picture, being well dressed, and in a somewhat southern-plantation-owner-like fashion, signifies both economic and racial ascendancy.

Between the two images, the Celt's visible racial transformation emphasizes the New World as a cauldron where whiteness proper is forged, no matter one's national origins. As perhaps the sole marker of Americanness, and in lieu of other points in common given class differences between newcomers, whiteness thus emerges to unite disparate immigrant groups. Divided by national origins, languages, and religions, they can come together on the basis of invented epidermal affinity, a process that signifies America as the space where the inferior Old World "stocks" of immigrants become improved, if not white-washed. Paradoxically, such an approach to visualized whiteness puts in question the essentialist notions of race and eugenic approaches to national origins that it has been invented to uphold in the first place. That is, by stressing the transformative nature of immigrant experience in America, the image proclaims race as a construct rather than an essence, and illustrates its workings through the appearance of the Celt who loses his darkness/racial markings of Irishness to become an Americanized white man.

The second image contains another element highlighting
the interdependence of economic advancement and fictions of
racial uplift in the after-immigration figure of the Irishman.
Perhaps not surprisingly, given the long and troubled history
of eclipsing the presence of "others" who are essential to the
mechanisms of producing whiteness in American culture,
an African figure visible in the second image has gone unnoticed in its several reproductions. In the background framing the successfully whitened Celt, partially hidden by a wall
and framed by the sky and boat sails, stoops an unmistakably
dark-skinned, African figure, a Mammy-like woman, who is
wearing light-colored clothing and a headscarf. To a careful
beholder, both racialized processes of separate and unequal
Americanization—of enslavement and descent into blackness/
invisibility and upward mobility and ascent into Americanness/
visibility/whiteness—are thus intertwined and inseparable in
the second image (as much as they are gendered and sexualized). Much like the narrative accounts of immigration, the
hieratic, allegorical space of the lithographs conveys racialized,
gendered, and sexualized processes of national-identity building through discursive and visual racial uplift of the Irishman
and degradation and erasure of the African woman. This is
amplified by architecture, as walls separate the newly whit-
ened/Americanized and the irrevocably black/displaced. The
image's hieratic perspective also makes the African woman
a mere "shadow" in the background and thus enlarges the
Irishman (she is literally an extension of the man's shadow).
Most important, in the racialized and gendered gaze of the
nation, the self-important Celt is supposed to be as unaware
of the African's existence as the African is supposed to be
unable to be noticed by or look at those placed above her in the
national racial hierarchy.

Because they cannot see each other, the two symbolic figures
in the lithograph cannot communicate; their stories cannot touch.
And yet the larger-than-life newly whitened Irish American male
needs the African, or African American, female rather desperately for the whole picture to make sense. Within what Henri
Lefebvre would term "representational" spaces—or the spaces

of interpreters, critics, and readers—the European-African interdependence in the visual and spatial frame of Americanization
must enlist the lithograph's viewers/consumers for its allegorical national dynamics to work successfully. The image's didactic
appeal relies on the viewers' having naturalized the architectural,
spatial, and epidermal hierarchies that make up their own social
space and that are reflected, symbolically and literally, in the picture they observe. This presumed complicity of viewers—and
critics—in Maguire's depiction of American national design can
help to explain why the African figure has gone unnoticed and
undiscussed among the reproductions of the lithographs for such
a long time. It also helps to explain why, as readers of American
literature, we have been reluctant to imagine a dialogue between
the stories written by the descendants of African slaves and white
European immigrants.

To remedy this, let us imagine Baldwin as a hypothetical reader/subject of Maguire's lithographs and lend his voice
to the African figure on whom the whiteness of the Irishman
depends. As his interlocutor, or the hypothetical "Irishman,"
we can enlist Oscar Handlin, the historian whose groundbreaking work helped to legitimize scholarship on immigration. In
short, I propose that we bring together Baldwin and Handlin in
the interdisciplinary—historical, visual, and literary—frame of
Americanization that I consider in this essay. Juxtaposing such
strange bedfellows—Baldwin, the artist, prophet/witness, and
civil rights activist, and Handlin, the immigration historian
and founding father of the "Ellis Island school of immigration
studies"—enables a productive interdisciplinary interrogation
of the spaces where the "black" and "white" narratives of displacement and national (up)rootedness intersect and clash, but
also come into fruitful dialogue.

Talking across the "Color Line"

Oscar Handlin's famous account of the lower-class European
crossing to the New World—that bible of immigrant studies,
The Uprooted: The Epic Story of the Great Migrations That Made the

American People proclaims: "Once I thought to write a history of the immigrants in America. Then I discovered that the immigrants *were* American history." James Baldwin's essay, "Many Thousands Gone," gives a different testimony: "The story of the Negro in America is the story of America—or, more precisely, it is the story of Americans" (65). Both texts were published in 1951.

Regardless of their literary, physical, and intellectual separation—if not spatial segregation—at the time of writing these works, James Baldwin and Oscar Handlin undertake a strikingly similar, profound, and complex project of defining the American people through history and experience of transatlantic migrants. Baldwin demands recognition of African Americans as subjects and citizens, whose ancestors lived through and passed on the story of the Middle Passage and whose presence has been crucial to constructing Americanness as an exclusionary racialized national identity. Handlin proclaims that it is the impoverished European immigrants' passage from the Old World to the New that constitutes a metonymic history of the nation. Handlin's book earned the Pulitzer Prize in history the year after its publication; Baldwin had to wait until 1963 and the publication of the *The Fire Next Time* for national prominence.

Baldwin's statement from "Many Thousands Gone" moves the story from an individual who stands in for his people (the ubiquitous and synecdochal "Negro") through the writing of the nation ("the story of America") to embracing all peoples of his country ("the story of Americans"). While doing so, he is also pointing at the ways in which the personalized vision of "America" often occludes the actual, various historical actors. On the other hand, Handlin's more autobiographic proclamation moves from his desire to represent immigrant peoples' experience as a scholar ("I thought to write a history of the immigrants in America") to his discovery of the foundational nature of his subject to his larger academic enterprise ("the immigrants *were* American history"). Despite their obvious differences in background, genre, approach, focus, and subject, both the black writer, who is a descendant of African slaves, and the white scholar, who is a descendant of East European Jews, emphasize narrative underpinnings of national history and racialized identity.

While doing so, they claim the exceptionality of their visions and approaches as spokespersons for distinct narrative traditions that represent national "history" or "story." They also utilize approaches that might be seen as somewhat unorthodox at the time. Baldwin, a fiction writer, uses the autobiographic essay to explore the historic background of contemporaneous politics of American racism in ways that transform the genre and make it all his own while giving us an unmatched vision of twentieth-century Americanness. Handlin, a historian, in a groundbreaking move dispenses with the formal apparatus of his discipline—archives, notes, references to other scholars—to narrate, validate, and make palpable the experience of lower-class immigrant transplantation by means of a collective narrative of the "huddled masses."

In his choice to focus on anonymous personal narratives of immigrant passage in *The Uprooted*, Handlin employed "story" in his accounts of removal, passage, arrival, and acculturation much more deliberately than "history" understood as a chronologically organized account of facts, deeds, and actors. It is interesting to note that Baldwin, who began writing on immigration at the same time, must have been compelled to perform a similar feat in the narrative designs of some of his major works, all of which employed autobiographic and sometimes vernacular elements. To Handlin, immigrants are the main focus of his work, whereas to Baldwin they are part of a much more complex human landscape. This does not mean that the former was oblivious to the issues of racism or the latter to his occasional privileging of the black or essentializing of the white perspective. Both, however, are aware of and grapple with—no matter their highly divergent results—the spatial/epidermal regimes that place them on the opposite ends of American racial hierarchies in the context of the early 1950s.

Twenty years after *The Uprooted*, in *A Pictorial History of Immigration* (1972), Oscar Handlin takes on the Middle Passage by including a brief chapter on "Immigrants in Bondage," in which he represents the transatlantic slave trade as a kind of involuntary migration between Africa and the New World. He writes: "Africa...made a substantial contribution to the American population.... The unique qualities of this migration had by then planted the seeds of *a difficulty that would permanently mark the nation"* (66). While Handlin is right to point at certain commonalities in the migration processes of various populations he studies, the oblique language in his last sentence is revealing. Handlin refers here to the "difficulty," or transatlantic slavery and the "problem of the color line," that preoccupied James Baldwin and many other black writers in disapora at that time. Besides making a hard-to-support case for treating Africans as merely one among other immigrant groups—nine years after Baldwin's acclaimed call to "end the racial nightmare" in *The Fire Next Time* (1963)—Handlin's statement surprises with its forced reticence and vagueness on the topic of racial strife that had raged throughout the United States for over two decades by then. Baldwin's reference to the black presence in the United States as the "shadow" in "Many Thousands Gone" seems to echo the lasting legacy of Maguire's racialized images and helps to contextualize Handlin's approach. In its deliberate eclipsing of African Americans so that the symmetries and schemes of his work on immigration would be upheld, Handlin's *A Pictorial History of Immigration* proves Baldwin right: "the Negro in America does not really exist except in the darkness of our minds" (*PT* 66).[8]

Unlike Baldwin, who included immigrant characters of all hues in his plays and fiction,[9] and who sees all Americans as burdened with the painful histories of the nation, Handlin in *The Uprooted* separates the passengers on his boat and demarcates immigrant stories according to skin color. He does so to establish the exceptionalism of the white European, whose origins he makes a stand-in for American history, thus performing the creation of the exclusionary myth of "immigrant America" (Ngai 5). He writes, "The experience of these men on the move [European immigrants] was more complex that that of eighteenth-century Negroes or of seventeenth-century Englishmen or of eleventh-century Normans." This is so because "[t]he participants in the earlier mass migrations had either wandered to unoccupied places, where they had only to adjust to new conditions of the physical environment, or they had gone under the well-defined conditions of conquering invader or imported slave" (5). While

Handlin certainly has a point when he claims that "the effect of the [European] transfer was harsher upon the people than upon the society they entered," he is wrong in embracing the whitened vision of American national identity. As historian of Asian American immigration Mae Ngai comments on his work, "Like most pluralists of his generation, Handlin imagined 'the descendants of immigrants' as white Euro-Americans" (246). By doing so, he deliberately centered the narrative of passage on them, despite his token, and often misguided, nods toward other groups, including indigenous peoples, comprising the nation.[10]

In contrast, Baldwin's explicit goal is not to separate peoples and cultures but to bring them all together in a much more comprehensive transatlantic perspective, albeit from an artistic, rather than a scholarly perspective. In "Encounter on the Seine," his hypothetical African American visitor deliberates the complexities of his status in Paris, where, on the one hand, he encounters his white and black compatriots, and, on the other, he meets French colonial Africans for the first time in his life: "Perhaps it now occurs to him that in his need to establish himself in relation to his past he is most American, that this depthless alienation from oneself and one's people is, in sum, the American experience" (*PT* 39). This discovery is not a confirmation of some universal American character, but rather an acknowledgment of a shared heritage of departures, passages, and arrivals—in short, of uprootedness, flux, and constant change as markers of national belonging beyond *and* because of race. When in 1952 Baldwin returned to New York for the first time since his departure for Paris, it was at the height of McCarthyism. He saw whites "lying about their motives and…blackmailed by their guilt." At the moment when the Cold War anticommunist witch-hunts reached a feverish pitch, these people were "nothing more than the respectable issue of various immigrants, struggling to hold on to what they had acquired" (*PT* 465). He remembers this historical moment in the introduction to his second essay collection, *Nobody Knows My Name* (1961), in which he also writes that he cannot escape the impact of race on his own immigrant identity: "In America, the color of my skin had stood between myself and me; in Europe, that barrier was down. Nothing is more desirable than to be released from an affliction, but nothing is more frightening than to be divested of a crutch" (*Nobody Knows My Name* 11).

By thus displacing the white-male American traveler of Mark Twain's or Henry James's America-to-Europe accounts with a black one (or by revealing their implicit dependence on whiteness as an unmarked racial category), Baldwin insists on the material consequences of race for all Americans everywhere. This lesson hits home to a similar degree for the characters in his novels, the white American David of *Giovanni's Room* (1956) and the black American Arthur in *Just above My Head*, when they confront love affairs with European men. The identities of these characters cannot escape the American "social forces" (135) of racism, homophobia, and heterosexism. Although not physically threatened by these forces while in Europe, Baldwin's migrant white and black characters bear their imprint in their minds and on their bodies; they have to negotiate and remake themselves as part of a larger project of changing national consciousness.

Because Handlin was invested in constructing Americanization as a myth of Euro-American identity, his work insists on one-way passages. His model does not allow for the possibility that we have seen in Maguire's image, or that the Celt/Irishman could be "homeward bound" following his immigrant stint in America. Interestingly, what we now consider as Handlin's rather recalcitrant vision came about as a result of linking "traditional" with "new" strategies to stress the radical importance of personal narratives and lower-class status of the majority of European newcomers. Conversely, Baldwin demonstrated foundational entanglements between the stories of the Middle Passage and white(ned) immigrant crossing in the larger context of transatlantic slavery and contemporaneous upheaval of the civil rights era. While Handlin's story traversed the Atlantic one way and circulated around Ellis Island and American urban centers, Baldwin's went back and forth along some of the same trajectories, but also triangulated toward colonized Africa, South America, and Asia, not to mention the North-South axis in the United States. Such an approach allows Baldwin to chart a more complex map of American identity and to posit it as transatlantic, transnational, as well as regionally, racially (and sexually) heterogeneous.[11] Regardless of their profound differences in vision and ideology, we should read Baldwin's and Handlin's works side by side. We should see the black writer and the white Jewish historian as traveling in the "same boat," as engaged in a kind of dialogue of strange immigrant bedfellows precisely because the narrative models they employ are indispensable for the design and making of transatlantic American identities and thus of the larger "American story," as Baldwin puts it. Such a reading of national identity, and the multidirectional narratives inscribing it, recognizes the profound differences in historic, cultural, and geopolitical circumstances of the passages into, and especially the dramatically divergent political, economic, and social outcomes of the arrival in, the New World for the respective populations of Africans and Europeans. At the same time, in the vein of Paul Gilroy's call for comparative and interdisciplinary study of transatlantic crossings, the reading I propose enables a cross-fertilization of narratives of passage to the New World that brings together formerly disparate races and ethnicities. As Gilroy stresses, while referring to the lessons of the Holocaust and transatlantic slavery, even unlikely stories can be "precious resources from which we might learn something valuable about the way modernity operates...about the claims of science, and...about the ideologies of humanism with which these brutal histories can be shown to have been complicit" (The Black Atlantic 217).

"Inseparability of Great Literature and Social Life"

While the majority of scholarship has positioned Baldwin chiefly between Harlem, New York City, and Paris, his works and life story add up to a much more complex picture as they draw on diverse population movements within and without North America and root themselves in a wide span of the Americas' history—from pre-Columbian and colonial eras, through Native American genocide, transatlantic slavery, colonialism, and the Cold War.[12] Baldwin's world stretches from Harlem and Greenwich Village in New York to the cities and towns in the southern United States, and across the Atlantic to France and to Turkey, where he wrote several of his major American works, as well as to the Soviet Union and other countries in Europe—not to mention places in Africa, Asia, the Caribbean, and South America where he traveled on occasion. Never comfortable with the label of "expatriate"—he argued that it was impossible to leave a country that was not one's true "patria"—Baldwin put a completely new spin on being an African American immigrant writer.

Let us return for a moment to the short story we started with. If Baldwin's protagonist from "This Morning, This Evening, So Soon" were allowed to arrive in his native land—that is, if we ventured to dramatically re-write the story that ends on the morning of his departure from France—he might be met by racist white customs officials, but then end up going to Hollywood to become a star. Such a revised ending would arguably place him in a better social and economic position than was the lot of the majority of poor white European emigrants depicted by Oscar Handlin. Baldwin was well aware of his privilege once he became famous and affluent, although as a black man in the street he would still not be able easily to hail that proverbial cab in New York City.

As it is, however, the ending of Baldwin's story has the protagonist-narrator locked in the cage of the elevator that is taking him downstairs in his Parisian building, on the first leg of his long journey back to the "house of bondage," or his home in the United States. Being floated back home again, "into danger," Baldwin seems to suggest, is the necessary condition for claiming his African American birthright. As a returned (black) immigrant and successful artist, both the writer and his protagonist are a curious hybrid, a "dangerous alien," one who affirms the power of the self to overcome places and stories proscribed by the state by turning his imprisonment into impulse for revolutionary creativity.

I speculate on this ironic displacement and the vagaries of Baldwin's migrant narratives' outcomes not only to bring the vessel of this paper back to the point where it started, but also to propose a somewhat unusual conclusion. As if anticipating Baldwinian rhetoric of the "house of bondage," not to mention Foucauldian heterotopias, C. L. R. James, closes his critical, political, and philosophical exploration of Herman Melville, *Mariners, Renegades, and Castaways,* with an autobiographic chapter that relates his unexpected imprisonment on Ellis Island as a "dangerous alien":

> Here was I, just about to write, suddenly projected onto an island isolated from the rest of society, where American administrators and officials, and American security officers controlled the destinies of perhaps a thousand men, sailors, "isolates," renegades, and castaways from all parts of the world. It seems now as if destiny had taken a hand to give me a unique opportunity to test my ideas of this great American writer. (126)

What used to be the mythical place of passage into America for millions of immigrants in the earlier decades of the twentieth century, by 1952 became a prison and space of suffering for the Trinidadian author. And yet it is from within this place that he constructs his highly dynamic and liberated reading of Melville's works as transoceanic scripts of American history and character that provide a fascinating blueprint for his own age of migration, totalitarianism, and Cold War.

While doing so, James is writing his own migrant story of arrival, interrogation, betrayal, and deportation into the study of the ways in which American literary imagination reflects the realities of power relations in the society that produced it. What Donald Pease attributes to James could be also said about Baldwin: "In writing as one of the persons the state has included within the category 'mariners, renegades, and castaways,' James derives his interpretive authority from his having lived the experience of their narratives" (xviii). And vice versa, Baldwin's heterotopia echoes in James's work and life story. Although he is West Indian, or Trinidadian, James becomes like Baldwin's African American returned immigrant from "This Morning, this Evening, so Soon," who is perpetually stranded on the boat/island of the immigration station that is a stand-in for the national "house of bondage."

Like Baldwin's, James's immigrant critical study can be read as reconstructing and affirming the "Americanness" that has been adulterated and betrayed by the "American administrators and officials, and American security officers" who attend to his confinement. As narrated in the conclusion to *Mariners, Renegades, and Castaways,* James's experience on Ellis Island counters his initial impression of the United States as having enabled his "sense of expansion which has permanently altered my attitude to the world" (159). And yet, despite his immobilization in the repressive frame of 1950s Americanization, he remains committed to his mission to "advance both the understanding of literature and the cause of freedom" (167). In thus linking literary practice to his politics of liberation, he voices a sentiment akin to Baldwin's desire to be a "good writer," who is changing the world book by book. For Baldwin and James—even for Handlin, whether he acknowledges it or not—narratives have material consequences for people's lives. Hence the "American," the (im)migrant, and the "Negro"—those allegorical personages posited on the multipolar ends of the richly hued American spectrum of humanity—find themselves sailing in the "same boat."

NOTES

I thank Arlene Keizer, Sarah Blair, Sarita See, Tobin Siebers, and the members of the Global Ethnic Literatures Seminar at the University of Michigan for their feedback on the first draft of this essay. June Howard and Justine Pas, both in the Program in American Culture, read later versions, while Douglas Field's editorial advice helped to shape the final.

1. For "immigrant narrative" as a genre see Boelhower's "The Immigrant Novel," Kasprzycki's "The Migrant Novel and Its Characteristics," and Hatzimanolis's "Immigrant Writing Coming of Age." See also Huttunen's "M. G. Vassanji's *The Gunny Sack,*" de Fina's *Identity in Narrative,* and Zaborowska's *How We Found America.* Lowe's *Immigrant Acts* summarizes typical elements of the

immigrant story as pertaining to the "terrain of national culture" through which "the individual subject is politically formed as the American citizen: a terrain introduced by the Statue of Liberty, discovered by the immigrant, dreamed in a common language, and defended in battle by the independent, self-made man" (2).

2. "American" refers to both Americas. Baldwin does not refer to Asian ethnics and racial groups in this story.

3. See Zaborowska, *James Baldwin's Turkish Decade*.

4. Scholars in immigration studies who deal with race in the fields of history and social sciences include, among others, Mary C. Waters, Vijay Prashad, David Roediger, Mathew Fry Jacobson, Lisa Lowe, Ramaswami Mahalingam, Mae Ngai, Louis Mendoza, and Karen Brodkin.

5. The concept of national "literary imagination" comes from Morrison's *Playing in the Dark* and evokes Bercovitch's references to "symbols," "allegories," and "cultural symbology"—a "system of symbolic meanings that encompasses text and context alike, simultaneously nourishing the imagination and marking its boundaries" (*The Office of the Scarlet Letter* xvii).

6. James was a West Indian immigrant from Trinidad, a communist, and political activist, who was deemed "dangerous." He was eventually deported from the United States.

7. Apart from the display at the Ellis Island Museum of Immigration, this image has been reproduced in Tifft's *Ellis Island* (10), in Jacobson's *Whiteness of a Different Color* (200–201), and in Handlin's *Pictorial History of Immigration* (98).

8. Handlin's 2002 paperwork edition of *The Uprooted* begins: "THE TEXT STANDS AS WRITTEN" (xi).

9. See *Blues for Mister Charlie* (1964), Parnell, the Irish American descendant of slave owners; *If Beale Street Could Talk* (1974), an Italian female shop keeper and a Puerto Rican rape victim; *Tell Me How Long the Train's Been Gone* (1968), Jerry, Leo and Barbara's Italian American roommate; and *Just above My Head* (1979), a Caribbean girlfriend of Hal Montana.

10. Handlin's notion that immigrants entered an empty space in the New World erases the indigenous presence in North America.

11. Handlin implies that immigrants did not bring culture with them; if anything, they "were" material culture as objects of study (*Pictorial History of Immigration* 321). He also marks them as challenged

in terms of high culture: "The foreign-born were less prominent in literature" and weak in "religious and secular music" (324).

12. Baldwin is aware of his own exclusions, and refers to Native Americans in "Notes on the House of Bondage" (*PT* 672–63), *Nothing Personal* (*PT* 382), in the novel *Giovanni's Room* (7), and in The Fire Next Time (1963), where he terms the "American Indian...the most despised creature in this country" (*The Fire Next Time* 115).

WORKS CITED

Avedon, Richard, and James Baldwin. *Nothing Personal. Photos. By Richard Avedon and Text by James Baldwin*. New York: Atheneum, 1964.

Baldwin, James. "As Much Truth as One Can Bear." New York Times Book Review, January 14, 1962, 11 and 38.

———. "Autobiographical Notes." In *Notes of a Native Son*. Boston: Beacon Press, 1984. 3–12.

———. "The Discovery of What It Means to Be an American" (1959). Reprinted in *The Price of the Ticket: Collected Nonfiction, 1948–1985*. New York: St. Martin's/Marek, 1985. 171–76.

———. "Encounter on the Seine: Black Meets Brown" (1950). Reprinted in *The Price of the Ticket: Collected Nonfiction, 1948–1985*. New York: St. Martin's/Marek, 1985. 35–39.

———. "Everybody's Protest Novel" (1949). Reprinted in *The Price of the Ticket: Collected Nonfiction, 1948–1985*. New York: St. Martin's/ Marek, 1985. 27–34.

———. *The Fire Next Time*. New York: Dell, 1963.

———. *Giovanni's Room*. New York: Dell, 1956.

———. "Introduction: The Price of the Ticket." In *The Price of the Ticket: Collected Nonfiction, 1948–1985*. New York: St. Martin's/ Marek, 1985. ix–xx.

———. *James Baldwin: Collected Essays*. Edited by Toni Morrison. New York: Library of America 1998.

———. "Many Thousands Gone" (1951). Reprinted in *The Price of the Ticket: Collected Nonfiction, 1948–1985*. New York: St. Martin's/ Marek, 1985, 65–78.

———. "Nobody Knows My Name: A Letter from the South" (1959). Reprinted in *The Price of the Ticket: Collected Nonfiction, 1948–1985*. New York: St. Martin's/Marek, 1985, 183–93.

———. *Nobody Knows My Name.* New York: Dell, 1961.

———. "Notes for a Hypothetical Novel" (1960). Reprinted in *The Price of the Ticket: Collected Nonfiction, 1948–1985.* New York: St. Martin's/Marek, 1985, 237–44.

———. "Notes on the House of Bondage" (1980). Reprinted in *The Price of the Ticket: Collected Nonfiction, 1948–1985.* New York: St. Martin's/Marek, 1985. 667–75.

———. *The Price of the Ticket: Collected Nonfiction, 1948–1985.* New York: St. Martin's/Marek, 1985.

———. "Stranger in the Village" (1953). Reprinted in *The Price of the Ticket: Collected Nonfiction, 1948–1985.* New York: St. Martin's/ Marek, 1985. 79–90.

———. "This Morning, This Evening, So Soon." In *Going to Meet the Man.* New York: Dial Press, 1965. 143–93.

Bercovitch, Sacvan. *The Office of "The Scarlet Letter."* Baltimore, Md.: Johns Hopkins University Press, 1991.

———. *The Puritan Origins of the American Self.* New Haven, Conn.: Yale University Press, 1975.

Boelhower, William Q. "The Immigrant Novel as Genre." *MELUS* 1 (Spring 1981): 3–13.

Darsey, James. "Baldwin's Cosmopolitan Loneliness." In *James Baldwin Now,* edited by Dwight A. McBride. New York: New York University Press, 1999. 187–207.

Fanon, Frantz. *Black Skin, White Masks.* Translated by Charles Lam Markmann. London: MacGibbon and Kee, 1968.

de Fina, Anna. *Identity in Narrative: A Study of Immigrant Discourse.* Amsterdam: John Benjamins Publishing, 2003.

Foucault, Michel. "Of Other Spaces and Others." *Diacritics* 16 (Spring 1986): 27.

Gilroy, Paul. *Against Race: Imagining Political Culture Beyond the Color Line.* Cambridge, Mass.: Belknap Press of Harvard University Press, 2000.

———. *The Black Atlantic: Modernity and Double Consciousness.* Cambridge, Mass.: Harvard University Press, 1993.

———. "It ain't where you're from, it's where you're at." In *Small Acts: Thoughts on Politics of Black Cultures.* London: Serpent's Tail, 1993: 120–45.

Handlin, Oscar. *A Pictorial History of Immigration.* New York: Crown Publishers, 1972.

Handlin, Oscar. *The Uprooted: The Epic Story of the Great Migrations That Made the American People.* Boston: Little Brown, 1973.

Hatzimanolis, Efi. "Immigrant Writing Coming of Age? The Getting of Genre in Angelika Fremd's Heartland." *Journal of Narrative Technique* 21.1 (1991): 24–31.

Hutner, Gordon. "Introduction." In *Immigrant Voices: Twenty-Four Narratives on Becoming American.* New York: Signet Classic, 1999: ix–xxi.

Huttunen, Tuomas. "M. G. Vassanji's *The Gunny Sack*: Narrating the Migrant Identity." In "Tales of Two Cities: Essays on New Anglophone Literature," edited by John Skinner. Special issue, *Anglicana Turkuensia* [University of Turku, Turku, Finland] 22 (2000): 3–20.

Jacobson, Matthew Frye. *Whiteness of a Different Color: European Immigrants and the Alchemy of Race.* Cambridge, Mass.: Harvard University Press, 1998.

James, C. L. R. *Mariners, Renegades, and Castaways: The Story of Herman Melville and the World We Live In.* 1953. Reprinted with an introduction by Donald E. Pease. Hanover, NH: Dartmouth College, published by University Press of New England, 2001.

Kaplan, Amy. "Violent Beginnings and the Question of Empire Today: Presidential Address to the American Studies Association, Hartford, Connecticut, October 17, 2003." *American Quarterly* Vol. 56. No. 1 March 2004: 1–18.

Kasprzycki, Nancy. "The Migrant Novel and Its Characteristics." *Commonwealth Novel in English* 7–8 (1997): 169–78.

Keizer, Arlene R. *Black Subjects: Identity Formation in the Contemporary Narrative of Slavery.* Ithaca, N.Y.: Cornell University Press, 2004.

Lazarus, Emma. *Songs of a Semite: The Dance to Death and Other Poems.* New York: The American Hebrew, 1882.

Lefebvre, H. *The Production of Space.* Oxford: Blackwell, 2000.

Lowe, Lisa. *Immigrant Acts: On Asian American Cultural Politics.* Durham, N.C.: Duke University Press, 1996.

Miles, Tiya. *Ties That Bind: The Story of an Afro-Cherokee Family in Slavery and Freedom.* Berkeley: University of California, 2005.

Morrison, Toni. *Playing in the Dark: Whiteness and the Literary Imagination.* Cambridge, Mass.: Harvard University Press, 1992.

Ngai, Mae M. *Impossible Subjects: Illegal Aliens and the Making of Modern America* Princeton, New Jersey: Princeton University Press, 2004.

Nwankwo, Ifeoma Kiddoe. *Black Cosmopolitanism: Racial Consciousness and Transnational Ideology in the Americas.* Philadelphia: University of Pennsylvania Press, 2005.

Roediger, David R., ed. *Black on White: Black Writers on What It Means to Be White.* New York: Schocken Books, 1998.

Sollors, Werner. *Beyond Ethnicity: Consent and Descent in American Culture.* New York: Oxford University Press, 1986.

———, ed. *The Invention of Ethnicity.* New York: Oxford University Press, 1989.

Stevens, Laura M. "Transatlanticism Now." *American Literary History* 16.1 (2004): 93–102.

Stokes, Mason. *The Color of Sex: Whiteness, Heterosexuality and the Fictions of White Supremacy.* Durham, N.C.: Duke University Press, 2001.

Tifft, Wilton S. *Ellis Island.* Chicago: Contemporary Books, 1990.

Trachtenberg, Alan. *Shades of Hiawatha: Staging Indians, Making Americans, 1880–1930.* New York: Hill and Wang, 2004.

Yezierska, Anzia. "You Can't Be an Immigrant Twice: An Interview with Anzia Yezierska," an interview with Richard Duffy. In *Children of Loneliness,* 261–70.

———. "How I Found America." In *How I Found America: Collected Stories of Anzia Yezierska.* New York: Persea Books, 1991. 108–27.

West, Cornel. "Black Strivings in a Twilight Civilization." In *The Future of the Race,* by Cornel West and Henry Louis Gates, Jr. New York: Knopf, 1996. 53–112.

Zaborowska, Magdalena J. *How We Found America: Reading Gender through East European Immigrant Narratives.* Chapel Hill: University of North Carolina Press, 1995.

———. *James Baldwin's Turkish Decade: Erotics of Exile.* Durham, N.C.: Duke University Press, 2009.

Illustrated Chronology

Baldwin's Life

1924 James Arthur Jones born (August 2) in Harlem Hospital, New York City, to Emma Berdis Jones. (Baldwin will never know the identity of his biological father.) Emma Berdis Jones marries David Baldwin, and she and James take the name Baldwin.

1929 Attends Public School 24 in Harlem.

1935 Graduates from Public School 24 and enters Frederick Douglass Junior High School in Harlem, where he is taught by Countee Cullen.

1938 Graduates from Frederick Douglass Junior High School and enters DeWitt Clinton High School.

1938–41 Writes for the school journal, *The Magpie,* and preaches at the Fireside Pentecostal Assembly.

1940 Meets the painter Beauford Delaney, who becomes his mentor.

1942 Awarded his high school diploma. Works as a laborer at the army depot in Belle Mead, New Jersey. Refused a hamburger for being "colored" at a restaurant in Princeton.

Beauford Delaney's portrait of James Baldwin. Courtesy of Engin Cezzar, Letters to a Friend.

1943   David Baldwin, Sr., dies (July 29). Meets Eugene Worth, who becomes a close friend and who commits suicide in 1946.

1943–4   Lives and works in Greenwich Village.

1944   Meets Marlon Brando and Richard Wright.

1945   Starts literary magazine with Brad and Claire Burch, *This Generation*. Awarded Eugene F. Saxton Foundation Fellowship after Wright's recommendation.

1947   Publishes reviews in *The Nation* and *The New Leader*.

1948   Awarded Rosenwald Fellowship. Publishes with *Commentary*.

1948   Sails for Europe (November 11). Meets Themistocles Hoetis and Asa Beneviste, friends of Richard Wright and editors of the literary magazine *Zero*.

1948–57   Lives in Paris, the south of France, and Switzerland.

1949   Publishes "Everbody's Protest Novel" in the first edition of *Zero*. (The essay would also be published in *Partisan Review* in June.) Publishes "Preservation of Innocence" in the second issue of *Zero*.
   Sets off to Tangiers, but falls ill and stays in Aix. Arrested for receiving stolen goods (December) and spends two weeks in Fresnes prison. Meets Lucien Happersberger a few days later.

1950   Publishes "The Death of the Prophet" in *Commentary* (March), a short story and draft of *Go Tell It on the Mountain*.

1951–52   Spends the winter with Lucien Happersberger in Loèche-les-Bains, Switzerland, where he finishes *Go Tell It on the Mountain*.

Contents page of the first edition of Zero (Spring 1949), the first magazine to publish "Everybody's Protest Novel." Photograph by Douglas Field. Courtesy of George Solomos (Themistocles Hoetis).

1952 Meets Bernard Hasell, a dancer, who becomes a lifelong friend. Borrows money from Marlon Brando to return to New York to sign the publishing contract on his first novel. Meets Ralph Ellison.

1953 Publishes *Go Tell it on the Mountain.* Beauford Delaney arrives in Paris.

1954 Returns to New York (June). Awarded a fellowship at the MacDowell colony, New Hampshire (August).

1955 Publishes *Notes of a Native Son.* *The Amen Corner* is performed at Howard University, attended by Sterling Brown and Alain Locke. Returns to Paris (October).

1956 Publishes *Giovanni's Room.* Takes overdose of sleeping pills. Covers the Congrès des Ecrivains et Artistes Noir (Conference of Negro Writers and Artists) for *Preuves* and *Encounter.*

ZERO

Cover of Zero (Spring 1949). Illustration by John Goodwin. Photograph by Douglas Field. Courtesy of George Solomos (Themistocles Hoetis).

*Harold Norse, close friend of Baldwin from the 1940s and one of the first people
to see a substantial draft of* Go Tell it on the Mountain *(San Francisco, 2007).
Photograph by Douglas Field.*

*James Baldwin in Loèche-le-Bains,
Switzerland, winter 1953. Courtesy of
Lucien Happersberger.*

1957   Publishes "Sonny's Blues"
in *Partisan Review*. Returns to the
United States. Visits the South for
the first time in the fall. Meets
Martin Luther King Jr. in Atlanta.
(Baldwin would publish two
essays about his trip: "A Fly in
Buttermilk" and "Nobody Knows
My Name: A Letter from the
South," collected in *Nobody Knows
My Name: More Notes of a Native Son*
[1964]).

1958   The Actors Studio performs
a workshop production of *Giovanni's
Room* with Engin Cezzar in the title
role. (Baldwin would remain close
friends with Cezzar for many years.)
Returns to Paris in the summer.

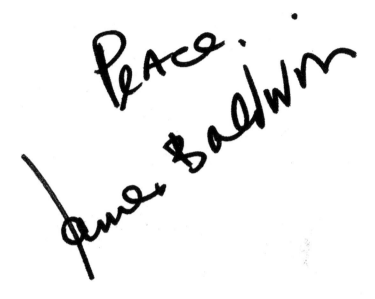

James Baldwin's signature. Photograph by Douglas Field.

1959 Travels to Sweden to interview film director Ingmar Bergman (October). Meets Jean Genet in Paris.

1960 Baldwin visits the South (May) and becomes directly involved in the Congress of Racial Equality (CORE). Interviews Martin Luther King Jr. Richard Wright dies.

1961 Publishes *Nobody Knows My Name: More Notes of a Native Son*. Stays at William Styron's guest house in Connecticut (where Styron wrote *The Confessions of Nat Turner*) and works on *Another Country*. Meets the Honorable Elijah Muhammed. Stays with Engin Cezzar in Turkey and meets David Leeming.

1961–69 Stays intermittently in Turkey (with lengthy stays from the end of 1964 through 1967). Becomes close friends with the novelist Yashar Kemal. (Baldwin will campaign for Kemal's release from prison in 1971.)

1962 Publishes *Another Country*. Travels to Senegal, Ghana, and Sierra Leone with his sister Gloria.

Engin Cezzar in Giovanni's Room, *Actor's Studio, 1958. Courtesy of Engin Cezzar,* Letters to a Friend.

James Baldwin. Courtesy of Engin Cezzar, Letters to a Friend.

James Baldwin with his brother David in Bodrum, Turkey. Courtesy of Engin Cezzar, Letters to a Friend.

James Baldwin in Istanbul. Courtesy of Engin Cezzar, Letters to a Friend.

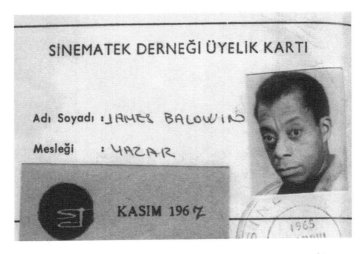

SİNEMATEK DERNEĞİ ÜYELİK KARTI

Adı Soyadı : JAMES BALOWINO

Mesleği : YAZAR

KASIM 196 7

1965

James Baldwin's membership card to the Turkish cinema-tek. Courtesy of Engin Cezzar, Letters to a Friend.

219

1963 Publishes *The Fire Next Time*. Meets with U.S. Attorney General Robert Kennedy (May 24). Participates in the March on Washington (August 28). Undertakes lecture tour for CORE and meets James Meredith, the first African American student to attend the University of Mississippi.

1964 *Blues for Mister Charlie* opens at the ANTA Theater on Broadway on April 23, closing on August 29. Baldwin's name is added to the "Security Index" by the FBI, and Baldwin complains to the Bureau about harassment. Publishes *Nothing Personal* (with Richard Avedon).

1965 Publishes *Going to Meet the Man*. Meets with Bertrand Russell in London to discuss American action in Vietnam.

1967 Meets the Black Panther leadership in San Francisco after Huey Newton's arrest for the murder of a policeman. Talks to Bobby Seale, chairman, and Eldridge Cleaver, minister of information. Baldwin strikes up a long friendship with Bobby Seale.

James Baldwin and Marlon Brando at the March on Washington, D.C, June 28, 1963. Courtesy of the National Archives and Records Administration.

1968 Publishes *Tell Me How Long the Train's Been Gone*. Works in Hollywood on a screenplay of *The Autobiography of Malcolm X* for Columbia Pictures. Hosts a birthday party/fundraising rally for Huey Newton in Oakland (February).

1969 *Baldwin's Nigger*, a documentary featuring Baldwin, directed by Horace Ové, is aired.

1971 Publishes *A Rap on Race* (with Margaret Mead). Moves to Saint-Paul-de-Vance, near Nice, France. (Baldwin will be based here until his death.)

1972 Publishes *No Name In the Street* and *One Day When I Was Lost: A Scenario Based on* the *Autobiography of Malcolm X*. Works with Ray Charles and is involved in the "Hallelujah Chorus—the Life and Times of Ray Charles" at the Carnegie Hall (July 1).

1973 Publishes *A Dialogue* (with Nikki Giovanni).

1974 Publishes *If Beale Street Could Talk*. Awarded centennial medal for "the artist as prophet" from the Cathedral of St. John the Divine, New York.

1976 Publishes *The Devil Finds Work* and *Little Man, Little Man: A Story of Childhood*.

1978 Teaches at Bowling Green University. (Baldwin will teach here again in fall 1979 and 1981.) Awarded honorary degree from the University of Massachusetts.

1979 Publishes *Just Above My Head*. Teaches at the University of California, Berkeley. Death of Beauford Delaney, painter and Baldwin's close friend.

1980 Participates in the meeting of the African Literature Association in Gainesville, Florida, with the Nigerian writer Chinua Achebe.

1981 Travels to Atlanta to write an article on the child murders that had occurred since 1979. The article becomes *The Evidence of Things Not Seen*.

1982 *I Heard it Through the Grapevine*, a film by Dick Fontaine about Baldwin revisiting the South, airs on U.K. and U.S. public television.

1983 Publishes *Jimmy's Blues: Selected Poems*. (The American edition will be published in 1985.) Musical version of *The Amen Corner* runs for six weeks at Ford's Theatre, Washington.

1983–6   Teaches five semesters at the University of Massachusetts.

1984   *Notes of a Native Son* is reprinted with a new introduction. Hospitalized in Boston for heart problems.

1985   Publishes *The Evidence of Things Not Seen* and *The Price of the Ticket: Collected Nonfiction, 1948–1985*. Film version of *Go Tell Tell It on the Mountain* is aired on the Public Broadcasting System.

1986   Presented with the French Legion of Honor by President François Mitterand. Publishes his last article, "To Crush the Serpent," in *Playboy*. *The Amen Corner* opens in London and is well received.

1987   Dies of cancer of the esophagus in St. Paul-de-Vence, France (December 1). Baldwin's funeral is held at New York's Cathedral of St. John the Divine (December 8). Buried at Ferncliff Cemetery in Hartsdale, New York.

1989   *James Baldwin: The Price of the Ticket*, a documentary directed by Karen Thorsen, is released. Posthumous publication of *Gypsies and Other Poems* (limited to 325 copies).

1998   The Library of America publishes *James Baldwin: Collected Essays* and *James Baldwin: Early Novels and Short Stories*, both edited by Toni Morrison.

1999   Berdis Baldwin dies at the age of ninety-nine.

2004   A James Baldwin stamp is issued by the U.S. Postal Service.

Historical Events

1924   Countee Cullen publishes *From the Dark Tower*. Calvin Coolidge is in his second year as the thirtieth U.S. president. V. I. Lenin (b. 1870) dies. George Gershwin's *Rhapsody in Blue* is first performed.

1925   Alain Locke publishes *The New Negro*. Josephine Baker leaves the United States for Paris. The *Scopes* trial.

1926   Carl Van Vechten publishes *Nigger Heaven*. Langston Hughes publishes *Weary Blues*. The National Broadcasting Company, America's first radio network, is founded.

1927   James Weldon Johnson publishes *God's Trombones*. Duke Ellington begins residency at the Cotton Club. Charles Lindbergh makes the first solo flight across the Atlantic Ocean. Marcus Garvey is deported from the U.S.

The James Baldwin U.S. postage stamp. Design (c) 2004 United States Postal Service. All rights reserved. Used with permission.

Langston Hughes, 1942. Photograph by Jack Delano. Courtesy of the Library of Congress.

Marcus Garvey in 1924, the year of Baldwin's birth. Courtesy of the George Grantham Bain Collection, Library of Congress.

1928   Nella Larsen publishes
Quicksand. Claude McKay publishes
Home to Harlem. Walt Disney
releases the first cartoon with
Mickey Mouse, "Plane Crazy."

1929   Nella Larsen publishes
Passing. William Faulkner
publishes *The Sound and the Fury*.
"Black Friday" stock market crash.
Herbert Hoover is inaugurated
as the thirty-first U.S. president.
Martin Luther King Jr. is born.

1930   Langston Hughes publishes
Not Without Laughter. Nation
of Islam is founded by W. D. Fard.

1931   George S. Schuyler
publishes *Black No More*. Scottsboro
Boys convicted of raping two
white women in Alabama.
Empire State Building opens in
New York.

1932   Sterling Brown publishes
Southern Road. Wallace Thurman
publishes *Infants of the Spring*.
James Chadwick discovers the
neutron.

1933   James Weldon Johnson
publishes *Along This Way*. Bessie
Smith makes her last recordings,
and Billie Holiday begins her first
recordings. Franklin D. Roosevelt
is inaugurated as the thirty-second
U.S. president and begins the New

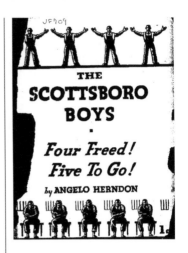

*"The Scottsboro Boys," by Angelo
Herndon. Courtesy of the Michigan
State University Library, Special
Collections Division.*

Deal programs. Adolf Hitler is
appointed as German chancellor.

1934   Zora Neale Hurston
publishes *Jonah's Gourd Vine*. Nancy
Cunard edits *Negro: An Anthology*
Elijah Muhammad becomes
leader of the Nation
of Islam.

1935   Zora Neale Hurston
publishes *Mules and Men*. George
Gershwin premieres *Porgy and
Bess*. Harlem riots. Roosevelt signs
Social Security Act. The Federal
Writers Project is established
(1936–39).

1936 William Faulkner publishes *Absalom, Absalom!* Jesse Owens wins four gold medals at the Berlin Olympics. Spanish Civil War begins (1936–39).

1937 Zora Neale Hurston publishes *Their Eyes Were Watching God.* Joe Louis becomes world heavyweight boxing champion. William H. Hastie is appointed as the first African American federal judge.

1938 Richard Wright publishes *Uncle Tom's Children.* The House Committee on Un-American Activities is established as a special investigating committee.

1939 John Steinbeck publishes *The Grapes of Wrath.* World War II begins (1939–45).

1940 Richard Wright publishes *Native Son.* Marcus Garvey dies. Germany occupies Paris. Leon Trotsky is assassinated.

1941 John Crowe Ransom publishes *New Criticism.* The United States enters World War II after attack on Pearl Harbor. FDR issues Executive Order 8802, banning racial, ethnic, and religious discrimination in all hiring for industrial facilities receiving federal contracts.

1942 First issue of *Negro Digest* is published. Albert Camus publishes *L'Étranger.* Internment of Japanese Americans begins.

1943 Paul Robeson stars in the Theatre Guild production of *Othello* on Broadway. The jitterbug dance becomes popular in the United States. Race riots in Detroit and Harlem. Zoot Suit Riots in Los Angeles.

1944 Gunnar Myrdal publishes *An American Dilemma.* FDR is elected for a fourth term. Supreme Court rules that voting restrictions against African Americans are unconstitutional.

Colored waiting room in Rome, Georgia, September 1943. Photograph by Esther Bubley. Courtesy of the Library of Congress.

1945   Richard Wright publishes *Black Boy.* FDR dies and Harry Truman is inaugurated as the thirty-third U.S. president. The United States drops atomic bombs on Hiroshima and Nagasaki. World War II ends.

1946   Ann Petry publishes *The Street.* Truman creates the Committee on Civil Rights.

1947   Léopold Senghor, Léon Damas, and Aimé Césaire found Présence Africaine. Jackie Robinson becomes the first African American in major league basketball. Truman Doctrine and Marshall Plan. The Central Intelligence Agency is founded.

1948   Norman Mailer publishes *The Naked and the Dead.* Alfred C. Kinsey publishes *Sexual Behavior in the American Male.* Equal treatment in the armed forces is mandated by Truman in Executive Order 9981.

1949   Gwendolyn Brooks publishes *Annie Allen.* Miles Davis records *Birth of the Cool.* Truman is reelected to a second term.

1950   Gwendolyn Brooks is the first African American to win a Pulitzer Prize (for *Annie Allen,*

George Solomos (Themistocles Hoetis), editor of Zero *and friend of Baldwin (Paris, 1948). Courtesy of George Solomos.*

1949). Ralph Bunche is the first African American to receive the Nobel Peace Prize. The Korean War (1950–53) begins.

1951   J. D. Salinger publishes *Catcher in the Rye.* United Nations Headquarters opens in New York.

1952   Ralph Ellison publishes *Invisible Man.* Samuel Beckett publishes *Waiting for Godot.* The Immigration and Nationality Act becomes law, restricting immigration to the United States.

1953 Arthur Miller publishes *The Crucible*. Simone De Beauvoir's *The Second Sex* is translated into English (originally published in 1949). Dwight D. Eisenhower is inaugurated as the thirty-fourth U.S. president. Execution of the Rosenbergs for espionage. Josef Stalin dies.

1954 Ernest Hemingway is awarded the Nobel Prize in Literature. The first annual Newport Jazz Festival is held. In *Brown v. Board of Education*, the Supreme Court rules unanimously that segregated schools are unconstitutional.

1955 Vladimir Nabokov publishes *Lolita* in France. Rosa Parks is arrested for not giving up her seat to a white man on a Montgomery, Alabama, bus. Emmett Till is murdered in Mississippi.

1956 Allen Ginsberg publishes *Howl and Other Poems*. Sudan becomes an independent state. Eisenhower is reelected to a second term. The first Congress of African writers is held in Paris.

1957 Jack Kerouac publishes *On the Road*. The Southern Christian Leadership Conference is organized. Ghana becomes an independent state. The Civil Rights Act of 1957 establishes the

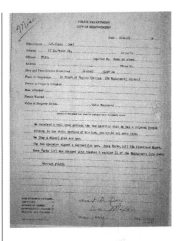

Police Report on the arrest of Rosa Parks (December 1, 1955). Courtesy of the National Archives and Records Administration.

Civil Rights Commission. Nine African American students at Little Rock High School, in Arkansas, are prevented from entering by the National Guard, prompting Eisenhower to send in federal troops to enforce desegregation orders.

1958 Chinua Achebe publishes *Things Fall Apart*. Arna Bontemps and Langston Hughes edit *The Book of Negro Folklore*. Guinea becomes an independent state.

1959 Lorraine Hansberry publishes *Raisin in the Sun*. Miles Davis records *Kind of Blue*. Fidel Castro assumes power in Cuba.

Dwight Eisenhower signing the Civil Rights Act of 1957. Courtesy of the Dwight D. Eisenhower Library.

1960   Harper Lee publishes *To Kill a Mockingbird*. Sit-in movement is initiated at a Woolworth lunch counter in Greensboro, North Carolina. The Student Non-Violent Coordinating Committee (SNCC) is organized. The Civil Rights Act of 1960 is passed by Congress. Numerous African countries achieve independence.

1961   Joseph Heller publishes *Catch 22*. John F. Kennedy is inaugurated as the thirty-fifth U.S. president. The United States launches the first astronaut into space. Frantz Fanon dies. The Berlin Wall is erected. Bay of Pigs.

1962   Edward Albee publishes *Who's Afraid of Virginia Woolf?* W. E. B. Du Bois dies. The Cuban Missile Crisis. Algeria wins independence from France. Race riots in Mississippi, following the admission of James Meredith to the University of Mississippi.

Eisenhower meets with Martin Luther King Jr. (left) and A. Philip Randolph (right) in the Oval Office on June 23, 1958. Courtesy of the National Archives and Records Administration.

awarded the Nobel Peace Prize. The Civil Rights Act of 1964 abolishes segregation in public accommodations throughout the South. Widespread race riots. Nelson Mandela is sentenced to life imprisonment in South Africa.

1965 Malcolm X and Alex Haley publish *The Autobiography of Malcolm X*. Amiri Baraka initiates the Black Arts movement. Race riots in Watts, Los Angeles. Malcolm X is assassinated. LBJ signs the Voting Rights Act. The United States sends troops to help the South Vietnamese government.

1963 LeRoi Jones publishes *Blues People*. Martin Luther King writes "Letter from Birmingham Jail." JFK is assassinated. Medgar Evers, head of the NAACP in Mississippi, is assassinated. The March on Washington culminates in Martin Luther King's "I Have a Dream" speech. Lyndon Johnson (LBJ) is inaugurated as the thirty-sixth U.S. president.

1964 LeRoi Jones/Amiri Baraka publishes *Dutchman*. Ralph Ellison publishes *Shadow and Act*. Martin Luther King Jr. is

Martin Luther King at the March on Washington, D.C., June 28, 1963. Courtesy of the National Archives and Records Administration.

1969   Half a million gather at a rock concert near Woodstock, New York. The Stonewall Riots mark the beginning of the gay liberation movement. Richard Nixon is inaugurated as the thirty-seventh U.S. president.

1972   Start of the Watergate scandal. Eleven Israeli athletes are murdered at the Munich Olympics.

Malcolm X waits at Martin Luther King press conference (March 26, 1964). Photograph by Marion S. Trikosko. Courtesy of the Library of Congress.

1966   James Meredith, the first black student admitted to the University of Mississippi, is shot (but not killed).

1967   Heavyweight boxing champion Muhammad Ali is arrested for refusing induction after being denied conscientious objector status (April 28). Boxing officials strip him of his title.

1968   Martin Luther King Jr. is assassinated.

Eldridge Cleaver, minister of information for the Black Panther Party and presidential candidate for the Peace and Freedom Party, speaking at the Woods-Brown Outdoor Theatre, American University (1968). Photograph by Marion S. Trikosko. Courtesy of the Library of Congress.

**CAPITALISM PLUS DOPE
EQUALS GENOCIDE**
By Michael "Cetewayo" Tabor (Political Prisoner, NY 21)
BLACK PANTHER PARTY, U.S.A.

"Capitalism Plus Dope Equals Genocide," by Michael "Cetewayo" Tabor. Black Panther Party, c. 1970. Courtesty of the Michigan State University Library, Special Collections Division.

1974 Richard Nixon becomes the first president to resign his office. Gerald Ford becomes the thirty-eighth U.S. president.

1977 Jimmy Carter is inaugurated as the thirty-ninth U.S. president.

1981 Ronald Reagan is inaugurated as the fortieth U.S. president.

1984 Reagan is reelected to a second term.

1985 Sonia Sanchez receives an American Book Award for her poetry collection *homegirls and handgrenades.* August Wilson's play *Fences* is produced and published.

1987 Toni Morrison publishes *Beloved.* Rita Dove is awarded a Pulitzer Prize for her poetry collection *Thomas and Beulah.* August Wilson receives a Pulitzer Prize for *Fences.* Public Enemy releases their debut album *Yo! Bum Rush the Show.*

Bibliographic Essay

The Price of the Ticket:
Baldwin Criticism in Perspective

Carol E. Henderson

> I believe that Baldwin's fate in literary
> history is more complex, and that it
> rests upon his refusal to attach himself
> to any single ideology, literary form,
> or vision.
> — D. Quentin Miller, *Re-viewing
> James Baldwin* (2000)

Baldwin's literary career is phenomenal. He published over twenty-two books, numerous essays and commentaries in magazines and newspapers, book reviews, and interviews. Across every piece of the global continental community, Baldwin has left a part of himself in the vivid syllables of the language he uses to speak the human condition. This condition—tormented by what he saw as the inconceivable arrogance of man's inhumanity to man—drives Baldwin to exclaim with brutal clarity in one of his earlier works, "the story of Americans... is not a very pretty story: the story of a people is never very pretty" (*Notes of a Native Son* 24).

Baldwin's willingness to tackle the perverse shadows of racism and classism, of gender and sexual oppression in the Americas puts him at the margins of a society grappling with the darkness of its own estrangement from itself. The chaos of the American psychology, its unwillingness to accept the reality of its social thinking toward the disenfranchised, the marginalized, the poor, and black means—as Baldwin would remark in *The Fire Next Time* (1963)—"a bill is coming in that I fear America is not prepared to pay" (378). Baldwin's prophetic message, contained in the annals of his plays, poems, essays, and fiction, constitutes his willingness to offset this debt. As he concludes, "If we—and now I mean the relatively conscious whites and the relatively conscious blacks, who must, like lovers, insist on, or create, the consciousness of the others—do not falter in our duty now, we may be able, handful that we are, to end the racial nightmare, and achieve our country, and change the history of the world" (*Price of the Ticket* 379).

But the price Baldwin would pay for this debt was high, and it is very evident in the critical reception of his work. As D. Quentin Miller concludes in the introduction to *Re-viewing James Baldwin*, Baldwin's literary career—while fleshed out in documentaries and biographical portraits or admired in anecdotal reflections by famous people and literary dignitaries—still remains unjustly overlooked (3). Baldwin's uneasy alliance with the press and with critics alike has as much to do with the rhetorical strategies within his work as it does with the boldness with which he speaks his literary subjects. Moreover, Baldwin's literary journey, shaped by the artistic vision of the tumultuous 1960s and 1970s, stands as a testament to the governmental and social pressures of a country intent on silencing dissent. Baldwin's well-known FBI file is full of "the symbolic consequences of the spectacular conditions of (gay) black male subjectivity," according to Maurice Wallace, and the bureau's obsessive tracking of Baldwin's international travels ("Jimmy's FBEye Blues," 140). Additionally, J. Edgar Hoover's compulsive curiosity about not only Baldwin's subject matters in his books (*Another Country* and *The Fire Next Time* among others), but also his sexual life and the sexual lives of other black men in general, led Wallace to determine that Baldwin's FBI file reveals, in the end, the systematic attempt to criminalize, indeed "'frame' the black male body . . . for the visual pleasures of whites" (139).

What is most relevant in assessing the critical reception of Baldwin's literary opus in light of these comments rests in the ways in which Baldwin's written works have been "framed" in the archives of literary studies both here and abroad. Baldwin's international appeal is striking. He has been studied for over forty years in France, Germany, and elsewhere; in France, according to critic Rosa Bobia, Baldwin is the most intensely studied post-war writer of African descent from any nation since Richard Wright. Such international interest merits, in her estimation, "systematic analysis" that does not relegate Baldwin studies to purely an American phenomenon, but that considers, to a large degree, the international context of Baldwin's work and influence (1). A number of Baldwin's works have been translated into other languages. Professors Yoshinobu Hakutani and Toru Kiuchi reveal, for example, that in Japan, *Another Country* was the most popular of Baldwin's novels. It was translated into Japanese in 1964, and reprinted twice in 1977 and 1980. *The Fire Next Time* was also translated into Japanese, but in 1963, and reprinted in 1968. Likewise "Sonny's Blues" and "Come Out the Wilderness" have been translated and reprinted as well ("Critical Reception of James Baldwin" 753). The same can be said for other countries like France, Italy, Spain, Africa, and various parts of Europe. Thus, the critical response to Baldwin's work must be understood in terms of not only the major historical moments that produced them in the United States (i.e., the Civil Rights Movement of the 1950s and 1960s, the Feminist Movement of the 1970s, and the Gay Power Movement of the 1980s and 1990s), but also the major theoretical synergies that continue to bring Baldwin's work to the forefront of American thought and world culture (i.e., African/Africana studies, African American studies, Caribbean studies, foreign languages and literatures, American studies, ethnic and/or cultural studies, film studies, and gender studies).

It should also be said that one could ascertain Baldwin's work in terms of the genres in which he wrote—plays, poetry, short stories, essays, and fiction—but such categorizations may focus more on style than on content, thereby miniaturizing Baldwin's creative gestures at "witnessing" about the truths of America's race relations. This alliance, a self-imposed covenant Baldwin shared with his reading public, meant that he was willing to speak the truth in whatever form necessary to enact change. This chapter will not only consider the phases of Baldwin's work wherein he spoke these truths, but also contextualize the critical reception of Baldwin's truth sayings across the myriad of cultural moments and social movements that are reflectively sketched in his work.

For manageability, I have chosen not to rework the critical terrain so aptly covered by my colleagues Fred L. Standley, Nancy V. Burt, Therman B. O'Daniel, David Leeming, Rosa Bobia, Jakob J. Kollhofer, and James Campbell. Each has produced stellar reference guides, bibliographies, and critical evaluations of Baldwin's work in the United States, France, and German up to the early 1990s. Standley, in particular, produced a very useful critical reference guide of writings (reviews and articles) about James Baldwin's primary texts from 1946 to 1978 entitled *James Baldwin: A Reference Guide*. In 1988, he and Nancy Burt followed that critical volume with *Critical Essays on James Baldwin*, another collection of essays on Baldwin's work that covers everything from Baldwin's role as an activist, artist, and "disturber of the peace" to his character development in his dramas and fiction. Standley and Burt's volume has a useful introduction that divides the critical reception of Baldwin's work into the following periods: (1) the early response to Baldwin's literary works published in the 1950s (primarily *Go Tell It on the Mountain* [1953], *Notes of a Native Son* [1955], and *Giovanni's Room* [1956]); (2) the 1960s and 1970s, which saw Baldwin publish sixteen creative works (four novels, five essay collections, two dialogues with other critics, two plays, one collection of short stories, one children's book, and one screenplay); and (3) the 1980s, which saw Baldwin publish three last works. I will begin my assessment of the critical reception of Baldwin's work with an overview of scholarship during these three periods. I will end by positing a fourth period, which I term the Baldwin Renaissance, the steady reclamation of Baldwin's work by black intellectuals and critics alike during the 1990s and beyond. Baldwin criticism in the four decades in which he wrote was definitely driven by the continuing literary production of the artist, but Baldwin's death did not dissipate the critical consideration of his work—as will be shown in our discussion of the Baldwin Renaissance. In this fourth period, certain continuities with earlier phases of Baldwin criticism are evident, as are the theoretical, critical, and cultural concerns of those charged with (re)viewing Baldwin's writing. Such elisions across time and space may make this exercise provocatively arbitrary. Yet it is in these capricious markers of critical inquiry that a discernible pattern of Baldwin scholarship reveals itself, evolving into a meaningful blueprint of Baldwin study.

When Baldwin published *Go Tell It on the Mountain* in 1953, little did he know that this work would become a foundational piece for Baldwin criticism. Baldwin had already established himself as an essayist and reviewer with the publications of "Maxim Gorki as Artist" (*Nation*, April 12, 1947), "Everybody's Protest Novel" (*Zero*, Spring 1949), "Many Thousands Gone" (*Partisan Review*, November-December 1951), "The Negro in Paris" (*The Reporter*, June 1950), and "Journey to Atlanta" (*The New Leader*, October 1948). Criticism on Baldwin's semiautobiographical first novel has been consistent for over fifty years, with numerous articles, dissertations, and book chapters examining the social significance of a book steeped in the cultural fervor of black religiosity. Bruce Cook in "Writers in Midstream" (1963) calls it "the most perfect Negro novel published in America" (35), while David Littlejohn in *Black on White* (1966) calls it Baldwin's "baptism of fire," a novel in which he (Baldwin) comes to terms with his boyhood experiences in a way that is vividly personal and transcending (72). Robert Lashley (2005) goes so far to say that "even in the realm of prodigious American literary giants, Baldwin casts a palpable shadow" with his "one and only truly brilliant work of fiction"(1).

Yet other critics felt that *Go Tell It on the Mountain* was a somewhat morbid reflection of the black family, and that the primary technical flaw of the book, as critic Riley Hughes argues in "Novels Reviewed" "is its striving after 'poetic effect' when the language of revivalism is not everybody's language" (393). J. Saunders Redding, a well-known critic and writer of the 1950s and 1960s, believed the novel was burdened with questions of black subjectivity and identity that continue to plague Baldwin's writing throughout his career ("James Baldwin Miscellany," 4), although Redding would later say that it was Baldwin's first and best novel ("Since Richard Wright" 21). Writer Wallace Graves goes so far as to question whether Baldwin is a major novelist, arguing that *Go Tell It on the Mountain*, while praised by most critics, may have been prematurely elevated to the status of creative prominence based on a clouded politeness "engendered by Caucasian guilt," and a need to fill an "experiential void in Negro life" ("Question of Moral Energy" 215). Regardless of the initial reception, Baldwin's literary stature grew steadily after the publication of *Go Tell It on the Mountain* as well as his collection of essays *Notes of a Native Son* (1955), *Nobody Knows My Name* (1961), and *The Fire Next Time* (1963). Respectively, these works sold over five hundred thousand, two million, and one million copies in the last quarter of the previous century—not an easy feat for a man bold in his assessment of America's social injustices, whom Fred L. Standley, Nancy V. Burt, and Benjamin De Mott consider indispensable to the revolutionary culture of the 1960s.

Baldwin's international appeal is driven as much by his acutely honest and paradoxical reflections of race relations in America as it is his indictment of man's inhumanity to man. Creative genius Sterling Brown credits Baldwin with belonging to the paperback revolution of the 1950s and 1960s, a movement spurred on by the likes of the Beat Generation's subculture and the social unrest of the 1960s ("A Century of Negro Portraiture" 74). Baldwin published *Notes of a Native Son* around the time that Allen Ginsberg published *Howl* (1956) and Jack Kerouac published *On the Road* (1957). This subculture of nonconformist and bohemian hedonists gave voice to the American angst of the time, as did Baldwin's narratives. Critic Clarence Major declares Baldwin is the "greatest American essayist since Ralph Waldo Emerson" ("James Baldwin" 73). With the publications of *Another Country* (1962), *The Fire Next Time* (1963), *Giovanni's Room* (1956), *Nobody Knows My Name* (1961), *The Devil Finds Work* (1976), and *Going to Meet the Man* (1965), Baldwin established his international reputation. He was thrust into the spotlight as

America's black spokesman. His writings, although personal to some, gave voice to the social revolutionariness of black intellectualism prevalent in the 1960s, framing what critic Leslie A. Fiedler calls "literary anthropolitical(ism)" ("Caliban or Hamlet" 23). This approach, a creative reinvention of nationalism and nativism, based its philosophy on the "experiences and values, the attitudes and idioms" of a mixture of ethnic and cultural groups. Unique and controversial, it reordered the American literary landscape of the 1960s, causing writers of all races to deal with the Caliban-Hamlet paradox at the heart of European American and African American cultural relations. This paradox reflects the dilemma of the dispossessed sons of America. That is, Hamlet—and more specifically his melancholy—represents those inherited histories and social commitments tied to the ideals of race in this country. Caliban is the monstrous Other—the African American son—who needs to be reshaped into a respectable citizen. Baldwin's literary reflections speak to this moral dilemma from Caliban's perspective, laying before the nation its hypocrisies. (23).

The cultural shifts of the 1970s and 1980s found the role of Baldwin and his work resituated and saddled with the responsibilities of the feminist movement and the economic complexities of poverty and Reaganomics. Many critics continued to focus their critiques of Baldwin on his essays, overlooking the significance of his novels and plays. Trudier Harris's *Black Women in the Fiction of James Baldwin* (1985) was a landmark for its treatment of a topic scarcely covered in previous studies. Harris found Baldwin's treatment of women lacking and one dimensional in his earlier works, but sees a progression in the conceptual view of women as wives, mothers, sisters, and lovers. However, the "nature" of black women in Baldwin's fiction is always subservient to the prominence of black male characters in the novels. As Jordan writes in her 1974 review of *If Beale Street Could Talk*, Baldwin's female narrator is not believable and, instead, reminds the reader of a inane man with no particular voice or purpose (33). Such assessments complicate the virtue of Baldwin's work. In some instances, these assessments do not leave room for other creative feminist readings of Baldwin's work. It should be noted that Harris's book is the last single-authored study to discuss each of James Baldwin's novels.

Although Baldwin continued to write well into the 1980s, reviews such as those by Jordan, Harris, Redding, and Hughes continued to alter his public role as activist and champion of human rights. Moreover, critics found Baldwin's later work inconsistent with the literary promise of his previous work. In "The Divided Mind of James Baldwin"(1979) for example, C. W. E. Bigsby found Baldwin double-minded, a "telling parabola . . . of contradictions" who was once "an articulate spokesman for black revolt, now living an expatriate existence in southern France" (94). Bigsby's comments direct attention to the complex critical conundrum Baldwin found himself in as an international citizen. Baldwin's novels were both lionized and criticized for their political and social impotence both here and abroad. His novels were summarily compared to the fiction of both Richard Wright and Chester Himes, whose focus on the social and political ills of America's economic systems differed starkly from Baldwin's portrayal of oppression in *Go Tell It on the Mountain*. As one French critic writes, Baldwin seems more interested in "the moral misery of men than by their social concerns. It seems that he did not know how to reconcile that moral misery and the state of material destitution and physical suffering. Nor [does] he understand the nature of alienation, of certain deprivations" (Sainville 177). Comments such as these reveal a portion of the African French response to Baldwin, but by no means defines the whole. Baldwin's transatlantic appeal certainly put him at odds with those individuals who felt he had abandoned not only the French and African Negritude movement of the 1950s and 1960s, but also the idealistic promise of his American country. But Baldwin has always been clear about his role as a writer: "I am a witness. That's my responsibility. I write it all down" (Georgkas 665).

It is this energy that has continued to undergird the next phase of Baldwin criticism, what I term the Baldwin Renaissance. From the 1990s into the present, over one hundred articles, book chapters, as well as a number of books dissertations have considered the significance of Baldwin as a transatlantic commuter and a political, social, and cultural writer. As Dwight McBride makes clear in the introduction to his seminal volume *James Baldwin Now* (1999), Baldwin's work is key to "understanding many of our contemporary societal problems" (1). Many of these issues, cloaked in the unrelenting strictures of race, class, gender, and sexuality, are explored in Baldwin's writing. Whether or not you agree with his assessment of the world, Baldwin's persistence at unlayering the traditional modes of literary training in the academy found a ready audience in a host of approaches during the height of interdisciplinary studies and the revolution of the cultural studies movement. This intersection allowed critics to consider Baldwin's views on homosexuality, gender, and race in ways that did not diminish the political impetus of his writing. As McBride concludes, "Baldwin was no more content to be simply a black writer, a gay writer, or an activist than he was to write exclusively in the genres of the novel, drama, poetry, or the essay. Baldwin was, continues to be, many things to many people" (2). This multiplicity of intersecting ideals has writers like Rosa Bobia considering the critical reception of Baldwin in France and writers like Rebecca Aanerud and Lawrie Balfour ascertaining Baldwin's critique of white liberalism and race consciousness in the new millennium.

Baldwin's body of work is expansive. Quincy Troupe, Toni Morrison, and others believe Baldwin published approximately 6,895 pages of material in his lifetime (Troupe 76). To these can be added the numerous interviews and film and visual documentaries that bear Baldwin's imprint. Such an outpouring of creativity warrants our most careful attention. Baldwin's gifts—multiple and vast—meant that he was unwilling to allow America to stay comfortable in its ignorant haze. Baldwin's contributions to humankind meant that he was willing to pay a price to free mind, body, and spirit. How we honor these gifts will depend on the numerous ways we respond to the witnessing in Baldwin's work.

WORKS BY JAMES BALDWIN

The Amen Corner. New York: Dial Press, 1968.

5 *Another Country.* New York: Dial Press, 1962.

Blues for Mister Charlie. New York: Dial Press, 1964.

The Devil Finds Work: An Essay. New York: Dial Press, 1976.

The Evidence of Things Not Seen. New York: Holt, Rinehart, & Winston, 1985.

6 *The Fire Next Time.* New York: Dial Press, 1963.

3 *Giovanni's Room.* New York: Dial Press, 1956.

Going to Meet the Man. New York: Dial Press, 1965.

2 *Go Tell It on the Mountain.* New York: Alfred A. Knopf, 1953.

9 *If Beale Street Could Talk.* New York: Dial Press, 1974.

James Baldwin: Collected Essays. Edited by Toni Morrison. New York: Library of America, 1998.

James Baldwin: Early Novels and Stories. Edited by Toni Morrison. New York: Library of America, 1998.

Jimmy's Blues. New York: St. Martin's, 1985. (British edition published in 1983).

10 *Just Above My Head.* New York: Dial Press, 1979.

Little Man, Little Man: A Story of Childhood. Illustrated by Yoran Cazac. New York: Dial Press, 1976.

H *Nobody Knows My Name: More Notes of a Native Son.* New York: Dial Press, 1961.

8 *No Name in the Street.* New York: Dial Press, 1972.

1 *Notes of a Native Son.* Boston: Beacon Press, 1955.

Nothing Personal. With photographs by Richard Avedon. New York: Atheneum, 1964.

One Day When I Was Lost: A Scenario Based on Alex Haley's The Autobiography of Malcolm X. London: Michael Joseph, 1972.

The Price of the Ticket: Collected Nonfiction, 1948–1985. New York: St. Martin's/Marek, 1985.

7 *Tell Me How Long the Train's Been Gone.* New York: Dial Press, 1968.

POSTHUMOUS WORKS

Gypsies and Other Poems. Edition limited to 325 copies. Leeds, Mass.: Gehenna Press/Eremite Press, 1989.

SELECTED CRITICAL BIBLIOGRAPHY

Works cited in this chapter can be found in the following bibliographic list.

Collections of Essays

Chametzky, Jules, ed. *Black Writers Redefine the Struggle: A Tribute to James Baldwin.* Amherst: University of Massachusetts Press, 1989.

Harris, Trudier, ed. *New Essays on* Go Tell It on the Mountain. New York: Cambridge University Press, 1996.

Henderson, Carol E., ed. *James Baldwin's* Go Tell It on the Mountain: *Historical and Critical Essays.* New York: Peter Lang, 2006.

King, Lovalerie, and Lynn Orilla Scott, eds. *James Baldwin and Toni Morrison: Comparative Critical and Theoretical Essays.* New York: Palgrave Macmillan, 2006.

Kollhofer, Jakob, ed. *James Baldwin: His Place in American Literary History and His Reception in Europe.* New York: Peter Lang, 1991.

McBride, Dwight A., ed. *James Baldwin Now.* New York: New York University Press, 1999.

Miller, D. Quentin, ed. *Re-Viewing James Baldwin: Things Not Seen.* Philadelphia: Temple University Press, 2000.

O'Daniel, Therman B., ed. *James Baldwin: A Critical Evaluation.* Washington, D.C.: Howard University Press, 1977.

Standley, Fred L., and Nancy V. Burt, eds. *Critical Essays on James Baldwin.* Boston: G. K. Hall, 1988.

Special Issues of Journals

College Language Association Journal 42.4 (June 1999).

Middle Atlantic Writers Association Review 19.1 (June 2004)—*James Baldwin's* Go Tell it on The Mountain *50 years later.*

Presence Africaine: Revue Culturelle du Monde Noir / Cultural Review of the Negro World 145 (1988)—*Tributes to James Baldwin.*

Parts and Chapters of Books

Auger, Phillip. *Native Sons in No Man Land: Rewriting Afro-American Manhood in the Novels of Baldwin, Walker, Wideman, and Gaines.* New York: Garland Publishers, 2000. Chapter 1, pp. 15–28.

Beemyn, Brett. "To Say 'Yes to Life': Sexual and Gender Fluidity in James Baldwin's *Giovanni's Room* and *Another Country*." In *Bisexual Men in Culture and Society*, edited by Erich Steinman and Brett Beemyn. New York: Harrington Park, 2002. 55–72.

Beliele, Kelvin. "The Prophetic Burden: James Baldwin as a Latter-Day Jeremiah." In *The Gift of Story: Narrating Hope in a Post-Modern World*. Waco, Tex.: Baylor University Press, 2006. 187–206.

Blair, Sara. "Photo-Text Capital: James Baldwin, Richard Avedon, and the Uses of Harlem." In *Harlem Crossroads: Black Writers and the Photograph in the Twentieth Century*. Princeton, N.J.: Princeton University Press, 2007. 192–238.

Butler, Cheryl B. "James Baldwin: Voice of Prophecy." In *The Art of the Black Essay: From Meditation to Transcendence*. New York: Routledge, 2003. 58–80.

Clark, Keith. *Black Manhood in James Baldwin, Ernest J. Gaines, and August Wilson*. Urbana: University of Illinois Press, 2002. Ch. 2, pp. 30–64.

Cobb, Michael L. "James Baldwin and His Queer, Religious Words." In *God Hates Fags: The Rhetorics of Religious Violence*. New York: New York University Press, 2006. 53–78.

Field, Douglas. "Passing as a Cold War Novel: Anxiety and Assimilation in James Baldwin's *Giovanni's Room*." In *American Cold War Culture*, edited by Douglas Field. Edinburgh: Edinburgh University Press, 2005. 88–105.

Gounard, Jean-François. *The Racial Problem in the Works of Richard Wright and James Baldwin*. Westport, Conn.: Greenwood Press, 1992. Chs. 6–10, pp. 149–256.

Hakutani, Yoshinobu. "No Name in the Street: James Baldwin's Exploration of American Urban Culture." In *Cross-Cultural Visions in African American Modernism: From Spatial Narrative to Jazz Haiku*. Columbus: Ohio State University Press, 2006. 60–71.

———. "If Beale Street Could Talk: Baldwin's Search for Love and Identity." In *Cross-Cultural Visions in African American Modernism: From Spatial Narrative to Jazz Haiku*. Columbus: Ohio State University Press, 2006. 72–82.

Harris-Lopez, Trudier. "Slanting the Truth: Homosexuality, Manhood, and Race in James Baldwin's *Giovanni's Room*." In *South of Tradition: Essays on African American Literature*. Athens: University of Georgia Press, 2002. 18–30.

Henderson, Mae G. "James Baldwin's *Giovanni's Room*: Expatriation, 'Racial Drag,' and Homosexual Panic." In *Black Queer Studies: A Critical Anthology*, edited by Patrick Johnson and Mae G. Henderson. Durham, N.C.: Duke University Press, 2005. 298–322.

Ikard, David. "Black Patriarchy and the Dilemma of Black Women's Complicity in James Baldwin's *Go Tell It on the Mountain*." In *Breaking the Silence: Toward a Black Male Feminist Criticism*. Baton Rouge: Louisiana State University Press, 2007. 49–80.

Jimoh, A. Yemisi. "Jazz Me Blues: Reading Music in James Baldwin's 'Sonny's Blues'." In *Spiritual, Blues, and Jazz People in African American Fiction: Living in Paradox*. Knoxville: University of Tennessee Press, 2002.

Johnson-Roullier, Cyraina E. *Reading on the Edge: Exiles, Modernities, and Cultural Transformation in Proust, Joyce, and Baldwin*. Albany: State University of New York Press, 2000.

Jothiprakash, R. *Commitment as a Theme in African American Literature: A Study of James Baldwin and Ralph Ellison*. Bristol, Ind.: Wyndham Hall Press, 1994. Chs. 3–4, pp. 56–114.

Lewis, Leslie W. "*Philadelphia Fire* and *The Fire Next Time*: Wideman Responds to Baldwin." In *Critical Essays on John Edgar Wideman*, edited by Bonnie TuSmity and Keith Eldon Byerman. Knoxville: University of Tennessee Press, 2006. 145–59.

Major, Clarence. "James Baldwin: A Fire in the Mind." In *The Dark and Feeling: Black American Writers and Their Work*. New York: Joseph Okpalca, 1974. 73–83.

Malburne, Meredith M. "No Blues for Mister Henry: Locating Richard's Revolution." In *Reading Contemporary African American Drama: Fragments of History, Fragments of Self*, edited by Trudier Harris and Jennifer Larson. New York: Peter Lang, 2007.

Margolies, Edward. "Struggles for Space: Stephen Crane, James Baldwin, Ann Petry, Bernard Malamud." In *New York and the Literary Imagination: The City in Twentieth Century Fiction and Drama*. Jefferson, N.C.: McFarland, 2008.

McBride, Dwight. "Straight Black Studies: On African American Studies, James Baldwin, and Black Queer Studies." In *Black Queer Studies: A Critical Anthology*, edited by E. Patrick Johnson and Mae G. Henderson. Durham, N.C.: Duke University Press, 2005. 68–89.

Pavlić, Edward M. "Follow Me into a Solo: Jazz, History, and Reckoning with Diasporic Dissociation in James Baldwin and David Bradley." In *Crossroads Modernism: Descent and Emergence in African American Literary Culture.* Minneapolis: University of Minnesota Press, 2002. 244–86.

Walker, Will. "After The Fire Next Time: James Baldwin's Postconsensus Double Bind." In *Is It Nation Time? Contemporary Essays on Black Power and Black Nationalism,* edited by Eddie S. Glaude, Jr. Chicago: University of Chicago Press, 2002. 215–33.

Wallace, Maurice O. "On Being a Witness: Passion, Pedagogy, and the Legacy of James Baldwin." In *Black Queer Studies: A Critical Anthology,* edited by E. Patrick Johnson and Mae G. Henderson. Durham, N.C.: Duke University Press, 2005. 276–86.

———. "'I'm not entirely what I look like': Richard Wright, James Baldwin, and the Hegemony of Vision: or, Jimmy's FBEye Blues." In *Constructing the Black Masculine: Identity and Ideality in African American Literature and Culture 1775–1995.* Durham, N.C.: Duke University Press, 2002. 133–146. Appeared in a different version in *James Baldwin Now. Ed. McBride (1999), pp. 289–306.*

Books

Balfour, Lawrie. *The Evidence of Things Not Said: James Baldwin and the Promise of American Democracy.* Ithaca, N.Y.: Cornell University Press, 2001.

Bobia, Rosa. *The Critical Reception of James Baldwin in France.* New York: Peter Lang, 1997.

Boyd, Herb. *Baldwin's Harlem: A Biography of James Baldwin.* New York: Atria Books, 2008.

Campbell, James. *Talking at the Gates: A Life of James Baldwin.* Berkeley: University of California Press, 1991.

———. *Exiled in Paris: Richard Wright, James Baldwin, Samuel Beckett and Others on the Left Bank.* New York: Scribner, 1995.

Champion, Ernest A. *Mr. Baldwin, I Presume: James Baldwin—Chinua Achebe, A Meeting of the Minds.* Landham, Md.: University Press of America, 1995.

Hardy, Clarence. *James Baldwin's God: Sex, Hope, and the Crisis in Black Holiness Culture.* Knoxville: University of Tennessee Press, 2003.

Harris, Trudier. *Black Women in the Fiction of James Baldwin.* Knoxville: University of Tennessee Press, 1985.

Lee, Robert A. *James Baldwin: Climbing to the Light.* New York: St. Martin's, 1991.

Leeming, David A. *James Baldwin: A Biography.* New York: Knopf, 1994.

Littlejohn, David. *Black on White: A Critical Survey of Writing by American Negroes.* New York: Grossman, 1966. 72–74, 110–37.

Porter, Horace A. *Stealing the Fire: The Art and Protest of James Baldwin.* Middletown, Conn.: Wesleyan University Press, 1989.

Rusk, Lauren. *The Life Writing of Otherness: Woolf, Baldwin, Kingston, and Winterson.* New York: Routledge, 2002.

Scott, Lynn Orilla. *Witness to the Journey: James Baldwin's Later Fiction.* East Lansing: Michigan State University Press, 2002.

Standley, Fred L. and Nancy V. Standley. *James Baldwin: A Reference Guide.* Boston: G.K. Hall, 1980.

Sylvander, Carolyn Wedin. *James Baldwin.* New York: Ungar, 1980.

Troupe, Quincy. *James Baldwin: The Legacy.* New York: Simon & Schuster, 1989.

Weatherby, William J. *James Baldwin: Artist on Fire: A Portrait.* New York: D. I. Fine, 1989.

Zaborowska, Magdalena J. *James Baldwin's Turkish Decade: Erotics of Exile.* Durham, N.C.: Duke University Press, 2009.

Articles and Reviews

Bell, Matt. "Black Ground, Gay Figure: Working through *Another Country*, Black Power and Gay Liberation." *American Literature* 79.3 (September 2007): 577–603.

Bigsby, C. W. E. "The Divided Mind of James Baldwin." *Journal of American Studies* 13 (1979): 325–42. Reprinted in *Critical Essays on James Baldwin*, edited by Fred L. Standley and Nancy V. Burt. Boston: G. K. Hall, 1988. 94–111.

Brown, Sterling. "A Century of Negro Portraiture in American Literature." *Massachusetts Review* 7.4 (1966): 63–96.

Champion, Laurie. "Assimilation versus Celebration in James McPherson's 'The Story of a Dead Man' and James Baldwin's 'Sonny's Blues.'" *Short Story* 8.2 (Fall 2000): 94–106.

Cook, Bruce. "Writers in Midstream: John Williams and James." *Critic* 21 (February/March 1963): 35–40.

Corber, Robert J. "Everybody Knew His Name: Reassessing James Baldwin." *Contemporary Literature* 42.1 (Spring 2001): 166–75.

Davis, Nicholas K. "Go Tell It on the Stage: *Blues for Mister Charlie* as Dialectical Drama." *Journal of American Drama and Theatre* 17.2 (Spring 2005): 30–42.

Field, Douglas. "Looking for Jimmy Baldwin: Sex, Piracy, and Black Nationalist Fervor." *Callaloo* 27.2 (Spring 2004): 457–80.

Fielder, Leslie A. "Caliban or Hamlet: An American Paradox." *Encounter* 26 (April 1966): 23–27.

Georgkas, Dan. "James Baldwin...in Conversation," Abraham Chapman, ed. New York: New American Library, 1968. Page 665 is the original citation in note 3 of the Standley and Pratt edited collection *Conversations with James Baldwin* (Jackson: University of Mississippi Press), vii.

Graves, Wallace. "The Question of Moral Energy in James Baldwin's *Go Tell It on the Mountain*." *College Language Association Journal* 7 (March 1964): 215–23.

Hakutani, Yoshinobu and Toru Kiuchi. "The Critical Reception of James Baldwin in Japan: An Annotated Bibliography. *Black American Literature Forum* 25.4 (Winter, 1991): 753–779.

Hughes, Riley. "Novels Reviewed." *Catholic World* 177 (August 1953): 393.

Jordan, June. "If Beale Street Could Talk." *Village Voice* (June 20, 1974): 33–35.

Kramer, Lloyd. "James Baldwin in Paris: Exile, Multiculturalism, and the Public Intellectual." *Historical Reflections/Re'flexions Historiques* 27.1 (Spring 2001): 27–47.

Lashley, Robert. *BC: Blogcritics Magazine* (November 30, 2005): 1–5.

Lee, Susanna. "The Jazz Harmonies of Connection and Disconnection in 'Sonny's Blues.'" *Genre* 37.2 (Summer 2004): 285–300.

Miller, Elise. "The 'Maw of Western Culture': James Baldwin and the Anxieties of Influence." *African American Review* 38.4 (Winter 2004): 625–36.

Moon, Sahng Young. "African Americans and Colonialism: James Baldwin's Essays in the Era of the Civil Rights Movement." *Journal of English Language and Literature*. 47.4 (Winter 2001): 941–57.

Nabers, Deak. "Past Using: James Baldwin and Civil Rights Law in the 1960s." *Yale* 18.2 (Fall 2005): 221–42.

Norman, Brian. "James Baldwin's Confrontation with U.S. Imperialism in *If Beale Street Could Talk*." *MultiEthnic Literatures of the United States* 32.1 (Spring 2007): 119–38.

———. "Crossing Identitarian Lines: Women's Liberation and James Baldwin's Early Essays." *Women's Studies* 35.3 (2006): 241–64.

———. "Reading a 'Closet Screenplay': Hollywood, James Baldwin's Malcolms and the Threat of Historical Irrelevance." *African American Review* 39.1–2 (Spring/Summer): 103–18.

Nowlin, Michael. "Ralph Ellison, James Baldwin, and the Liberal Imagination." *Arizona Quarterly* 60.2 (Summer 2004): 117–40.

O'Hara, Daniel T. "Toward Global Democracy: James and the Stoic Vision of Amor Fati." *Boundary 2* 33.3 (Fall 2006): 61–72.

Ohi, Kevin. "'I'm Not the Boy You Want': Sexuality, 'Race,' and Thwarted Revelation in Baldwin's *Another Country*." *African American Review* 33.2 (Summer 1999): 261–81.

Pavlić, Ed. "I Just Don't Know How to Move on Your Word: From Signifyin(g) to Syndetic Homage in James Baldwin's Responses to William Faulkner." *Mississippi Quarterly* 53.4 (Fall 2000): 515–31.

Powers, Kerry. "The Treacherous Body: Isolation, Confession, and Community in James Baldwin." *American Literature* 77.4 (December 2005): 787–813.

Redding, J. Saunders. "Since Richard Wright." *African Forum* 1 (Spring 1966): 21–23.

———. "James Baldwin Miscellany." *New York Herald Tribune Book Review* (February 26, 1956): 4.

Reid, Robert. "The Powers of Darkness in 'Sonny Blues.'" *College Language Association Journal* 43.4 (June 2000): 443–53.

Robinson, Angelo R. "The Other Proclamation in James Baldwin's *Go Tell It on the Mountain*." *College Language Association Journal* 48.3 (March 2005): 336–51.

Ryan, Katy. "Falling in Public: Larsen's *Passing*, McCarthy's *The Group*, and Baldwin's *Another Country*." *Studies in the Novel* 36.1 (Spring 2004): 95–119.

Sainville, Leonard. *Anthologie de la literature negro africaine I: romancier et conteur* (Paris: Présence africaine, 1963): 177. As quoted in Rosa Bobia's *The Critical Reception of James Baldwin in France*.

Stuckey, Sterling. "Foreshadowings and Fulfillment: The Ring Shout, the Blues and Jazz in the Works of Douglass, Melville, and Baldwin." *Letterature d' America: Rivista Trimestrale* 21.86 (2001): 45–61.

Tackach, James. "The Biblical Foundation of James Baldwin's 'Sonny Blues.'" *Renascence: Essays on Values in Literature* 59.2 (Winter 2007): 109–18.

Wright, David. "No Hiding Place: Exile 'Underground' in James Baldwin's 'This Morning, This Evening, So Soon.'" *College Language Association Journal* 42.4 (June 1999): 445–61.

Interviews and Conversations with James Baldwin (National and International)

Astre, Georges-Albert. "Meeting with James Baldwin." *Lettres françaises,* 1047 (September 30, 1964): 1, 4.

Baggett, James. "Going to Meet the Man: An Interview with James Baldwin." *New York Native* (December 21, 1987): 20–23.

Bobia, Rosa. "The James Baldwin Interview." In *The Critical Reception of James Baldwin in France,* by Rosa Bobia. New York: Peter Lang, 1997. 69–71.

Combettes, Jean-Marie. "Meeting with James Baldwin." *Les Masques* 12 (Winter 1981).

Conversations with James Baldwin. Edited by Fred Standley and Louis H. Pratt. Jackson: University Press of Mississippi, 1989.

Duflot, Jean. "An Interview with James Baldwin Concerning 'No Name in the Street.'" *Politique hebdomadaire* (May 18, 1972): 21–22.

Estes, David C. "An Interview with James Baldwin." *New Orleans Review* 13.3 (1986): 59–64.

Fossey, Jean-Michel. "An Interview with James Baldwin." *Combat* (August 10, 1972): 6.

Gates Jr., Henry Louis "An Interview with Josephine Baker and James Baldwin." *Southern Review* 21.3 (1985): 594–602.

Giovanni, Nikki. *A Dialogue.* Philadelphia: J. B. Lippincott, 1973.

Goldstein, Richard. "Go the Way Your Blood Beats: An Interview with James Baldwin." In *James Baldwin: The Legacy,* edited by Quincy Troupe. New York: Touchstone/Simon & Schuster, 1989. 173–85.

Hadley-Garcia, George. "Removing Barriers: To James Baldwin, the Goal is 'To Sail Through Life on at Least One Smooth Tide of Unity.'" *New York Native* (October 14, 1985): 28.

Holloway, Clayton G. "When a Pariah Becomes a Celebrity: An Interview with James Baldwin." *Xavier Review* 7.1 (1987): 1–10.

"James Baldwin: Racism Has the Same Origin Everywhere, Slavery." *L'Unite'* (January 24, 1986): 34–36.

Karmel. "James Baldwin: Discovers the Orient." *Combat* (March 3, 1970).

Leeming, David Adams. "An Interview with James Baldwin on Henry James." *Henry James Review* 8 (Fall 1986): 47–56.

Lescaut, Sonia. "James Baldwin: In France Your Color Does Not Stick to Your Skin." *Arts, Lettres, Spectacles* (September 30, 1964): 4.

Mead, Margaret. *A Rap on Race: James Baldwin and Margaret Mead.* Philadelphia: J. B. Lippincott, 1971.

Monga, Ce'lestin and Renaud de Rochebrune. "An Interview with James Baldwin: Freedom for Black Americans Will Make It Possible for the Liberation of Whites." *Jeune Afrique* (October 2, 1985): 60–63.

Pache, Andre' "An Interview with James Baldwin." I *La Voix protestante* (August 16, 1968): 1, 7.

Raynal, Patrick. "James Baldwin in Atlanta: I Have Been Terrified by the Souvenirs of My Youth." *Le Matin* (September 10, 1985).

Troupe, Quincy. "The Last Interview." In "James Baldwin, 1924–1987: A Tribute." *Essence* 18 (March 1988): 53, 114ff. Reprinted in *Conversations with James Baldwin,* edited by Fred L. Standley and Louis H. Pratt. Jackson: University Press of Mississippi, 1989.

Troupe, Quincy. "Last Testament: An Interview with James Baldwin." *Village Voice* (January 12, 1988): 36. Reprinted in *Conversations with James Baldwin,* edited by Fred L. Standley and Louis H. Pratt. Jackson: University Press of Mississippi, 1989.

"Vantage Point on America: An Interview with James Baldwin." *Mensuel* (January 1986).

Vianey, Michel. "James Baldwin Speaks." *L'Express* 637 (August 29, 1963): 8–9.

Films and Documentaries on James Baldwin

Biography: James Baldwin: Witness. Written and directed by Angie Corcetti and Helen Hood Scheer. Peter Jones Production, February 20, 2003.

Go Tell It on the Mountain. Directed by Stan Lathan. California: Monterey Video, 1985. Reissued on DVD, February 3, 2004.

I Heard it Through the Grapevine. Directed by Dick Fontaine and Pat Hartley. Living Archives, 1982.

James Baldwin. Produced by Jerry Baber and Amy A. Tiehel. Directed by Amy A. Tiehel. Bela Cynwyd, Pa.: Schlessinger Video Production, 1994.

James Baldwin: From Another Place. Directed by Sedat Pakay, 1973.

James Baldwin's Harlem. Narrated and directed by James Baldwin. January 1, 1964.

James Baldwin: Patience and Shuffle the Cards. Written and directed by James Baldwin. Reissued by Benchmark Media, 1998.

James Baldwin: Price of the Ticket. Directed by Karen Thorsen. A Nobody Knows Production, Maysles Film. San Francisco: California Newsreel, 1989.

Pressure/Baldwin's Nigger. Directed by Horace Ové. Bfi Video, 1969. Reissued on DVD, September 26, 2005.

Contributors

DOUGLAS FIELD is Senior Lecturer in Contemporary Literature and Culture at Staffordshire University, U.K. He is the editor of *American Cold War Culture* (Edinburgh University Press, 2005) and has written on James Baldwin, jazz, and religion for a number of publications, including *Genre*, *Wasafiri*, *Callaloo*, *Literature and Theology*, and the *Guardian*. He is the book review editor for *Callaloo* and is the author of the forthcoming book *James Baldwin* in the *Writers and Their Work* series (Northcote House Publishers). He is also completing a monograph on Baldwin that focuses on the writer's religious and political work.

CLARENCE HARDY is an assistant professor in the Department of Religion at Dartmouth College, New Hampshire. He has written several articles in the *Journal of Religion*, *Church History*, and *American Quarterly* and is the author of *James Baldwin's God: Sex, Hope, and Crisis in Black Holiness Culture* (University of Tennessee Press, 2003). He is currently working on a book, *"'We Grappled for the Mysteries': Black God-talk in Modern America."*

CAROL E. HENDERSON is Associate Director of Black American Studies and Associate Professor of English and Black American Studies at the University of Delaware, Newark. She has published extensively on African American literature and culture, and her articles and books on Baldwin include "Knee Bent, Body Bowed: (Re)Memory's Prayer of Spiritual Re(new)al in Baldwin's *Go Tell It On The Mountain*," *Religion & Literature* 27.1(Spring 1995); "Refiguring the Flesh: The Word, The Body, and the Process of Being in *Beloved* and *Go Tell It On the Mountain*," in *James Baldwin and Toni Morrison: Comparative Critical and Theoretical Essays*, edited by Lovalerie King and Lynn O. Scott (Palgrave, 2006); and *Scarring the Black Body: Race and Representation in African American Literature* (University of Missouri Press, 2002). She is the editor of *James Baldwin's* Go Tell It On the Mountain: *Historical and Critical Essays* (Peter Lang, 2006).

JUSTIN A. JOYCE is a doctoral candidate in the English Department at the University of Illinois at Chicago (UIC) and a three-time NCAA Academic All-American as a competitor for the UIC men's gymnastics team. His publications include a coedited collection of essays, *A Melvin Dixon Critical Reader* (University of Mississippi Press, 2006), and the essay "Fashion, Class, and Gender in Early Modern England: Staging *Twelfth Night*," in *Styling Texts* (2007). He is completing a dissertation that reads Hollywood Westerns against uniquely American legal paradigms to assess the legal, social, and ideological conflicts that have been addressed in the cowboy-hero's gunplay.

RANDALL KENAN is a professor of Creative Writing at the University of North Carolina, Chapel Hill. His first novel, *A Visitation of Spirits*, was published by Grove Press in 1989. His collection of stories *Let the Dead Bury Their Dead* (Harcourt, Brace, 1992) was nominated for the Los Angeles *Times* Book Award for Fiction, was a finalist for the National Book Critics Circle Award, and was included among *The New York Times* Notable Books of 1992. He is also the author of a young adult biography of James Baldwin (1993) and several other works of fiction and nonfiction. His latest book, *The Fire This Time*, a personal response to Baldwin's 1963 essay, was published by Melville House in 2007.

DWIGHT A. MCBRIDE is Dean of the College of Liberal Arts and Sciences and Professor of African American Studies, English, and Gender and Women's Studies at the University of Illinois at Chicago. His published essays are in the areas of race theory and black queer studies. He is author of *Impossible Witnesses: Truth, Abolitionism, and Slave Testimony* (New York University Press, 2001) and *Why I Hate Abercrombie and Fitch: Essays on Race and Sexuality* (New York University Press, 2005), both of which were nominated for the Hurston-Wright Legacy Award. The latter was also a nominee for the Lambda Literary Award. He is the editor of *James Baldwin Now* (New York University Press, 1999); coeditor of a special issue of the journal *Callaloo* titled "Plum Nelly: New Essays in Black Queer Studies" (Winter 2000); coeditor of the Lambda Literary Award–winning fiction anthology *Black Like Us: A Century of Lesbian, Gay, and Bi-Sexual African American Fiction* (Cleis Press, 2002); and coeditor of *A Melvin Dixon Critical Reader* (University of Mississippi Press, 2006). He is currently at work on two new book manuscripts, tentatively titled "Poetics, Politics, and Phillis Wheatley" and "White Lies in the Republic: Race, Sexuality, and the Law."

D. QUENTIN MILLER is Associate Professor of English at Suffolk University in Boston. He is the editor of two collections of essays, *Prose and Cons: Essays on Prison Literature in the United States* (McFarland, 2005) and *Re-Viewing James Baldwin: Things Not Seen* (Temple University Press, 2000). He is also the author of *Drawing the Iron Curtain: John Updike and the Cold War* (University of Missouri Press, 2001) and the editor or coeditor of three textbooks, *The Heath Anthology of American Literature, The Generation of Ideas: A Thematic Reader,* and *Connections: Literature for Composition. He has published eight reference-volume entries on Baldwin and a number of essays on Baldwin and other American writers, including Toni Morrison, John Edgar Wideman, Leonard Peltier, and Ernest Hemingway. He is currently working on a book on Baldwin in the context of the law.*

LYNN ORILLA SCOTT is a visiting assistant professor at James Madison College, which is a Residential College of Public Policy within Michigan State University. Her publications on Baldwin include *James Baldwin's Later Fiction: Witness to the Journey* (Michigan State University Press, 2002); "James Baldwin," in

The Greenwood Encyclopedia of Multiethnic Literature, edited by
Emmanuel Nelson; and "Baldwin's Reception and the Challenge
of His Legacy," in *Bloom's BioCritiques: James Baldwin*, edited by
Harold Bloom (Chelsea House, 2006). With Lovalerie King, she
coedited *James Baldwin and Toni Morrison: Comparative Critical and
Theoretical Essays* (Palgrave MacMillan, 2006), which includes
her essay "Revising the Incest Story: Toni Morrison's *The Bluest
Eye* and James Baldwin's *Just Above My Head*."

RANDAL KENAN is a professor of Creative Writing at the
University of North Carolina, Chapel Hill. His first novel, *A
Visitation of Spirits*, was published by Grove Press in 1989. His collection of stories *Let the Dead Bury Their Dead* (Harcourt, Brace,
1992) was nominated for the Los Angeles *Times* Book Award for
Fiction, was a finalist for the National Book Critics Circle Award,
and was included among *The New York Times* Notable Books of
1992. He is also the author of a young adult biography of James
Baldwin (1993) and several other works of fiction and nonfiction. His latest book, *The Fire This Time*, a personal response to
Baldwin's 1963 essay, was published by Melville House in 2007.

MAGDALENA J. ZABOROWSKA is Associate Professor in the
Program in American Culture and the Center for Afroamerican
and African Studies at the University of Michigan in Ann Arbor.
Her main publications on Baldwin include *James Baldwin's Turkish
Decade: Erotics of Exile* (Duke University Press, 2009); "Racing
Transatlantic Passages: James Baldwin's African 'America' and
Immigrant Studies," *Cultural Psychology of Immigrants*, edited by
Ramaswami Mahalingam (Lawrence Erlbaum, 2006); "From
Baldwin's Paris to Benjamin's: The Architectonics of Race and
Sexuality in *Giovanni's Room*," *Architectural Theory Review* (2005)
updated and revised as "Reading Benjamin's Paris through
Baldwin's: The Architectonics of Race and Sexuality in *Giovanni's
Room*" in *Walter Benjamin and Architecture*, edited by Gevork
Hartoonian (Routledge, 2009); and "Mapping Transcultural
Masculinities: James Baldwin's Innocents Abroad, or *Giovanni's
Room* Revisited," in *Other Americans, Other Americas: The Politics
and Poetics of Multiculturalism*, edited by Magdalena J. Zaborowska
(Aarhus University Press, 1998).

Index

27003064R00154

Made in the USA
Middletown, DE
09 December 2015